PRENTICE-HALL EDUCATION SERIES

Dan Cooper, *Editor*

SCHOOL B

SCHOOL BOARDS

Their Status, Functions
and Activities

by

CHARLES EVERAND REEVES, Ph.D.

Consultant in Educational Administration

New York

PRENTICE-HALL, INC.

1954

Library of Congress
Catalog Card Number:
54-7461

PRINTED IN THE UNITED STATES OF AMERICA

A Tribute

To the American School Board:

> *Agent of the state in preserving the social heritage,*
>
> *Acting for and in the interest of all people of your district,*
>
> *Provider of educational opportunities for all children,*
>
> *Provider of foundation education—basic to development and progress,*
>
> *Conservator of America's most important resource—developing children,*

America salutes you with gratitude and praise.

C.E.R.

Preface

In the United States, school board members devote a total of more than twenty million hours a year to the maintenance and control of the public schools. Entering upon their duties as laymen in education, they have no single source from which to get information concerning the status, functions, and activities of school boards. This book provides a general comprehensive treatment of the work in order to give information essential to the more effective performance of board functions.

It not only can be used by school board members as a basis for short courses, but it should be useful to school superintendents and graduate students of school administration in helping them to understand more fully the viewpoints and problems of the controlling boards in determining school policies.

It is hoped that *School Boards* will help inspire school board members to act in accordance with the importance of their office, and to develop increased appreciation of the opportunities for service inherent in their positions of community trust.

In preparing this volume, I have drawn freely upon twenty years of close experience with school boards and school board members as a consultant and director of studies for their school systems. I am grateful to Griffenhagen and Associates for affording me the opportunity of making these studies, in the course of which many of the examples cited have been observed, and to colleagues in the firm for encouraging me to write this book. However, neither the firm nor its members are responsible for the ideas expressed or implied. That responsibility is mine alone.

To the National Education Association and to the authors of several doctoral dissertations, I am indebted for facts presented in their scientific research. Credit should also go to various state school boards associations and their officers and to various authors of articles and books for confirmation of some of my opinions. For suggestions concerning the contents of a part of this volume, I want to thank Mr. Edward M. Tuttle, Executive Secretary of the National School Boards Association. My sincere thanks also to my brother, Dr. Floyd W. Reeves, Professor of Educational Administration and Consultant to the President, Michigan State College, and Mr. Raymond F. Lane, who has assisted me in rendering consultation services, for their critical reading of the manuscript.

CHARLES EVERAND REEVES

Contents

SCHOOL BOARDS

CHAPTER 1

The Importance of School
Board Control

Education engages the time of more citizens of the United States than does any other occupation. There were, in 1950, nearly one million teachers and more than twenty-five million pupils in the public schools and, since then, the numbers have been rapidly increasing. The United States Bureau of the Census[1] estimates that the number of public school pupils will increase to more than thirty-four million by 1958.

Total current expenditures for schools, in 1949–1950, amounted to nearly six billion dollars, of which almost four and three-fourths billion were for current expenses.

Public school systems range in size from the one-teacher school system, in a district of its own, to the mammoth public school system of New York City with hundreds of thousands of pupils and thousands of teachers. From the standpoint of the number of persons (adults and children) engaged in different activities, the schools are usually the largest single enterprise in any community.

There are many methods for computing the value of public property, such as original cost, original cost minus depreciation, replacement cost, appraisal value, insurance value, and the like. The original cost value of public school property was over eleven billion dollars in 1950, according to the Biennial Survey

---

[1] Hecht, George J. "Our Desperate Need for More Schools—and What Can Be Done About It." (Reprinted from *Parents' Magazine*) New York. The American Parents' Committee, Inc.

of Education in the United States, 1948–1950. It has rapidly increased since that time, and many school buildings are still under construction or are planned for construction during the next few years. A study by the United States Office of Education shows a present estimated need for additional school buildings amounting to ten billion, seven hundred million dollars. As for property valuation, the public schools are also among the larger enterprises in a community. With regard to expenditures for current operation, the public schools are often the largest single enterprise in the community.

Scope of the Influence of Public Schools

Public schools have evolved into active institutions. Their curricula have been expanded beyond the fundamental tools of reading, writing, and arithmetic into the fine and practical arts, such as music, painting, homemaking, and various kinds of shop construction activities; health and physical education have been developed; and the content subjects, such as history, citizenship, geography, and the sciences, have been vitalized. The people are interested in pupil activities, many of which have been absorbed by the curriculum. The schools have become, in many areas, the centers of community life. Learning activities have been extended into preschool and adult years. The schools are no longer being operated only for a few brilliant scholars, but for pupils of all levels and characteristics of ability. The public schools are more nearly the peoples' schools now than they have ever been in the past. Their activities reach into almost every home in the United States at some time, and into most of them from the time the oldest child enters the kindergarten or first grade until the youngest child has been graduated from the twelfth or fourteenth grade. There is no one in the United States who has not felt the influence of the public schools, directly or indirectly, and most persons have attended them for many of their childhood years.

School Board Designations

The term "school board" will be used in this book to designate any board in control of public schools. Such boards have specific legal titles, and the term "school board" is rarely used as such. The title of school boards most commonly used, particularly in city and county school systems, is "board of education." Other legal titles are "board of school directors," or "school directors," "board of school trustees," or "school trustees," "board of school commissioners," or "school commissioners," "board of school inspectors," or "school inspectors," and "school committee." Although the term "school board" is occasionally used as a specific title, it is more commonly used in a generic sense than is any other of the titles of boards in control of public schools.

Number of School Boards and Board Members

In 1950, the United States Office of Education showed in its biennial survey that there were 83,237 basic administrative units (school districts or their equivalent) and about 280,000 school board members. The number of units declined 12 per cent, from 1948 to 1950, indicating much consolidation of school districts.

The maintenance of good schools in the United States, at reasonable cost, will require still further reduction in the number of school districts and school boards. Some states have few school districts. Maryland has 24; Utah, 40; West Virginia, 55; Louisiana and Florida each have 67; and some states have 100 to 200 school districts. On the other hand, four states had more than 6,000 school districts in 1950. Consolidation of small school districts and an accompanying reduction in the number of school boards have been proceeding in recent years in Illinois, Kansas, Oklahoma, California, New York, Washington, and other states, but there is need for more drastic measures for consolidation and reduction in the number of school districts in order to secure efficient control and administration of the public schools.

Distinction between School Boards
and Other Municipal Boards

In the United States the public schools are almost universally conducted under the direction and control of school boards, usually under some such title as "Board of Education of . . . School District." School boards are different, in some respects, from other municipal boards. A school board usually governs a school district. By law, it is a government unit distinct from that of a city, township, or county, a part or all of which may be included within the boundaries of the school district. The school district is usually a separate corporate unit of government. Its board is usually a corporate body with legal authority to hold and dispose of property in the name of the board or the district, to sue and defend itself and the district against suit, and to make and execute contracts in the name of the board or school district. The board is usually vested with the authority, responsibility, and functions that, under state law, make it independent as a governing body and sovereign in performing its legal functions. In some of the larger school districts, particularly if city and school district boundaries are coterminous, certain specified powers over school district affairs are granted to city authorities, but such is not generally the case. As a rule, school boards are subject to more control by the state legislature than are other local boards, and the state usually furnishes more of the financial support for public schools than for the functions performed by other local boards.

Other local governing boards do not, as a rule, govern separate districts, but are a part of the city, town, or county governments. They are usually not corporate bodies, but their authority and functions are a part of the regular municipal government, subject to the authority of the council or other legislative body. Usually, they do not have the power to hold and dispose of public property, to sue and be sued, or to make and execute contracts. These functions are performed for them by the municipal authorities.

Proposals for the Discontinuance of School Boards

About twenty years ago, several prominent educators proposed that school boards be abolished and city schools be operated more directly by the professionally trained superintendents of schools. These superintendents would be appointed by the mayor and serve under him or a nonprofessional commissioner of education. It was held that such control would cause less interference with professional management of the schools than was being caused by boards of education.

Educators generally agreed, and were upheld by the decisions of the courts of many states, that education was a state rather than a local function. Also, it was shown that the legislatures have the right to use any agency available to perform their constitutional public education functions and that they have the power to abolish any or all school boards which they have created and assign the functions to regularly constituted municipal authorities. It was argued that appointment of the superintendent of schools by a mayor or city manager would place him more directly in charge of the schools than would his appointment by a board of education.

A number of other educators sprang to the defense of boards of education as co-ordinating agencies between the community interest and the self-interest of the professional staff. They concluded that boards should be retained but made nonpolitical and, in some cities, improved in quality. The movement for discontinuing school board direction and control of the public schools was generally not popular with either educators or the public, and the proposal has not been pressed. However, many political scientists have advocated that schools be operated by superintendents under the general direction of a city commissioner or city manager as a part of the government of the municipality.

Until recently, St. Paul and Chattanooga had a commissioner of education in charge of public schools, but they have since changed to boards.

The principal fear of educators and the public is that a mayor, commissioner, or city manager placed in authority over the superintendent of schools will make the schools even more subject to the changing fortunes of political parties than do boards of education, or that school issues will be confused with local municipal issues. It is feared that the control of school finances will be removed from school authority and placed under the city financial authority and that a political party in control of both school finances and school personnel will have control of a rich political plum tree which it can use for the reward of party workers and in the maintenance of its own power.

Responsibility of the School Board for the Quality of the School System

Responsibility for the quality of education in a community rests largely on the school board. The board alone has the power to provide public schools under authority delegated to it by the lawmaking body of the state. Its members have been selected by the community to determine the expenditure of the moneys appropriated by both the community and the state for the support of public schools. The quality of the schools depends, basically, on how well this is done. Of course, a board cannot immediately make a school system good if it has an incompetent or partly incompetent staff. But within necessary financial limitations and the provisions of state tenure laws for teachers, the board is also responsible for the quality of the staff. It selects the superintendent of schools and approves the staff selections he makes. If the superintendent is well qualified to select administrative assistants, teachers, janitors, and other staff members for the board to approve, and is not restricted by too rigid financial or other limitations in doing so, it is likely that a school system will, in the main, have a well qualified and capable staff.

Hence the selection of a superintendent of schools is a very important act of the board in determining the quality of the school system.

As the policy-making body for the operation of public schools, the school board determines important additions to, deletions from, or changes in the school system. It adopts rules and regulations and determines policies that apply to the school system in general; it even determines policies by setting precedents in its actions on specific cases. The actions of the board are therefore very important in determining the quality of public education in a community.

Responsibility of School Boards for America's Future

The work of school boards in the United States is of the greatest possible importance to both the individual and society. So far as we, the people, have the power to determine our collective destiny, the future of our nation rests with the children, and depends on their development. The kind of adults the children will become depends largely on the public schools. The type of school provided is determined largely by the board that controls and directs it. That school boards, as representatives of the people of their communities, have made progress toward extending education in the past is attested by the fact that the average education level attained by young adult men drafted into the army for World War I was several grades below the average attainment in World War II.

The school and the home carry most of the responsibility for the physical, intellectual, and social development of children. Among other institutions that educate children are churches, community centers, playgrounds, young people's organizations, motion pictures, and, in fact, all other community agencies that furnish experiences to youth. However, the homes and schools carry most of the responsibility for good or mediocre education, for they are the only institutions in which practically all youth spends large proportions of its time, and the schools are the only institutions organized specifically for the purpose of furnishing educational experiences to children. The home and the school help children to develop health habits and attitudes, provide means for their recreation, give them the opportunity for some measure of appreciation of the fine arts, develop in them skills in the language arts, mathematics, and the sciences, help them to develop characteristics of good citizenship and social living, train them in a vocation, and assist them in other ways to develop as individuals and members of society.

Conservation of the Human Resources of the Community

The nation and state need to conserve many natural resources, but the most important resource in any community is the developing children. Everywhere, they constitute the greatest potential asset. Whether or not this asset is developed to its maximum capacity by the application of scientific principles of education depends largely on the quality of the public school. The school is dependent upon the quality of the school board. However, the board must be supported by the community in its effort to maintain as good schools as the financial ability of the community will permit. Public schools are the most important factor in determining the quality of the civic, social, and economic life of the future. In fact, the public schools, to a considerable degree, decide the future. Each community's future is being largely determined by the kind of schools it maintains in the present. However, it is not only the local community that benefits from good schools, but also the state and nation.

It is the school board that is important in the conservation of the human resources of a community. None realize better the importance of such conservation than the board. A defective road or water system might, at high cost, be removed and reconstructed; an uneducated or poorly educated child has completely lost the opportunities for educational experiences in childhood years. At best, the only possibility for the correction of his early defective education is a patching job in later years if he has enough initiative to desire it and can spare the time from earning a living to work for it.

Conservation of the Social Heritage

The public schools are responsible for transmitting from generation to generation the vast accumulations of the social heritage that, in many instances, cannot be effectively transmitted by other institutions. This inheritance includes not only the developed tools of learning, but also much of the scientific, political, economic, and other scholarly parts of the social inheritance; the traditions and customs of civilization; and the vast endowment of fine and practical arts. It is the function of the public schools to transmit the fundamentals of these inheritances. Without the public schools as a conservator of the better elements of the social inheritance, much of modern civilization would be lost in a few generations.

Further Development of American Culture

Education is an economic asset in a community and a state. It creates not only greater needs for goods, services, and activities, but provides the ability to satisfy them. It is the satisfaction of socially desirable wants of individuals that constitutes what is known as a high standard of living. Education not only creates the desire, but furnishes the criteria and develops the judgments necessary for selecting the satisfactions that will be beneficial to the individual and to society. The number and quality of wants and the ability to satisfy them in ways that are good constitute the differences between primitive and civilized societies, between backward and progressive peoples, and between the more poorly developed and the more highly developed states of the nation. Many studies have shown high positive correlation between the average level of education attained and the standard of living maintained. Whether cause or effect, the fact that education and a high standard of living go together, makes education highly desirable.

The creating of desires, the developing of abilities that enable people, by individual and group efforts, to satisfy desires in ways that are accepted as good, and the satisfying of new, good desires constitute progress. In the modern age, education is basic to inventions, discoveries, and to additions to the cultural inheritance. The schools must develop as well as preserve this social heritage.

School Boards as Bulwarks of Democracy

Control of the schools by local school boards has been a product of development over many years. The Federal Government, having no original control over public schools, has authority only in establishing the requirements for eligibility for federal financial aid, which the several states and school districts are, theoretically, free to accept or reject. Subject to the requirements of state law, local school boards control the public schools. It is important to the sound maintenance of our representative form of government that school control continues to reside, in large measure, in the representatives of the local communities.

In seizing power, a dictator demands control of the schools and usually places them under the authority of a minister of propaganda and education—two terms that, as we know them, are mutually incompatible. Both Mussolini and Hitler, two tyrants who openly hated the meaning of the word democracy, quickly grasped control of the schools. It was the course also taken by Lenin and Stalin, tyrants who gave lip service to democracy but permitted no practice of it. It is still the practice of the dictators of the Soviet Union and its satellites. Dictators understand that their control can be maintained only by control of the schools and the indoctrination of the young into the forms of political, economic, and social thinking that will produce the bias and prejudice necessary to the continuance of their power. The training of the young, if completely controlled by a dictator, can distort the thinking of a nation in a generation by moulding the minds of developing and trusting children.

The free education system of the United States, operated under the direction of many school boards, has avoided political control. Because of this, the school board system of control is a bulwark of democracy.

The Soviet Union and some other countries rival the natural resources of the United States. However, they are backward in their political, social, and industrial development because the education they provide is biased and not designed for free and open-minded people. The level of education attained is low on the average. No country can develop far unless its children are taught to think and act honestly and fearlessly and are free from indoctrination into the forms of thinking desired by the adherents of some political party or other group or person, however wise.

In our country there are variations within and among the states in the freedom of learning allowed and the levels of education attained. Consequently, there are corresponding variations in the enlightenment and progress of the people, but nowhere is there the rigid control of thought practiced in despotic nations. The responsiveness of local boards of education to the will of their communities has prevented such control of the public schools. The school boards, with varying composition, have protected education in the United States from subservience to false political ends.

School Boards as Community Balance Wheels

School boards must serve as balance wheels between those factions in the community holding differing opinions on matters concerning the public schools. Probably the most common difference pertains to the amount of money required for their operation. If the school tax is increased, many taxpayers will be displeased; if taxes are reduced by curtailment of expenditures, many parents and members of the school staff will object. It is incumbent on the board to maintain an adequate system of schools and, at the same time, to protect the taxpayers against exorbitant taxes. It is the board's obligation to expend public moneys to the best advantage possible even if it results in complaints about high taxes or unfulfilled needs.

Many other matters are sometimes subjects of contention in the community. Some of these are the kind of school building to be constructed, the location of the building, elementary school subdivisions of the district, transportation of pupils, qualifications of teachers, expansion or curtailment of the high school curriculum, the administration of athletics, the discharge of a superintendent or principal, the quality or extent of pupil health service, and scores of other problems that, dividing community opinion, need to be settled fearlessly by the board.

In making its decisions the board must be mindful of the fact that it represents the whole people of the school district. It will soon find itself in trouble if it tries to placate vociferous groups or to base its decisions on temporary public notions that may not be in the interests of the children of the schools. Such actions will leave the board holding the responsibility for the public's whims. The board must act with considerable independence. It must bend its efforts toward keeping public opinion balanced. To be successful, it must serve the interests of the whole public rather than the special interests of groups, small in proportion to the whole, that pour forth "much smoke but have little fire," so far as the interests of the schools are concerned.

Discriminative judgment requires well-balanced board members. Such will be the case if they can understand the place of the schools in the community and are able to base decisions on ultimate benefits rather than on immediate pressures. To act for the best interests of the people of the community, board members must be able to visualize the community in the projected future. They must be able to see the boys as men and the girls as women. Members lack balance when they are swept first one way and then another by the opinions of various small groups, when they form opinions on the basis of emotion instead of logic, when they seek to favor friends or political cronies, or when certain members make decisions on important matters and the others are indifferent and accept such decisions without question. Any such board fans the flames of community dissension instead of assuaging them.

School Board Membership as a Community Service

The office of school board member is a trusteeship for an important community function. In some places the school board is known as the board of trustees, and the members as trustees. The services rendered are vital to the well-being of community, state, and nation. They are worthy of the best efforts of men and women of the highest intelligence and the most self-sacrificing qualities of citizenship the community affords. In spite of occasional public failure to appreciate the services rendered by members of school boards, the work performed is as important as that performed by any other public servants. No public service is so productive of personal satisfaction as that of membership on a school board when the office is accepted by a person genuinely wishing to render service to the community and its young, developing citizens.

It has been the author's observation, over a period of more than twenty years devoted to advising boards on school problems, that most school board members accept or seek the responsibilities with a sincere desire to help their respective communities, for which they have real affection. The hours of arduous work required for preparation for board meetings (personal reflection on the possible solutions of school problems and the formulation of desirable school policies) must be subtracted from the member's allotment of time for his own occupation or recreation and given freely to his community. The more intelligent and generous part of the community usually appreciates this. It is often the selfish and ungrateful persons in the community, unable to conceive of altruistic motives, who are unreasonably suspicious of the free services rendered by school board members.

Of course, not every school board member is a model of altruism, unselfishness, and courage in fulfilling his voluntarily assumed obligations. Cases have been known in which motives were selfish, and school board membership was sought for the purpose of private gain. However, such motives are rarely those that impel persons to accept membership.

Anyone who accepts membership on a school board should realize that he is entering an important position of trust and responsibility that will require much of his time and energy. If this is clear to him, he will no more prove faithless to his trust than he would embezzle funds from his company. He will, to the best of his ability, fulfill his functions by attending board meetings, by studying school problems, by discussing in board meetings questions affecting the schools, by participating with other members in determining policies for the school system, and by approving or disapproving the way the adopted policies are being executed.

Public Appreciation of School Board Service

People work for pay, but monetary compensation seldom motivates a person to give his best to an activity. A person will put forth even greater effort and carry an even heavier load of responsibility to discharge a trust placed in him by his friends and neighbors. The time and energy donated by board members to the work are unrewarded financially, and sometimes there is inadequate expression of appreciation by the public.

However, the public often does express appreciation for the hours of service and the heavy responsibilities. It is only by such appreciation that school board membership can be made attractive to those persons of the community best qualified to perform the function. In spite of the time and responsibility involved, it is usually not difficult to induce the best qualified persons to accept school board membership in a community in which the public expresses its appreciation.

Tributes are sometimes paid to worthy school board members by the press. A few years ago the *Springfield* (Massachusetts) *Union* published the following editorial:

> After serving for 20 years as a member of the school committee, Chester T. Neal will retire at the end of this year. He has set a high standard for his successors and an excellent example of fine public service. Mr. Neal has had no political ax to grind. His great concern has been the good of the public school system. No measure has received the support of Mr. Neal unless he has been convinced that it was right and would benefit the school children.
>
> Mr. Neal has done much to help safeguard the Springfield public school system from politics. He was a leader in the movement to make merit the sole basis for the selection and promotion of teachers; he did much to bring about the adoption of the single salary schedule. He made a study of trade school practices and was among the first to urge the establishment of a trade school here. It is fortunate for the city that Mr. Neal has served on the committee during a period when a great many important school posts have been filled.

Sometimes the public is fickle and, at election time, may forget long and faithful service. The majority of voters may allow some incident of the moment to determine their selection. Sometimes the public may suspect self-interest on the part of board members when none exists. Public silence when acclaim is due may be interpreted by the board members as a lack of appreciation. In spite of delinquency by the public in expressing its appreciation, membership on a school board is a distinction which should arouse pride in any man or woman. It means that the people in a person's own community, where he is known best, have enough confidence in his ability, good judgment, and integrity to entrust to him the responsibility for decisions on matters affecting the future of their children, an expression of great faith. Membership on a school board, with a reasonable amount of enthusiastic public support for the improvement of the schools, can be one of the most satisfying public services a person can render.

CHAPTER 2

The Development of the Local Board
System of School Control

Historical Perspective

School boards of the United States, under their various appellations, have developed gradually as experience has demonstrated the need for changes. The strengths and weaknesses of existing school board forms, organization structures, functions, procedures, and activities for the maintenance and control of public schools, can be best appreciated by consideration of their origin and development. Only a brief chapter can be devoted to a recapitulation of a few of the more salient and pertinent facts to serve as historical perspective for an understanding and evaluation of school board control of public education. It will be obvious that existing school boards differ in various ways from one another and that some boards have been developed in certain respects for more effective performance of their functions than have others.

Early Control of Public Schools

In the original thirteen colonies the first schools were usually established by religious bodies, and education was generally considered to be a function of the church. Some were established and maintained by charitable groups, formed for that purpose, and, in some cases, schools were maintained as private enterprises. The public school system of the United States, in many of its basic features, originated in New England. In most of colonial New England, particularly in Massachusetts, the people were generally of a common religious faith; and it was not unnatural that they should entrust to their local governments the performance of functions then usually relegated to the church.

A Massachusetts law, enacted in 1647, less than a generation after the first settlement, made the maintenance of a school in each town mandatory and left to the selectmen the decision as to the means to be used for its support. The public schools were made a function of town government. Policies and administrative matters were determined in town meeting or by the selectmen of the town, who performed both legislative and administrative functions for the schools and other town agencies. Some of the policies dealt with in this way concerned such matters as the levy of town taxes, the selection of teachers and determination of their wages, the length of school terms, the provision of one or more school buildings, and other matters relating to the public schools.

School Committee Assumption of Responsibilities

As the number of teachers increased and public interest in the schools grew, and as the nonschool problems of local government multiplied, the selectmen appointed temporary committees to report to them or to perform various approved functions, such as selecting a schoolmaster or providing a schoolhouse. In 1721, a permanent committee on school visitation was appointed in Boston. Similar committees, without legal status, were appointed in other cities and towns. At first an agency of the selectmen or other governing body, the school committee was later given separate status. The school board in Massachusetts is still officially known as the School Committee, even though it acts largely independently of the local governing body of the city and of other governing authorities. The municipal authorities have gradually lost their control over school committees. Now, most of them consist of members elected by the people. This is a brief statement of the beginning and early development of school boards.

In the middle colonies there were both charity schools and schools maintained by rate bills assessed against parents according to the number of children they sent to school. Later, taxes were levied for the support of schools on all of the property within the separate school districts of the city or town, and the charity schools were absorbed into the tax-supported school system. As schools in the various towns and cities increased in number, each school often constituted a school district of the municipality, and a school board was appointed to manage it. When additional school buildings were constructed, the boards sometimes had more than one school to manage.

In the southern colonies the early schools were either maintained by the church or by private individuals who charged tuition. The county and independent school districts, under the control of school boards, were developed largely after the Civil War.

As new states were admitted to the union, their constitutions eventually provided for tax-supported public school systems and, often, local school boards to govern them. The constitutional provisions were supplemented by statutory enactments. In all states except Indiana the respective state constitutions or statutes now provide for the governing of all public tax-supported schools by school boards. In Indiana, township school systems are governed by a single trustee, city systems by boards.

For many years school boards performed both legislative and administrative functions. Their members actively managed the schools. They personally examined and selected the teachers and decided upon their salaries, determined the length of school terms, secured wood for fuel, had school buildings repaired, visited classes, and even examined pupils. In fact, they rendered most of the basic services performed by both the school board of today and the superintendent with his staff of principals, supervisors, and business personnel.

Development of State Authority over Schools

State authority over public schools began in Massachusetts soon after the settlement of the colony. The law of 1647 required all towns to maintain public schools under penalty of a five pound fine for failure to do so. In 1693, state authority was further affirmed by a law jointly charging the towns and their selectmen with the duty of maintaining schools and requiring the selectmen to levy taxes for school support if so directed by vote of the people in town meeting. These laws and later ones in other colonies made the colonies responsible for maintaining schools. When the colonies became states and, later, when new states were admitted to the union (in the central, western, and southern parts of the United States), it was natural that state constitutions should provide for a state system of education and that their legislatures should create school districts and provide a method for the support and control of public schools. Thus, the school board is a creature of the state and subject to its laws. However, the board is also responsible, within the provisions of law, to the people of the school district who, directly or indirectly, select its members.

Most school boards are empowered to act entirely or almost entirely under the provisions of state law and are not subject to city, county, or other outside local authority. In some cities an intermediate authority such as the city governing board or executive officer has been granted financial or building powers by city charter, which supersede those of the school board.

State legislatures gradually assumed increasing authority over local public schools, but even after the passage of laws fixing requirements and restrictions on school boards and delegating to state departments of education the authority to assist and often to control certain of their actions, the legislatures left considerable discretionary powers to the school boards. In recent years state controls have been increased by those requirements imposed as conditions for eligibility for financial aid or reimbursement for school expenditures.

The courts are generally agreed that education is a state rather than municipal function and that school boards serve as agents of the state. Some political scientists and a few courts, in decisions, have disagreed with this thesis. They maintain that the states have delegated certain fundamental controls to the cities instead of directly to the school districts, but this seems to be true only where provisions have been made by special legislation, like those to be found in some city charters.

All are agreed that education in the United States is not a Federal function. The Federal Constitution makes no mention of education or of schools. Matters not specified for Federal control or prohibited to the states by that document are reserved to the states or the people thereof.

Development of Board Control under State Authority

In 1798, the school committees of Massachusetts were recognized by law as separate governing bodies of the city or town, but some of the selectmen or members of other town governing boards sometimes were included in their membership. It was required by a Massachusetts law passed in 1826 that school committees be entirely separate from other governing authorities and that they be authorized to have "general charge and superintendence of all the public schools" of the town. Some authorities point to the Massachusetts law of 1826 as the official beginning of the school committee or board of education operating as the governing body for the public schools, separate from the governing body of the city or town. The duties of the independent school commitee included all of those previously mentioned. With school committees of large membership, in the bigger cities, it was natural that subcommittees should be appointed to perform various administrative functions and report to the whole school committee.

Gilland [1] calls attention to the large size of school boards even prior to the twentieth century. At the time of the Civil War, New York had a board of 44 members selected by wards. There were eight additional trustees and two inspectors in each ward, who had responsibility for the local administration of the schools. Near the beginning of the present century, Philadelphia had a board of 37 members, who were appointed by certain judicial officers. They lived in and represented the wards of the city in determining general policies for the schools of the city. In addition, each ward had a board of 12 school directors to administer its schools. In all, according to Gilland, there were 444 persons in charge of the public schools of Philadelphia. Cubberley [2] states the number as 533 members in 1900 and 559 in 1905. The ward directors selected school personnel and arranged for fuel, but reported to the central board. It is said that this was the largest number of persons in general control of the schools of any one city. In Cincinnati prior to 1873, the city council exercised control over business matters, school buildings, and even such things as the school calendar, and it made an annual examination of the schools.

School boards, under varying state appellations, have now become separate governing bodies responsible, within the provisions of state law, directly to the people of the separate school districts. The members are usually elected by popular vote, but in a few of the larger cities they are appointed by the city council, mayor, or some other agency of municipal government. In a few cases, Maryland for example, they are appointed by an agency of state government. School boards have been developed largely to provide an agency for the control of public schools that would be wholly distinct from municipal governing bodies and would neither be a part of nor subject to municipal political control or interference. School boards are creatures of the legis-

[1] Gilland, T. McD. *The Origin and Development of the Power and Duties of the City School Superintendent.* Ch. IV. Chicago: University of Chicago Press, 1936.

[2] Cubberley, E. P. *Public School Administration.* Revised. Boston: Houghton Mifflin Co., 1929.

latures of their states. They are established for the specific purpose of making effective, within the respective school districts, the laws of the state pertaining to public schools.

Consolidation of City School Districts and Their School Boards

In many cities and towns each city ward, or otherwise formed school district, had a school board. With occasional exceptions the schools were maintained separately from those of other districts. Sometimes they employed a common superintendent of schools or shared a high school. Often the poorer residence wards paid higher school taxes than the wealthier ones or those having valuable business properties. The less fortunate wards could afford only the poorest kind of schools for only a few months of the year. The unfairness of the plan was apparent, and movements were started to consolidate the city wards into a common, city-wide school district. In some cities this was done all at once; in others it was a gradual process of absorption with the outlying wards joining the consolidation when it was to their advantage. This was likely to occur when a new school building was needed. Separate school districts were abolished in Chicago in 1857, but they were not abolished in Philadelphia and Pittsburgh until 1905. It is only within the last quarter century that Hartford has become a completely consolidated city school district. The last of the outlying independent school districts of Waterbury joined the consolidated city school district not many years ago. At this time, the city of Phoenix, Arizona, is included in twelve different elementary school districts and one high school district, each with a separate school board. In this instance, the city and not the original Phoenix school district absorbed a great deal of territory outside the original city limits. However, this is an unusual practice.

The consolidation of city school districts and boards reduced their number, but increased the number of members on each board. Becoming cumbersome, the boards were finally reduced to one member from each ward or component school district. Each was expected to serve the interests of the school or schools in his area. Ward representation has persisted in some cities, but the trend has been toward the elimination of selection of members to represent wards and toward reduction of their number.

Appointment of a School Executive Officer

The early school boards performed executive and administrative as well as legislative functions. In many of the small school districts in the United States (from one to three teachers) and in some larger ones, they still perform executive and administrative functions except when some assistance is received from county or state school administrative offices. The early school boards were unqualified for co-ordinating the work of the different teachers, sometimes of several separate schools. Also, their members' own occupations did not allow them sufficient time for school administration. Some of the boards adopted the practice of appointing one of the teachers as principal teacher and authorizing him to act for the board in administering the schools. One of the functions of the principal teacher was to help the others maintain discipline.

At first the boards relinquished to the principal teacher only minor executive and administrative functions, usually those requiring immediate attention. At length, the principal teacher became the principal, but even now, the officer who performs the functions of superintendent of schools in the smaller and medium size municipalities of Pennsylvania and some other states is known as a supervising principal.

Even though all school systems, except for the very small, are now administered by superintendents of schools, the laws of the states vest nearly all executive and administrative functions in school boards. Frequently the state laws either do not mention the position of superintendent of schools or provide only that he shall be the executive officer of the board. Sometimes there is provision for the election or appointment of a county superintendent of schools for the school districts within the county. Even if appointment of a superintendent of schools is required by law, the board is usually still charged with all or most of the specified executive and administrative functions of the school district, and the superintendent merely acts as the agent of the board in administering the schools. Usually, the superintendent of schools is even now only legally what the early principal and later superintendent of schools used to be—an assistant to the board, delegated to administer the schools as directed by the board. This should always be the legal status of the superintendent of schools because the schools are maintained for and at the expense of the people of the school district. The administration and operation of schools can be safely entrusted only to professional personnel fully responsible to representatives of the people.

The position, superintendent of schools, is of fairly recent origin. The first superintendents of city school systems were appointed in Louisville and Buffalo in 1837. In 1870, there were only 29 city superintendents of schools in the 226 cities of the United States above 8,000 population.

Trend toward the Elimination of Committee Administration

When school boards were large, it was necessary for them to conduct much of their business through standing committees, which reported to the full board for approval of their actions. Gilland shows that in 1890 the Baltimore board of education had 26 standing committees as follows: Baltimore city college, female high school, grammar schools, primary schools, English-German schools, manual training schools, colored schools, normal schools, textbooks, furniture, music, discipline, accounts, expenditures, examinations, bi-weekly reports, conferences, buildings, printing, health, drawing, interstate estates, heating apparatus and fuel, rules, public school library, and nonresident pupils.

In some cities there were a still larger number of standing

committees. In 1861, Chicago had 10 functional committees plus "committees of one" for the component school districts. By 1872, it had 19 functional committees. By 1885, it had 70 such committees and at one time, 79. The names of committees differed among the school boards of the various cities. By 1912, the Chicago school board had reduced the number of its standing committees to 13, by 1922, to 7, and it now has only one, a committee on finance.

Other city boards had large numbers of standing committees at one time. There were 50 in the Cincinnati board. As late as 1929, the New York City board of education had 16 standing committees; they were finance and budget, buildings and sites, day schools, evening schools, departmental organization, special schools, law, continuation schools and speech improvement, physical training, supplies, care of buildings, bureau of attendance, lectures, local school boards, nominations, and retirement.

One can only conjecture from their titles what the probable duties of committees in various cities were. There seems to have been no consistent pattern of standing committee titles. The use of standing committees to conduct school board business seems to have been adopted as a means of enabling school boards of large membership to fulfill all their functions. As a rule, the smaller the boards, the fewer were the standing committees. In general, the number of standing committees has been greatly limited as boards have been reduced in size. Now most school boards have no standing committees at all. Even in many of the larger cities, control by means of standing committees has either been discontinued or the number of committees reduced to one or two.

Development of Public School Control in a Large City

In 1947, the author of this book was engaged in directing a study for the reorganization of the administration of the public school system of Chicago with recommendations for adoption. He therefore had occasion to investigate the development of control and administration in the school system of that city. Some of the principal events in that history may be briefly listed as follows:

1837. The common council of the City of Chicago appointed ten persons to act as a board of school inspectors. This board did not function, and held no meetings.

1840. The common council appointed a new board of school inspectors, consisting of seven members, which met the same year and organized.

1853. The common council established the offices of superintendent of schools and secretary of the board of school inspectors.

1854. Chicago's first superintendent of schools assumed office.

1857. The title of the board of school inspectors was changed to board of education, and the number of members was increased from seven to fifteen. The separate school districts of the city were consolidated.

1872. By action of the state legislature, the fifteen members of the board of education were to be hereafter appointed by the mayor with the approval of the common council and at large, instead of by wards.

1917. At some time prior to this year, the number of members had been increased from fifteen to twenty-one. In 1917, the number was reduced from twenty-one to eleven, and their term of office was increased from three to five years.

1946. By legislative action, a unified system of educational administration was established by the consolidation of the separated functions of instruction, business, and physical plant under the direction of an officer designated as general superintendent of schools.

1947. The school system was reorganized in such manner as to make effective the unification of administrative functions under the direction of the single administrative head.

The present eleven members of the board of education of the Chicago school system are still appointed by the mayor, subject to approval of the common council, but recently new members have been appointed from a list of nominees furnished by a committee of disinterested persons. The board of education is independent of fiscal control by the common council and mayor. Though the council levies taxes for school purposes, it does so only as directed by the board of education. The board of education adopts the school budget in final form.

Trend in the Size of School Boards

In 1849, Boston had 214 members, elected by wards, on its various committees in charge of primary and advanced schools. In 1875, there were 116 members; this number was reduced to 25, including the mayor. In 1906 the number was further reduced to five members.

Gilland shows that in 1865 the Providence school committee had 45 members, 42 of whom were elected by wards and three of whom were city officers serving *ex officio*. In 1886, the wards were divided, and the number of members was increased to 63. In 1889 the number of members was reduced to 33 and in 1925 to seven, elected by divisions of the city to represent the people residing in them. In 1889, Milwaukee had 36 members on its board of education. The number was increased to 42 members in 1896 and then reduced to 23 in 1897. In 1905, the number was reduced to 12 and in 1907 was increased to 15 members. Other examples are cited by Gilland.

The trend in St. Louis, San Francisco, Baltimore, Rochester, Albany, Lowell, Grand Rapids, Scranton, Pittsburgh, and most other cities has been toward smaller school boards. In a 25-year period, from 1904 to 1929, the average reduction in the size of school boards was 50 per cent. In 1902 the average size of school boards in cities above 100,000 population had declined to 14 members; by 1917, to 10 members; by 1927, to 8 members; and by 1945 to 7 members.

Present Size of School Boards

The numbers of school board members in the 13 largest cities of the United States are as follows:

Philadelphia	15	New York	7
Pittsburgh	15	San Francisco	7
Milwaukee	15	Detroit	7
St. Louis	12	Los Angeles	7
Chicago	11	Cleveland	7
Washington	9	Boston	5
Baltimore	9		
		Median	9

A study of school districts in 1,892 cities, made by the National Education Association,[3] showed that 40 per cent of the school boards had 5 members and 88 per cent had from 5 to 9 members. The average number of school board members in school districts of cities of more than 500,000 population was 9.9; in cities from 100,000 to 500,000 population, 6.9; and in cities from 30,000 to 100,000 population, 7.0. School systems in still smaller school districts usually had either 5 or 7 members. The prevailing size of school boards seems to be 5, 7, or 9 members, except in very small population school districts where it is often 3.

Desirable Size of School Boards

Some states fix the requirements for the number of school board members in proportion to the population size or class of city or school district. There might be 3 for very small rural school districts, 5 for school districts of a larger specified size, and 7 for school districts that contain the larger cities.

Boards of 5 to 9 members have the advantage of furnishing the opinions of a number of persons; yet they are not so large as to make the dispatch of business difficult. If boards are large, it often becomes necessary to divide them into a number of standing committees, each with the function of studying questions in a particular field. The committee acts independently as a small board. This system encourages lack of co-ordination and inconsistency in legislation recommended to the full board for action.

Small boards need no committees and are less likely to de-

---

[3] National Education Association. Research Division. "Fiscal Authority of City Schoolboards." In *Research Bulletin*, April 1950.

velop factions or to form internal cliques. Much factional strife will be avoided in boards of 5 or 7 members. Many members of large boards often lose interest in their work and fail to assume the individual responsibility that is necessary for wise action. The amount of interest each member will have in the board usually appears to be in inverse ratio to the number of members on the board. Business is also expedited when the board is small. Meeting around a table, a board of 5 or 7 members can discuss problems without the need for speeches and other formal procedures. A small board can easily meet as a committee of the whole for discussion of matters in detail or those of a delicate nature, since a committee-of-the-whole session is closed to the public. Also, it is easier to find convenient times to hold special meetings with a small board. However, boards should not be as small as 3 members, except in very small school districts. Three are not enough to insure the presentation of different viewpoints on some of the more troublesome questions, and actions may often be taken without the more thorough consideration given by boards of 5 to 9 members.

Advantages of an Odd Number of Members

There should always be an odd number of members. Seven is a desirable number for a large city, and the largest American city, New York, has a 7-member board. Five members may be fully adequate for a small city. An even number of school board members sometimes becomes a barrier to the passage of certain legislation. In order to pass a motion by a majority vote of such a board, it must have the assent of 4 of 6, or 5 of 8, members. Four of 6 members constitutes a two-thirds vote as well as a majority. A motion fails to pass if the vote is 3 to 3. There is sometimes considerable dissatisfaction in losing a motion by a tie vote, which means that the same number of members favor as oppose a motion's passage. In such a case, it is not always the best policy for both sides to give up in favor of a new solution. An example of this would be the selection of a third candidate to fill a position when the board is deadlocked on the two best ones. Compromise is often worse than either solution. In a Massachusetts city, it once happened that a board with an even number of members became deadlocked over the selection of a school principal. After 192 ballots the board was still unable to agree, and a compromise on a third candidate was effected.

CHAPTER 3

The School District as
a Governing Unit

Development of School Districts

In Massachusetts and other New England states the public schools developed to fulfill a function of local town or city government and the school committee developed as an arm of the town or city governing body. Though the operation of public schools in New England is still largely a local town or city function, two changes have occurred in that part of the United States: (1) by legislation the states have arrogated to themselves a great deal of control over the schools and (2) the state legislative bodies have made the school committees largely independent, fiscally and otherwise, of other municipal authorities. In Massachusetts, for example, school committees now conduct school business largely independently of city, town, or other control by nonschool authorities. In spite of these developments the school committees are still a part of town and city government, and there are few separate governing units for schools such as the school districts which have been created in most other states.

In New York and most states to the west and south, a form of governing unit, designated as a school district, has been formed. School districts were established as government units, usually separate and distinct from county, city, town, and township government units. Sometimes the school district had common boundary lines with a city, county, or other government unit, but often it contained part or all of two or more such units or one such unit contained several school districts. School boards were established to govern the school districts and as agencies for enforcing the state laws relating to public schools. They were given the express or implied powers and duties necessary for making state laws effective.

School districts have developed in various forms to meet the needs or traditions of various states or special requirements of the districts themselves. Some school districts contain large cities such as Cleveland, Los Angeles, or Chicago; some contain all of the area within counties as in Florida, Maryland, and West Virginia, or these areas less those of certain independent city school districts as in some counties of Kentucky and Tennessee; some encompass the area of congressional townships, as in parts of Indiana, Illinois, and South Dakota; some are not identical geographically with any other unit of government, as in parts of Illinois, California, Missouri, and New York; and some are so small geographically or in population as to contain a one-teacher school only. Some years ago, in making a study of public school education in a mountain state, the author noted a school district having a single school. The school board consisted of a rancher, his wife, and his ranch hand. The wife was the teacher and held school in the ranch house. Her three children were the only pupils.

Many school districts have been continued in their original form though they do not meet present needs for the organization, administration, and operation of schools. The school district that was formed for a small pioneer settlement without highways or means of rapid conveyance and with pupils attending school during short winter terms of five or six months, is not suitable for a metropolitan center nor for a rural community having improved highways, possible bus transportation, and sufficient pupils for a high school.

Patterns of School District Organization Structure

County School Districts. In the southern states, the prevailing form of organization for the control of schools is the county school district, usually with considerable independence from the general county government. This is also true of the border states, Maryland, West Virginia, and Kentucky, and of Utah, in the West. In some southern states the members of school boards are elected from and represent magisterial districts or other subdivisions of the county, sometimes serving also as trustees of those districts for performing minor functions, subject to ratification by the whole board. Also, in some southern states, cities of specified population or class may be designated as independent school districts and operate their schools by separate boards from those of the surrounding county.

In most of the southern states considerable authority for school control is vested in the state board of education or the chief school executive officer of the state, or both. In Delaware this is the case to the extent that the system is often considered to be a state school system except for the one principal city, though there are also boards that exercise limited control over the schools in about sixteen other communities designated as districts. In Maryland the board members are appointed by the governor; in Virginia, by the city or town council or by a county electoral board appointed by the county circuit court. Utah has a county school district system except for five districts that are governed by separate boards.

Single Trustee System. In Indiana there are county school boards having limited control of schools not included in cities, but the control of township school systems, often having municipalities in them, is vested in a single school trustee who may exercise almost dictatorial powers over the schools and other township affairs. While the trustee sometimes uses the schools for the purpose of maintaining his political power, he is subject to election or re-election by the people of his township. Trustees who abuse the exercise of their powers are often voted out of office. Indiana's school system is not considered to be a county school system, for the county school board is not a board exercising major control over the schools. In the cities and many towns of Indiana, the districts are under the control of independent school boards.

Absence of Separate School Districts. In the New England states there are no school districts designated as separate corporations. Rural areas are included in the city or town organizations, and the school boards are a part of the city or town government. In spite of the fact that school boards are not in charge of separate corporations, court decisions have usually favored the independence of school committees from control by local town and city officers in matters relating to finance, school buildings, instruction, and curriculum unless city charters specifically provide for control of finances or school buildings by city or town authorities. The relative freedom from control by municipal authorities has been an evolutionary process that has come with the development of more specific and detailed state legislative requirements applicable to the school committee.

District Control with County Supervision. Each school district in the states between New York and California had a separate board for the control of each separate school, sometimes even a one-teacher school. (This is still the case in some areas.) It is by no means uncommon for school districts to have 3 school board members for only one teacher. In these states, there is usually an elected superintendent of schools for the county who is expected to perform certain professional functions for all schools of the county but who is often untrained and inexperienced in the administration of school systems and is very poorly qualified for his duties.

Overlapping High School Districts. Sometimes there is a variety of organization forms in use within a state. Such is the case in Illinois where there are small one-teacher elementary school districts, city school districts, community and township school districts, and overlapping high school districts under separate boards from those in control of the elementary school districts included in them. Most of the states do not have overlapping high school districts but have instead a common board for elementary and high schools. In such cases, school districts too small to warrant the operation of a high school depend on the larger school districts of cities and towns to furnish instruction to their high school pupils. The home school district usually pays tuition to the larger one for the number of pupils it takes each year. In a few cases no tuition charge is made, and in many cases the tuition charges are less than the actual average operating cost per pupil.

Trend toward the Consolidation of School Districts

There are wide differences in the size and number of school districts in different states. In 1950 there were only 24 school districts in Maryland, but there were 7,117 in Minnesota. In 1932 Illinois had 12,070 school districts. The number dropped to 11,061 in 1947 and has since been reduced to 4,580, but the process of consolidation has not been completed. Missouri had 8,520 school districts in 1947, and the number has since been reduced to 6,267, with the same incomplete reduction. The number of school districts is being reduced in many of the other states. In 1932 there were 127,529 school districts in the United States, in 1947 there were 104,074, and in 1950 there were 83,237 such units. These numbers include the administrative units in the New England states and in Virginia, which are not officially designated as school districts. The decrease for all states was 34.7 per cent from 1932 to 1950. Many of the school districts are small and rural, having only one or several one- or two-room schools. However, these conditions are being rapidly eliminated in the United States.

Reasons for and Obstacles to Consolidation of School Districts. Small school district administrative units are not suitable for effective administration. The employment of superintendents in school districts having 1, 10, or even 20 teachers is not warranted, and their employment in districts having even 50 or 100 teachers results in high overhead costs unless the superintendent doubles as a principal or teacher. Curriculum and instruction supervision, art and music supervision, pupil guidance, visual education, provision of special classes for atypical pupils, and even high school education cannot be furnished in very small school districts, and to furnish even poor facilities in fairly large districts is often very costly. It is only large school districts, like those including cities within their borders or those coterminous with counties, that can provide an administratively efficient and well co-ordinated school system. If a state had more than 7,000 road districts (the number of Minnesota school districts), each constructing its own roads with materials its local administrators fancied and each often disregarding the needs of the state, the road system would lack co-ordination. The operation of small school districts is almost as serious.

Small school districts should be consolidated at a much more rapid rate and in much larger units than they are at present. It has been argued that small school districts are needed to create interest in public schools, but this reasoning is fallacious. That interest in the small, inefficient schools of these districts is largely nonexistent is shown by their neglect. The greatest interest is usually manifest in the schools of cities, large towns, and large rural or combined rural-urban consolidated school districts, in which there are better school buildings, more complete library, science, music, art, and other equipment, a better educated corps of teachers, and more nearly adequate administration and supervision.

Some of the obstacles to the merging of school districts are: (1) the vested interest arising from differences in taxable wealth and the reluctance of the people in wealthier school districts to have their low tax rates increased to reduce the high taxes of poorer school districts; (2) differences in the status of the indebtedness of school districts that should be merged and the settling of the question of what jurisdiction shall pay existing debts; (3) differences in the relative values of existing school plants and needs for new plants; (4) the size, location, and quality of existing school buildings which may not be adaptable to consolidation of schools in the proposed consolidated school district; (5) city controls over some school district boards which may prevent the merging of suburban school districts with city ones as long as they obtain; and (6) the fact that a common tax rate for rural and city property represents a higher per cent of income of rural than of city property owners.

Encouraging the consolidation of school districts are: (1) a desire to improve school opportunities for children by the addition of a high school or by the provision of other advantages that a consolidated school system can afford; (2) refusal of a city to accept outside high school tuition pupils because of its own increase in school population; (3) the need of two or more school districts for additional school plant; (4) a desire to secure more high school pupils as a step toward producing better athletic teams; and (5) the desire of overburdened taxpayers from poorer school districts for an equalization of school financial support.

In any state there is need for equalization of both educational opportunity and tax support. Thousands of cases can be cited in which wealth is concentrated in one school district having few children and children are concentrated in another having little wealth. Two examples will suffice. (1) A small school district adjoining a western city has within its borders large oil storage tanks worth millions of dollars and about 40 children in its schools. School taxes are extremely low in that school district. Another adjoining school district includes a city without large property valuation. The tax rate is consequently high. (2) A school district in a central state has a one-teacher school, supported by the low rate taxes of a large manufacturing plant, part of one of the largest corporations in the United States. Two thousand workers in that plant are transported by the company six miles daily from a small city having very little property except the homes of the workmen and the shops they patronize. The tax rate is high and the families are large.

The movement for consolidation of school districts, making them large enough for economical and efficient administration and better equalizing both educational opportunity for children and the taxes paid for school support, needs to proceed more rapidly than at present.

Foundation of School District Control

Constitutional and Legislative Basis for Control. Public education is of concern to more people than are the several departments of local city or county government. It is important not only to the local community but also to the state and nation. The Federal Government abrogated any right it might have had to control education by omitting any such provision from the constitution and thus leaving control of the public schools to the states. The constitutions of the states usually provide for the specific control of public schools by their legislative bodies. Certain excerpts from state constitutions may be cited as examples of these specific provisions:

> The general assembly shall provide for the maintenance and support of a thorough and efficient system of public schools, wherein all the children of the Commonwealth above the age of six years may be educated, and shall appropriate at least one million dollars each year for that purpose. (Pennsylvania)
> A general diffusion of knowledge being essential to the preservation of the liberties and rights of the people, it shall be the duty of the Legislature of the State to establish and make suitable provisions for the support and maintenance of an efficient system of public free schools. (Texas)
> The Legislature shall provide for a uniform system of public free schools and shall provide for the liberal maintenance of the same. (Florida)

The original authority for the control of public schools lies in the states—not the nation or the local communities. School districts, as constitutional creations of the respective state legislatures, are clearly agencies of the state, created by it to make effective its education program. They are not subject to the authority of other governing units except as the legislature may determine in certain specific respects.

Delegation of Authority to Local School Districts. The legislatures of different states have delegated varying kinds and degrees of authority to their local school districts. To be successful, our form of government depends on an enlightened citizenry whose education cannot be left entirely or even largely to the whims and occasional neglect of local communities. With the exception of two or three states, school boards are selected by the people of the local school districts, or are appointed by a mayor or other local official or governing body, to represent and act for the state in maintaining public schools. Usually school districts are independent of city corporations or other government units. Except as provided specifically by law, officers of a city government have no more authority over the public schools than school boards have over city government officials.

School districts, like cities, counties, and other units of local government, have no original governing powers; they are subject to state control. They are agencies for effectuating state plans in a particular field of endeavor. The legislature of a state, except as limited by the state's constitution, has authority to regulate the power of school district officers or to destroy the school districts it has created. It may provide for the maintenance of public schools by the creation of school districts (the common practice), by the assignment of education functions to a department of a local governing agency, or by providing for the operation of public schools by the state.

In a sense, school board members may be considered to be state officers with school district jurisdiction. They are first responsible to the state for making effective the school laws of the state within the school district, and second, to the people of the school district for providing their children with the best public schools possible at a cost within the financial means of the community to supplement funds furnished by the state. Through their legislative body, the people of the state have the right to control all public schools in great detail. They control important matters such as prescribing the curriculum, certificating teachers, determining the salaries and tenure of teachers, determining how moneys shall be obtained and expended, requiring pupil attendance at school, and the like, and relatively trivial ones as well. (The relation of the school board to the state is developed further in Chapter 5.)

Place of the School District in the Hierarchy of Government Authority

The Constitution of the United States does not provide that the Federal Government shall exercise any control over public education and, therefore, its control resides in the states, but the actions of state legislatures, school authorities, and others, like the actions of all officers and private individuals, must conform to the general provisions of the Federal constitution.

Federal laws do not control education, but they sometimes impose requirements on school districts that must be met as conditions of qualification for Federal financial aid to public schools.

State constitutions usually require that the state maintain a public school system and sometimes make general or even detailed provision for the obtaining and apportioning of funds for distribution to school district authorities.

State statutes usually specify in considerable detail how public schools shall be maintained and conducted; they generally provide for school district organization and school board control; sometimes they delegate certain limited functions to city or other local government executive or legislative authorities.

Court decisions and attorney generals' opinions determine the meaning of state school laws as a basis for their enforcement.

State board of education regulations or state chief school officials' directives, varying in kind and degree according to state law, provide for the direction and control of public schools.

The rules and regulations of various state boards like those pertaining to health or motor vehicles, or the directives of state officers, such as the state treasurer or the state building inspector, impose limited controls on the school system.

The rules and regulations of local agencies (like those relating to health, police, fire, and streets) often apply to schools as well as to other public and private agencies and persons.

Local board of education by-laws, rules, and adopted policies within the framework of, and limited by, the higher controls already listed, constitute the principal bases for the control and direction of public schools.

Executive directives of the superintendent of schools and his staff are exercised within the framework of all of the preceding controls.

The authority and power of the school board are determined by the requirements and restrictions imposed on it by higher authorities. However, many of the school laws of a state are permissive and the school board may exercise discretion in making them effective in its school district. There are wide differences in the amount of state board of education or department of education control exercised over public schools, or allowed by law, ranging from very little in some states like Illinois, Iowa, Arizona, and Colorado to a great deal in other states like New York, Delaware, Louisiana, and Kentucky.

Relation of the School District to State Agencies

Within its jurisdiction, the district school board is responsible for the enforcement of state school laws, board of education rules and regulations, and the chief state school official's administrative directives. As a quasi-corporation of the state and its agent in the school district, the local board is responsible for making effective the will of the people as expressed through state laws and state agencies. The school board may employ a superintendent of schools as its executive officer, but the board is responsible for his administration. School boards should be cognizant of the fact that they are state agencies and as such must enforce the state school laws and regulations regardless of the reaction of their community.

School boards are required to enforce and observe state school laws relating to such matters as the following:

Teacher qualifications

Employment of certified teachers

Teachers' salaries

Permanent tenure of teachers

Retirement of teachers

Employment of school custodians

Inspection of school buildings and boilers

School building construction

Insurance of school buildings and busses

Consolidation of schools

Pupil transportation

Education of the blind and partially sighted

Education of the deaf and partially hearing

Education of mentally retarded children

Education of public charges

Pupil guidance and counselling

School curriculums

Vaccination of pupils

Issuance of employment certificates

Exclusion of pupils from school

Attendance of children at school

Classes for adults

School census enumeration

Employment of school medical staff

Medical inspection

Occupational placement of graduates

School lunches and cafeterias

Vocational education

Use of courses of study

Display of the flag

Observance of holidays

Minimum number of days in the school year

Closing of schools for teachers' conventions

Free textbooks and school supplies

Obtaining money for the financial support of public schools

School budgeting

Payment and collection of tuition

Uniform accounting procedure

Issuance of school bonds

State reimbursement of expenses to school districts

Reports as a basis for distribution of state funds

Maintenance of kindergartens and junior colleges

Reports to the state department of education

There are many other laws of both major and minor significance. All of them must be enforced by the school board or be applied at the board's discretion, according to the provisions of law.

States vary widely in the provisions they make for the enforcement of school laws above the district level, but most of them have established a state board of education and a position of chief state school executive, under various titles. Appropriate funds for the support of a state department of education headed by the state school executive help to make the state's control of the public schools effective. In some states the legislative body or constitution has delegated a considerable quantity of power to the state agencies and the district boards. In other states the legislatures have attempted to enact many controlling laws and to leave less discretion to the state and local agencies. Because some educational conditions change, it is much better in many areas for a state board, administrative officer, and department to make the rules and regulations relating to school control than for them to be enacted into law. As an example, the school laws of many states are cluttered with obsolete provisions concerning the certification of teachers.

Usually, state education agencies require reports from local school systems on various fiscal, vital, personnel, and other matters. These agencies compile and disseminate statistics and other information concerning the schools of the state, apportion state school moneys, administer laws relating to requirements for reimbursements from federal and state funds, issue teachers' certificates, furnish general supervision for the curriculum and instruction, disseminate information concerning the applications of the laws of the state, furnish visual education material, library books, textbooks, and supplies, and render many other services to the public schools.

District school boards must maintain certain relations with such state boards and offices as the board of health, the state auditor, the state treasurer, and the state librarian. They should also be willing to co-operate with teachers colleges and other institutions of higher education in providing public school facilities for research and practice teaching. Alternatively, they should secure the services of these institutions as aids in the inservice training of new teachers. Above all, school boards will find it advisable to maintain contacts with their state senators and representatives; to discuss school legislation with them; and to lend them whatever help they can in the preparation of educational bills for legislative action.

CHAPTER 4

Autonomy Versus Dependency
for School Boards

Derivation of School District Authority

After what has been shown in preceding chapters, it is clear that school district authority as exercised by the school board is derived from the state legislature and in no sense from city, county, or other local governments. Educators generally accept this view, and it is widely accepted by the courts. Political scientists, in their desire to co-ordinate under centralized control what appear to them to be local government functions, sometimes question the fact that education is a state function and the school district an agency of the state. More often, they question the desirability of the existing relationship between the school district and city governments. They sometimes argue that educa- tion should be a function of local city or county government and that separate school districts should be abolished. They point to the fact that cities and counties as well as school districts are creatures of state constitutional or statutory law and maintain that there is no need for duplicated government units. They maintain that the legislatures should have made public educa- tion a function of local government.

Some courts have argued that education should be a general government function. One court held that "the board of educa- tion, although invested with certain limited corporate powers, should be one of the departments of city government, much like a board of public works or park commissioners."[1] However, it will be noted that even this court did not hold that the board was such a department. Hundreds of courts have held that the board was not such a department. In those cases in which the legislatures have seen fit to grant limited powers over school boards to city, county, or other local government authorities, the boards are subject to dual control—state and local government authority. Service under dual authority is extremely undesirable.

Fiscal Autonomy in School Districts

The *Dictionary of Education* distinguishes between fiscally independent and fiscally dependent school systems as follows:

> *Fiscally independent system:* a school system in which the state has delegated to the board of education complete authority in all matters pertaining to the financial management of public schools, the board having the power to determine the amount of the budget and to levy or cause to be levied taxes to raise the required funds.[2]
>
> *Fiscally dependent system:* a school system in which the board of education cannot make estimates and decisions in financial matters without the approval of and control by municipal authorities.[2]

A study was made by the National Education Association[3] of 1,892 cities above 2,500 population, about one-half of the total number of such cities. In 54 per cent of these cities budgets were made and adopted by the school boards without review by any city, county, or other local government authority. In 18 per cent the review by the council, mayor, manager, auditor, treasurer, or other local government authority was found to be a mere formality, and the authority had no power to modify the budget as submitted. Thus, in 72 per cent of the city school districts reporting, the school board had final authority to adopt its budget. In the thousands of noncity school districts, there

[1] Winona v. School District, 40 Minn. 13; 14 N. W. 539.
[2] By permission, from *Dictionary of Education,* Carter V. Good, Editor. Copyright, 1945. McGraw-Hill Book Co., Inc.
[3] National Education Association. Research Division. "Fiscal Authority of City School Boards." In *Research Bulletin,* April 1950.

is seldom outside control over school budgets. In fact, many small school districts make no formal school budgets.

Most school boards, even in cities, are fiscally independent. This is even more generally true in small city and rural school districts. The courts usually hold that the school board has full authority to determine its budget and expenditures unless the laws of the state provide otherwise. Even in Massachusetts, where there are no school districts and the town school committees are considered to be a part of local government, no town authority may revise the school committee's budget, though it is submitted to a finance or advisory committee which makes recommendations for action by the people in town meeting.

The school board usually directs the tax levying authority of the county, city, or town to levy the school tax at a rate high enough, when applied to the total valuation of taxable property within the school district, to yield the amount required from property taxes (as shown by its adopted budget) for the support of the schools. School boards seldom either levy or collect taxes. It is not necessary for them to perform such mechanical functions to be fiscally independent. The fact that a school board can determine its expenditures budget and its actual expenditures without the amounts being subject to modification or approval by any authority of another local government unit makes the board fiscally independent.

Often the schools will be better served if the members of a fiscally independent school board are elected by popular vote instead of being appointed by the mayor. Then they will be truly independent and the board can be held fully responsible by the people for both the quality of the schools and the amount of money expended for their support. On the other hand, a fiscally dependent board is sometimes better able to serve the schools if the members are appointed on a nonpolitical basis, by the mayor with the approval of the council. In this instance, the mayor and council will have more confidence in the estimates of budget requirements presented by their appointees than would be the case if the members were popularly elected.

Then responsibility for the schools and expenditure requirements can be located in the city authorities who, in a fiscally dependent school district, finally adopt the budget and also appoint the school board members.

Property Ownership and Management
Autonomy in School Districts

School districts or their boards usually hold title to real estate: (1) on which school buildings have been constructed; (2) that has been obtained for the purpose of school use, such as playgrounds or athletic fields; (3) that has been obtained for possible future school building sites; and (4) that has served as sites for abandoned school buildings. Usually deeds are held by the school district unless they have been lost, as is sometimes the case. In any event, title is generally registered in the name of the school district or its board. In some school districts, usually embracing cities or towns, real estate is held in the name of the city or town for school use. In such instances, the municipal officials sometimes select the sites and contract for the construction of the school buildings. Mistakes in the location and construction of buildings for school use are often made in any case, but they seem to occur more often when school buildings are located and planned by city authorities.

An example of an extremely bad plan for physical plant construction and management is that of a certain Massachusetts city. Bonds are issued and school building construction contracts are let by city authorities. The property is held for school use in the name of the city. The need for repairs is determined by a city building inspector, and school buildings are maintained by a city maintenance department. The operation and care of school buildings is under the direction of the school board but not of the superintendent of schools. Such decentralized and unco-ordinated controls result in: friction between the school janitors, who sometimes ruin building parts with the wrong kind of cleaning materials, and the maintenance department of the city that has to repair or replace the parts; between principals and janitors as to jurisdiction and limits of authority; and between the school board and the city authorities over requirements for school building maintenance, location of school buildings, and features of school building plans.

Such disorganization and dispersal of authority over related and interdependent activities is costly both in money and educational results. No one can be held responsible for the resultant bad relationships, least of all the superintendent of schools, who controls no activity connected with school buildings except their use during the school day. The fault lies in poor organization for control and poor location of responsibility. The school authorities should have autonomy in all matters pertaining to the physical plant. This covers the issuance of voted bonds by the school board, the ownership of property by the school district, and complete management of the physical plant by persons responsible to the superintendent in accordance with policies adopted by the school board.

In the National Education Association study,[4] it was shown that the title to school property was vested in the school district in 80 per cent of the 1,892 school districts responding and in the other 20 per cent, in the cities and towns. In 76 per cent, the school board selected school building sites; in another 10 per cent it did so subject to approval by some local government agency; and in another 11 per cent it did so subject to approval by the voters. In only 3 per cent of the school districts were sites selected by an authority other than the school board. In 91 per cent of these school districts the school board had full authority to plan school buildings, and in 4 per cent it had such authority subject to approval by some local government agency. In 99 per cent of the cases school plants were maintained by the school board. In 62 per cent of the districts the school board was authorized to issue school bonds on its own authority; in 13 per cent it might do so after approval by the voters; in 6 per cent it might do so after approval by some local agency; and

[4] *Ibid.*

in 19 per cent the authority to issue school bonds resided in some other local government authority, with no power vested in the school board.

Education Autonomy in School Districts

Almost invariably, the school laws of the state give school boards autonomy, subject to the requirements of law, in matters relating directly to instruction, such as the authority to determine school curricula, to decide upon teacher qualification requirements above state requirements, to fix teachers' salaries, to select teachers, and often to furnish free textbooks.

Arguments for School District Autonomy

The proponents of full autonomy for school boards argue that the board should be entirely free from control by officers or agencies of city, town, county, or other government unit. Some of these arguments are as follows:

Public Education a State Function. Since public education is a state, not a local, function, to vest authority over the public schools in a city council or other agency extraneous to the school district places a barrier between the school board and the state. This may make it difficult for the school board to perform fully the state function for which it exists. It is the school board, not the city council, that is responsible for enforcing the state school laws. Furthermore, the state furnishes a large proportion of the funds required for the financial support of public schools. State school funds should not be made subject to possible indirect diversion from school support to other local government purposes. There might be a tendency for city authorities to reduce the amount of local school support and increase the amount of support for nonschool government functions when state funds for public schools are increased. This would defeat the purpose of the state in increasing the amount of state support of schools.

The state's interest in the separation of the school district from city or county government has been expressed in two of many similar court opinions as follows:

> Such boards are agencies of the state for the organization, administration and control of the public school system of the state, separate and apart from the usual political and governmental functions of other subdivisions of the state. The fact that certain officers of other subdivisions may be delegated some duties of authority in relation thereto does not change the status or destroy the separate identity of the school district.[5]

> The decision is by no means controlling upon the question of whether the repairs of school buildings constitute a local municipal affair. It does, however, indicate that through all the years the legislature has zealously guarded against a merger of school affairs with ordinary municipal affairs. It clearly indicates a legislative understanding that there was nothing in common between school matters and the ordinary municipal affairs, but, on the contrary, they constitute distinct and separate fields. . . . If the field of legislation upon the subject of education belongs to the state, it belongs to it entirely. If the cause of education is not a subject of municipal regulation, the municipality cannot touch it or interfere with it in the slightest degree. School buildings are an essential agency of the state's educational scheme, and to allow municipalities a voice in the construction, repair, control, or management of the school buildings within their borders is to yield to them the power to frustrate the state's plan in promoting education throughout the state. . . . These considerations lead irresistibly to the conclusion that, although the boundaries of a school district may be coterminous with the boundaries of a city, there is no merger of the school district affairs with the city affairs.[6]

If education is a state function, there should be no local government authority between the school board and the state or the board cannot be held responsible to the state for making effective its school laws.

Education Planning and Continuity of Policies. Complete independence of control from city or town governing agencies permits a school board to plan and more fully to realize its plans for the provision and improvement of schools. If a school board

---

[5] Cline v. Martin, 94 Ohio 420; 115 N. E. 37.

[6] State ex rel. Harback v. Mayor et al. of the City of Milwaukee, 189 Wis. 84; 206 N. W. 210.

must depend on a city council or other agency, it cannot expect to realize plans it may desire to make. Of necessity, it must operate its schools on a monthly or yearly basis, because any plans may be frustrated by the agency upon which such a board has to depend. The school budget represents the board's education plan in terms of expenditures. If it can be changed by persons not responsible for the education of children the school board may be frustrated in making its plans effective. Continuity of policy cannot be secured without plans and ability to make them effective. Without control of its budget or of the construction and management of its school buildings, a school board cannot plan for the future.

Full Autonomy Necessary for the Exercise of Education Authority. Most school boards have full fiscal and physical plant authority. This is necessary if they are to exercise the educational authority vested in them by law. Only if they have full authority can they accept complete responsibility for educational results, for school taxes levied and expenditures made, and for furnishing and maintaining appropriate physical plant facilities. Full educational autonomy is impossible if another agency controls either finances or the physical plant.

Fixing of Responsibility. Just as the school board cannot accept responsibility without authority, neither can it be held fully responsible for its decisions or results if its actions are made in deference to those of a city authority exercising higher control. For example, if the school board should request funds to establish kindergartens and the city council should strike out the item, or even deduct it from the budget total, the board would be unable to establish kindergartens. Or it could do so only by substituting expenditures for kindergartens for some other budget item or items. If an outside agency is authorized to eliminate amounts from the budget, it, rather than the school board, determines curricula, the qualifications and pay of teachers, when out-of-date textbooks can be changed for new ones, and the like. For example, if it does not have fiscal independence, the board may not be able to add a course in automobile driving for pupils 16 years of age, to pay salaries high enough to employ teachers with masters' degrees, or to install visual education equipment. It is impossible for a board to exercise educational authority without fiscal and property autonomy.

Whom should the people hold responsible for the conduct of the schools? There can be responsibility only if there is authority. If a board is permitted to determine the school budget, finally and irrevocably, and the tax levy to support it, and to construct its budget in the light of the professional advice it deems wise to accept and the desires of the people as it interprets them, and if it has full control over the school plant, then it can be held fully responsible for the quality of the schools, the adequacy of the facilities, and the tax rate and school expenditures. If school finances are controlled by city authorities the school board will be encouraged to, and logically can, "pass the buck" to the city authorities. The city authorities may pass the blame back to the school board. Thus, there can be endless attempted shifting of responsibility. It is fortunate that, in most school districts, school boards have fiscal, property, and educational autonomy and assume full responsibility for the conduct of the schools under their jurisdiction.

Incompetency of Outside Authorities to Determine School Budget Requirements. City and town councils or other authorities are not competent to determine budgetary requirements for a school system. They do not have the background of school experience and do not know the relative importance of items requiring the expenditure of school funds. A board elected for the control and direction of public schools should be more competent to pass on expenditure requirements than a body or person selected for the control of the functions of city or town government.

Action on Professional Advice. The superintendent of schools is the executive officer of the school board. The members of the board are accustomed to evaluating his recommendations and advice and acting on them as they see fit. A city or town legislative board or executive authority does not have the services of this professional education authority and his staff of administrators. If it does call upon him, it cannot secure full information as to the reasons for his recommendations in a half day conference. Moreover, the superintendent is not the executive officer of such a person or group and his recommendations are likely to be viewed with suspicion by a municipal authority because of its incompetence to make valid judgments on matters relating to the public schools. City authorities are inexperienced in weighing relative values in the field of public education.

Keeping the Schools Free from City Politics. It is important that the schools be kept free from the evil influences that city politics sometimes exert and that they be exempt from the promotional schemes of political parties. It is even more important that the schools are not used by political parties for patronage or graft. Incompetent and "hard boiled" teachers should not be appointed on the basis of political party affiliation. The influence of such a teacher is a permanent loss to the pupils who attend his classes. A school board which is subservient to a city council or mayor may be impelled to appoint as teachers or principals poorly qualified relatives and friends of politicians.

Preparing a True School Budget. Lack of school board responsibility, arising from failure to vest full authority in the school board, leads to the making of extravagant budget requests. A board dependent on a city agency expects whatever budget it submits to be reduced regardless of its soundness, because that agency will be incapable of evaluating the school requirements. It is natural under such conditions for the school board to increase requests for selected items or to include items that are educationally less essential than others but which may appeal to the city evaluating authority. The city council believes the school budget to be loaded, whether or not such is the case, but it does not know in what items or by how much. It arbitrarily reduces the budget from the amount requested. The whole process is unbusinesslike. Only the fixing of all responsibility in the school board, as is the practice in most school districts that include cities and in practically all others, will make businesslike procedures possible.

Economy in Expenditures. It is sometimes maintained that action on a school board's budget request forces economy, but cutting off the fat from a budget request that has been constructed to allow for such cutting is not real economy, even if the council, mayor, or board of estimates could distinguish fat from sinew. Such blind reduction may lead to extravagance. In explaining its reductions, the city authority shows what amounts requested it considers to be excessive or unnecessary. This makes it difficult for the school board to transfer amounts from less essential items to those that have been eliminated or reduced by the city authority. Real economy requires that the essentiality and desirability of competing materials or services be weighed and that expenditures be made for those most needed.

Without full authority and responsibility, a school board may be inclined to "play to the grandstand" and to plan more than the school district can afford and more than the city authority can permit it to achieve. The reduction is only false economy. School boards that act independently have less reason to be extravagant than boards that depend on an outside authority to curb them. Responsibility makes a school board more careful in determining the objects of expenditures. It is logical to assume that there will be greater economy if the spending agency is also the tax determining agency, responsible to the people for its expenditures.

Competition with City Departments for Funds. In the pressures brought by spending agencies for funds, the schools are at a disadvantage compared with city departments. The school "department" is larger than any of the others and, in number of employees and expenditure requirements, sometimes as large as all of them combined. Yet each agency has equal voice in presenting its budget to the city approval agency. The full significance of the difference in size is seldom appreciated by a city council or other agency that passes on all budget requests.

It is often easier to make a reduction in the budget of a large spending agency than in those of many small ones, though the large agency may actually be less extravagant than the small ones.

Control beyond Jurisdiction. Those who advocate that school boards should be dependent fiscally or otherwise upon city authorities neglect to consider the fact that city and school district boundary lines are usually not coterminous. A part of a city is often in one or more outlying school districts. In such a case it would have to be determined whether the city authority would exercise control over one school district or over two or more. Also, a school district often includes areas outside the periphery of the city, extending into suburban areas that may be essentially a part of the metropolitan area but have not been incorporated into the city.

In such cases a question may be raised regarding the propriety and fairness of a law that places a city council, mayor, or other city authority in control of areas outside the city. The people of these areas have no voice in the selection of city officials. The right of city authorities to determine school taxes and school expenditures in the areas outside the city might well be questioned. Yet the budget must be for the whole school district because the schools near the city boundary line serve pupils outside and inside the city limits. Persons living outside the city but within the school district might well challenge the right of city authorities to determine their school taxes. This may be one of the important reasons that most school districts are governed independently of the cities and towns included in them.

Kansas City, Missouri, may be cited as an example of the differences in territory included in city and school district corporations. In 1940 there were about 57¾ square miles in the city and about 58 square miles in the school district, but, in spite of the approximate equality of the areas, there was a considerable difference in them. The school district included parts of the suburbs at various places and frequent changes were made in these areas. The district operated schools for pupils outside the city limits but within the school district. On the other hand, a fairly large area of the city was not in the school district and was operated under a separate board as School District 15.

Arguments against School District Autonomy

Some of the arguments advanced for making the school board a regular department of city, town, or county government, subject to the same fiscal and physical plant control as the other city departments, are as follows:

Education a Local Function. It is maintained that education is historically (and in theory ought to be) a local function, just as police, public health, and public works are such. It is maintained that the work of these agencies affects the whole state just as does education. They are concerned with local people and have local financial support just as do the public schools. Public schools are administered by boards from the local community just as are some other local government agencies.

Education in a Commission or City Manager Form of Government. If the public schools were in a commission or city manager form of government, they would be removed from the undesirable influences of city partisan politics, as would be the case for all departments. The superintendent of schools would be selected by a commissioner in charge of education or the city manager. Such a man would be more able than an elected school board to select a superintendent, qualified not only in the field of education but also in business and physical plant management.

Department Status for Education Theoretically Sound. There is no reason to believe the schools will be better if school boards have complete autonomy. They might be equally good as a department of the city government, but, assuming that schools would be better under independent boards, that would not be a controlling reason for such boards. The same argument for independence from city, town, or county government might

as logically be applied to all local functions of government—
health, parks, public works, fire, police, and others. Carried to
its logical extreme, each function of local government would be
operated directly under the legislature as a state function and no
local government would remain.

Application of Business Methods to School Administration.
If the schools are a department of city government, there will be
closer co-operation with other city departments, thus promoting
economy. The city health department would be better able to
serve the schools and there would not need to be a duplication
of health services. The city purchasing agency could purchase
for the schools more economically than a separate school agency,
thus avoiding more duplication. The same could be done for
storage of supplies, centralized accounting, building maintenance, and other duplicated functions.

Duplication of Taxing Agencies. There should be but one
tax determining authority in a city. With two such authorities
independently requiring the levy of separate taxes, one or the
other may levy an unjustifiable proportion of the tax upon the
assessed property of the city. When there are two city taxing
authorities there is competition for tax moneys, and the total
taxes levied may be so high as to constitute an unwarranted burden on the property of the city. The same argument applies to
separate school and county tax determining authorities.

*Prevention of Educational Encroachment on the Financing
of Other City Functions.* It is often held that a single authority
can better weigh the needs of local agencies to determine their
relative budgetary requirements. The argument for making
the operation of public schools a local function to prevent its
encroachment upon the requirements for financial support of
other city functions may be stated in a quotation of the following court opinion:

> The board of education is dealing with a special subject.
> It is necessary for it to visualize the future educational neces-
> sities of the city and to plan to meet such necessities. On
> the other hand, the common council is the fiscal authority of the
> city. It knows and understands the financial conditions of the

city and the general municipal problems imposing burdens upon the taxpayers. Exorbitant demands on the board of education might very well make it impossible to carry forward other municipal undertakings of the greatest importance. There is sound policy in centralizing the taxing authority where a proper balance and proportion may be fixed and maintained in the matter of tax levies for all municipal purposes. . . . All of these provisions and others might be cited to indicate the legislative purposes that school affairs shall constitute a municipal function in cities, and that the board of education is merely a city agency the same as is the board of public works.[7]

Organization Trend. The general trend in organization of government agencies is toward the elimination of special boards, taxing units, and separate tax levies for separate government functions such as libraries, streets, parks, and the like. The principle that applies to these agencies also applies to separate tax levies for schools. There is much interdependence between the public schools and various departments of local government.

Co-operative Relations of School Districts with Other Local Government Units

Even though the boundary lines of cities or towns and school districts may not be coterminous, the major part of one is usually the major part of the other with regard to population, property, and often area. In spite of the independence of school corporations, they must comply with city or town ordinances and the regulations of other local government departments in the particular areas in which each exercises authority. Even though the school and the city, town, or county governments are usually separate, there are many services the local government units must or can render for the school system and some that the school system must or can render to local government units or to the people who are common to both. (The necessarily close relationships between city agencies and the school system could

[7] State ex rel. Board of Education v. City of Racine et al., 205 Wis. 389; 236 N. W. 553.

be considered as an additional argument for the school district's being made a department of city government.)

The schools sometimes furnish certain services to the people of the city or town. Among these are programs of athletic, music, dramatic, and forensic entertainment; occupational placement service for high school students or graduates; one or more adult education programs; school building facilities for elections; adult recreation programs and meetings of community groups; summer playgrounds on school property or in city parks; and above all, their main function of conducting schools for the education of the children and youth of the municipality.

Among the many ways in which cities or towns sometimes perform services for the public schools are the following:

The city health department often furnishes to the children of the schools physical and medical examinations, disease prevention services, and to some extent, treatment services, including dental, optical, and other special, as well as general, ones.

The city welfare department often supplies medical services, clothing, food, and sometimes school lunch tickets for children referred to it by the school attendance and health departments.

School facilities are not only used by the city recreation department, but facilities such as swimming pools, athletic fields, and parks adjoining school grounds are often made available for school use.

City libraries often furnish special services to the schools, such as traveling libraries, book reserve shelves, children's reading rooms, and circulating audiovisual materials. Museums and zoological parks are sometimes used by schools for instruction materials.

The police department often furnishes policemen to guard busy corners at times when pupils are coming to or leaving school. They sometimes provide special night guard service for school buildings and often are on hand to prevent disorder at athletic contests.

The fire departments of some cities hold fire drills in schools and inspect school buildings for fire hazards. They recharge fire extinguishers, inspect sprinkling systems and fire escapes, and have fire plugs and fire alarms located in or near school buildings.

Streets, sidewalks, and sewers along school property are sometimes constructed and maintained at city or county expense, though often the school district is charged for the expenditures. Sometimes the cities and counties help the schools by constructing or maintaining roads needed for school bus routes. Sometimes departments of streets remove snow from roads and sidewalks on school grounds.

In the few cities in which property used by schools is deeded to the city instead of to the school district, it is usual for the city to insure the school property, in a blanket policy, along with other city property, as a charge against the city.

In some school districts water and electricity are furnished free to the schools.

Sometimes garbage and trash are removed from school grounds by city departments without charge against the school district, as is also the case for taxpaying residents.

City planning commissions often assist in the location of school buildings, as should be the case, and they should always be consulted. Sometimes they determine locations which are not always advantageous to the school district since they may give more weight to factors other than location for proper school use or may not provide adequate ground area for school uses.

School board rooms and administration offices are often furnished in city or county buildings without charge to the school district.

Sometimes civil service agencies of cities classify custodial, maintenance, clerical, and similar positions for the school district.

Usually the city pays most or all of the expense of holding school elections within the city limits when held at the same time as city and other elections. The elections in any school district territory outside the city limits or at different times from the general elections may be held at the expense of the school board.

The office of the attorney of the city or county sometimes provides the school board with legal services, such as interpretation of the law and advice, drafting and reviewing contracts and other legal papers, and, if the school system is a department of the city government, conducting suits for the board.

In some cities purchasing, accounting, and some other school business functions are performed by the city for the school district. To be successful for the schools, the city purchasing department must purchase school supplies in accordance with specifications prepared by the professional education staff. City accounting for the school system should be such as has been designed for furnishing information for the required Federal and state school reports so that it will not have to be duplicated by the school authorities.

The city or county tax collector usually collects taxes for the school district as well as for other government units. Assessing of property for taxation is also performed by city or county assessors.

The treasurer of the city or county often serves as the treasurer of school district funds, to the advantage of the school system.

Some of the services listed as being performed for the schools are really performed for the agencies themselves. The departments of health, welfare, library, recreation, and some others merely find the schools convenient places to perform their own functions—places where these functions need to be performed. On the other hand, charges should be made against independent school districts for the construction of streets and sidewalks along or on school property, for electricity and water used, for use of city buildings for administrative offices, and the like. This should be done to secure proper allocation of expenses and for cost accounting, if for no other reason. It is difficult to draw a line between what should be furnished free and what at cost, but allocation should be made as accurately as possible.

CHAPTER 5

The Legal Status of School Boards

Limitation of Treatment of the School
Board's Legal Status

A chapter on the legal status of school boards obviously cannot deal with all phases of the subject. The subject is so vast as to defy complete treatment in any single volume. There are the varying provisions of the laws relating to public schools in the different states; the vast bodies of court decisions and legal opinions relating to public schools, school boards, and school districts in each of the forty-eight states; and books dealing with particular phases of the legal status of schools and their administration, operation, and control. Particular reference is made to several doctors' dissertations on the legal phases of these matters. Many of the handbooks and manuals of state school board associations deal with the legal status of school boards applicable to a particular state. Anyone especially interested in the legal status of school boards should pursue the subject beyond the limitations of this chapter. Some of the legal provisions that are valid in one state may not necessarily apply to another. Exceptions to court decisions and laws and fine points of discrimination cannot be indicated in a chapter presenting only a brief statement of the subject, though they may be important. This chapter is only a statement of some of the important elements of the legal status of school boards in general and not an exhaustive or authoritative treatise for all states, under all conditions.

Foundation of the Board's Legal Status

The first basis for the legal status of school boards is the constitution of each state which vests public school control in its legislative body. Some constitutions also contain certain detailed provisions for functions of public school operation and control, such as: the formation of county, town, and other types of school districts; the election of a state superintendent of public instruction; the appointment of a state board of education; restrictions on the investment of certain permanent school funds; the method of distribution of state funds for operation of schools or capital outlays; and various others.

The second basis for the legal status of school boards is the body of state school laws. These vary widely with regard to the amount of detail in which the state exercises legal control. The nature and degree of statutory controls vary: (1) according to the traditions of the state in the development of its public schools, such as that of town control in the New England states or of county control in the southern states; (2) according to the number and size of school districts, from the relatively few districts in states that have county units to the thousands of single school units in some of the central states; (3) according to provisions made for flexible control by a state board of education and a popularly elected or appointed state school executive; and (4) according to particular problems that have arisen in the past, due to geographic, economic, social, or other features of the state.

The third basis for the legal status of school boards concerns the decisions of courts, particularly within the same state where they were rendered. There are many court decisions relating to school boards, school districts, and the public schools. As a rule there is fairly good agreement among the decisions on closely similar matters, but there are sometimes varying opinions due to differences in statutory laws, differences in the circumstances and origins of cases on which decisions have been rendered, and, in spite of the attempts of judges to make decisions objectively, sometimes due to experiences or biases of judges.

It is the duty of the courts to interpret the laws. It is their purpose to be fair and just on grounds of reason and logic. They try to protect the interests of the public in so far as such action is consistent with law. They respect the discretionary powers of school boards and do not, themselves, determine educational policies, even though a board's action may appear to have been inadvisable. For example, a court will not overrule a board's decision respecting qualifications or salaries of teachers or of subjects to be taught if the decision is in conformity with the laws of the state. The decisions of the board are regarded as final by the court unless it is shown that the board has abused its discretionary powers or has acted outside the limits of its legal authority.

The courts aim to give full recognition to the authority which the legislature has vested in the board and require only that the board shall have acted in good faith under the terms of the law and in the interest of the public. When there is any doubt as to the application of a law, the courts usually construe it as favoring public rather than private interest. When a question of the meaning of the law is at issue, they try to discover its purpose from the events that called for its enactment and from those events to determine its meaning. They interpret the meaning with the objective of making effective the intent of the legislature.

The constitution, statutes, and court decisions on matters relating to public schools, school boards, and school districts constitute the foundations of the legal status of school boards.

School Board as a State Agency

It was previously shown that school districts are often considered to be agencies of the state of which they are a part and that they have been created by the state legislature for the specific purpose of making effective that body's plan for fulfilling the state's constitutional obligation to provide public schools for its children. Though the board members are elected by the people of the school district, or sometimes appointed by city officers, their duty as a board is to make effective the state laws relating to public schools and the rules and regulations of the state education agencies. The school board has authority to transact business only within the limits authorized by law and to perform the actions necessary to make the laws effective. The school board has no other legal function than to act for the state in providing the kind of education required or permitted by the state within the school district.

Even if a city charter provides that city officers shall be empowered to exercise certain control over the school board, those officers can exercise only such authority as is specifically delegated to them by the legislature, and the school board is still an agent of the state. The fact that in some cities the members of school boards are appointed by the mayor or city council does not lodge control in such officer or agency and has theoretically nothing to do with the independence of their actions. In practice, however, it sometimes produces subserviency of the board to the appointing authority.

The view that school boards are agents of the state, rather than of a city, town, or county, has been upheld in numerous court opinions upon which decisions have been based. It has been held that "A board of education is a distinct corporation and not an agent of the city," [1] and that "The board of education and municipal government are distinct entities." [2] In Connecticut[3] it was maintained that the state has the duty of providing for the education of children and in an Arkansas case[4] that the mandate of the constitution of that state, requiring the maintenance "of public schools throughout the state, is directed to the legislature of the entire state and not to any political sub-

[1] Titusville Iron Co. v. New York, 207 N. Y. 203; 100 N. E. 806.
[2] Wichita v. Board of Education, 92 Kan. 967.
[3] Walsh v. Hine, 59 Conn. 50.
[4] State v. A. T. & S. F. R. R., 28 Ark. 84.

division." One court[5] very emphatically held that the election of board members by the electors of a city does not make them "city officers," and that "when seated . . . they become, and thenceforward are, officers of a political subdivision of the state, separate and distinct from the municipality within the boundaries of which the school district is located." A Kentucky court[6] held that "every common school district in the state, whether it be located in a populous city or in a sparsely settled rural district, is a state institution, protected, controlled, and regulated by the state, and . . . the fact that the state has appointed agencies such as fiscal courts, school trustees, and municipal bodies to aid it in the collection of taxes for the maintenance of these schools does not deprive them of their state character." It has been held[7] that school taxes are raised "for state purposes, viz., public education" and that[8] "all common schools are state, not local institutions, and the people of the whole state are concerned in everything that affects any one of them either for good or evil." In a Michigan case[9] it was held that, even though the city treasurer collects school taxes, he does so, not for the city, but for the school district as a matter of convenience and to avoid a "multiplicity of officers." It was held in an Indiana case[10] that "every school that has been established owes its existence to legislation; and every school officer owes his authority to the state."

School Board as a Corporation or Quasi-Corporation

In most respects school boards are corporations or "artificial persons" having limited, specified powers of action. They have

[5] Ward v. San Diego School District et al., 203 California 712; 265 Pac. 821.
[6] City of Louisville v. Board of Education of the City of Louisville, 154 Ky. 316.
[7] North Vernon Lumber Co. v. City of Louisville, 161 Ky. 467.
[8] Williams v. Board of Education of Stanton Common School District, 173 Ky. 708.
[9] School District of the City of Lansing v. City of Lansing, 260 Mich. 405; 245 N. W. 449.
[10] State v. Howarth, 122 Ind. 462.

perpetual succession, employ persons, make contracts, may sue and be sued on contracts, may usually purchase and hold title to property in the name of the school district, may sell and give deed to property, may rent or lease property, and may make rules and regulations to govern their own procedures and those of the schools under their jurisdiction. As a corporation, a school board is a continuing body, and, even though membership frequently changes, such changes do not negate any prior obligations the board may have assumed. The statutes sometimes designate school districts as public corporations or the board as a corporate body. For example, in Maryland, the law provides that "The county board of education [is] hereby declared to be a body politic and corporate. . . ."

The school district and its board constitutes a peculiar kind of corporation, more properly designated as a quasi-corporation, or a body that acts as a corporation, according to numerous court opinions. For example, it was held by a court[11] that "Trustees of schools are a corporation, or more strictly a quasi-corporation, for the purpose and with the sole and only power of acting on matters pertaining to the public schools . . . and all other business is foreign to the object for which they were created a body corporate." It was held by another court[12] that "A city school district comprising the outlying territory of the city and certain contiguous outlying lands is a distinct corporate entity of quasi-municipal character, which is not lost or merged in that of the city." A Pennsylvania court[13] expressed the opinion that a school district constitutes a body corporate as a municipal quasi-corporation; it is the agency of the state for the performance of prescribed government functions; it was created and is maintained for the sole purpose of administering the state's system of public education.

Quasi-corporations are political divisions of a state, created by the state legislature to carry out some specified purpose of the

[11] People v. Dupuyt, 71 Ill. 651.
[12] Los Angeles School District v. Longdon, 148 California 380; 83 Pac. 248.
[13] Borough of Wilkinsburg v. School District of Wilkinsburg, 74 Atlantic Reporter 2d. 138; 365 Pa. 254.

state with authority to exercise only such specific powers as have been granted to them by law and such general or discretionary powers as they find to be permitted by law and necessary in fulfilling the special purpose for which they exist. One court[14] stated as its opinion that "quasi-corporations are created for a public purpose as an agency of state through which they can most conveniently and effectively discharge the duties of the state, as an organized government, to every person and by which they can best promote the welfare of all." Quasi-corporations are not permitted to exercise authority or powers unrelated to or unnecessary in performing the functions of the state for which they were created. As a quasi-corporation, a school board has the limited powers granted to it by statute or required of it to carry out its statutory powers. Within the limits of the state constitution, the legislature can exercise almost unlimited authority over its creature, the school board. As a state agency the school board possesses no inherent powers and, being unable to add to or deduct from its responsibilities, powers, and limitations, a school board is strictly the state's agent.

Structure of the School District Corporation

The structure of the school district corporation may be compared with the structure of an industrial corporation. The people of the school district, or more properly of the state, are the stockholders; the school board is the board of directors, representing and acting for the stockholders; the superintendent of schools is comparable to the president or other executive officer of the industrial corporation; the assistant superintendents, supervisors of instruction, business manager, physical plant manager, and other members of the administrative staff have their counterparts in the industrial corporation; the teachers, custodians, mechanics, and other employees are the workers; and the product is educated boys and girls. Of course the school district corporations do not all have equally high standards of produc-

[14] Galveston v. Posnornsky, 62 Tex. 118.

tion, and they are not operated for monetary profit as are industrial corporations. If the school system is a good one, the product will have a sound basic preparation for life physically, socially, emotionally, and intellectually. Some school districts will produce more or less inferior products. The responsibility for the quality of the products rests largely with the board of directors, the abilities of its executive and administrative staffs, and the skills of the workers employed.

School Board—a Continuing Body

A school board is a continuing body with changing membership. The board has the power to execute contracts and they are binding not only on the board as constituted at the time the contract is made but also on the board as it may be constituted in the future, after membership has been changed. The contract is with the board, as the representative of the people, in charge of the school district and not with the members thereof. This is true even if the entire membership of the board should be changed by the election of an opposing faction. The contract of a board, whose members have been replaced, is enforceable against succeeding boards until the terms of the contract have been satisfied. Also, adopted policies or rules and regulations are valid and must be observed by the board, employees, and patrons of the schools so long as they have not been repealed by the board. There have been some contrary opinions by the courts in the case of the lapse of a considerable period of time, but these opinions hinged on the time element rather than the change of membership.

Legal Status of the Powers, Duties, and Authority of School Boards

The powers, duties, and authority of school boards differ somewhat from state to state, but in general they are much alike. In some states more are specified than in others where the functions are performed under laws of more general application or with fewer restrictions. The statutes of the states specify many major and minor duties, functions, powers, responsibilities for, and restrictions on, the actions of school boards. Many such functions are administrative in character, thus making the board responsible for school administration even though it has the power to delegate administrative functions to its selected executive officer. The laws place on the school board the responsibility for making decisions as to the control and management of the public schools within the restrictions of law, the legally authorized rules and regulations made by the state board of education, and directives announced by the chief state school executive. The district (or local) school board may exercise such powers as are assigned to it by state law or as are necessary for it to use in exercising its legal powers. The courts refuse to recognize that a school board has any other powers and refuse to interpret implied and intrinsic powers broadly enough to place themselves in a position of assuming legislative functions.

The courts determine the meaning and application of the provisions of the statutes when cases are brought into court to settle differences of opinion as to the powers, duties, authority, and responsibilities of school boards with respect to specific, concrete cases involving school board actions and procedures, tort liability of boards or their members, contracts, employment of teachers, and the like. The resulting decisions often seem to vary among states due to differences in their statutes. They sometimes vary within a state due to varying case circumstances, and they sometimes turn one way or another on a fine point of law.

The functions of school boards are too complex to be treated in detail. More detailed treatment may be found in a book entitled *The Courts and the Public Schools* by Newton Edwards. In that book, court decisions relating to the duties, powers, and authority of school boards are briefed, analyzed, and interpreted.

School boards have the power to make rules and regulations

relating to the conduct of schools if not violative of state laws and if they are reasonable in the opinion of the courts. These may supplement state laws but cannot take precedence over nor contradict them. If regularly adopted, the rules and regulations of a school board are the school district's laws and are binding on the board, its employees, and the school patrons.

The superintendent of schools and his staff may make such rules and regulations or "administrative laws" as seem to them to be necessary, but only if they are reasonable and in harmony with state laws and other state requirements and also the rules, regulations, and other policies that have been adopted by the school board.

Legal Limitations on School Boards

School boards are limited in their actions by restrictions of state law and by absence of specific authorizations of law. They are also limited by court decisions which interpret the constitution and statutes and apply the principles of common law, where appropriate. The limitations on school boards are too many to be enumerated, but a few examples may be given.

It is a well established principle that public moneys should not be expended for private purposes. Under this principle the school board is not permitted to expend moneys for the support of private schools. In fact, some of the state constitutions expressly forbid such use of public school moneys.

A school board must observe the laws of the state with respect to tax limits for school purposes, the issuance of school district bonds, the construction of school buildings, the qualifications for state aid or financial reimbursement, the holding of school elections, and many other functions served by the board.

A school board is prohibited from employing any teacher not holding a valid certificate for performing the work required by the position to be filled. A contract to employ a teacher not properly certificated is void, and the teacher cannot recover for services rendered under it. Courts have often held that marriage is not valid ground for voiding a teacher's contract, either written or continuing under a permanent tenure law. A Pennsylvania court held that a school board has no power to adopt a rule that a woman teacher shall be dismissed for the reason of marriage. On the other hand, some courts have held that if a provision requiring the resignation of a woman teacher upon marriage is made in the contract or is included in the adopted rules and regulations of a school board, it may be valid and such resignation can be required. Teacher tenure laws usually provide that a teacher may be dismissed for certain causes, such as incompetency, neglect of duty, insubordination, or immorality, but they usually require that the school board give the teacher a hearing, with representation by counsel, if such is desired by the teacher. The burden of proof of the charge rests on the school board.

Legal Relations of a School Board Member to the Board

School boards are corporate bodies and can act only as such. Except for duties relating to their office, such as calling special meetings by the chairman and keeping records by the secretary, and except for performing duties previously authorized by the board, no board member has the right to make decisions or to act for the board. Without specific authorization by the board, no member can make legal contracts in its name though the board may legalize an action by one of its members after its consummation, or may authorize him to act in the future as its agent.

On whatever matter a school board may act, its action will not be valid unless taken in a legal board meeting. For example, if the chairman secures the oral or written consent of all the members to a proposal, it will not be legally binding on the board. A contract signed by all members without formal action by the board would have no validity so far as the board is concerned, though the members might be liable as individuals for the damages caused by its breach. The board is a corporation composed of the members, but the members as individuals or in concert outside a legal meeting are not the board. Even though the board is a continuing body, it exists for legal decisions only when in session. It cannot act legally as a board at other times. It is the formal action of the board in meeting and as a unit that makes a contract binding on the board.

It is usurpation of authority for any one member such as the chairman (or president) to assume authority for acting in the name of the board without specifically delegated authority to do so from the board. An officer of the board has no more authority than any other member.

Contracts that are illegal due to lack of school board authorization or approval are invalid and the board is not liable under them. The person making such a contract takes a chance that the board may not later ratify it. If actions or decisions of individual members of the board are later ratified, they become valid. If they are repudiated or no action is taken by the board, they remain invalid. They may be validated either specifically by motion or by acceptance of goods or services if all specifications and requirements have been fully met. Ratification is often secured by specific board action but may be implied if the board, while still in session after being informed of the action, does not raise formal protest. Much of the business of the board, such as the purchasing of goods or the employment of teachers, is often conducted by later approval of actions performed by its authorized agent—the superintendent or a member.

Written contracts should specify that it is the school board that is party to the contract. The mere signatures of board members may not indicate the action is that of the school board as a corporate body, but only that the contract is with the signers as individuals. The members and not the school board may be held under the terms of such a contract. It is important that board actions be in the name of the board.

Some state laws make it illegal for a school board member, or any firm in which he has an interest, to sell goods or services to, or enter into contract with, the board of which he is a member. Other state laws make it illegal for a school board to employ a near relative of a member, though this is not usually the case.

School Board Liability for Torts and Other Noncontract Actions

A school district is a legal subdivision of a state, and, under the common law, a state is sovereign and cannot be sued on noncontract actions and torts without its consent, though its contracts are enforceable. Of course statutory law may make the school district, its board, or its members liable for damages, as in the case of workmen's compensation laws. In general, the same conditions with respect to liability apply to other municipal corporations. A suit against a subdivision of a state is equivalent to a suit against the state. School boards are not required by law to exercise infallible judgment, and they are not liable for errors of judgment when acting in good faith. They are not liable, at common law, for the negligence of school employees in performing their duties nor to pupils for accidents on the school grounds, but statutory law or the board's own regulations may make them liable.

A school board is permitted to raise money by taxes or other methods only for the purposes provided by law. To expend tax money for the payment of claims for injury would divert tax funds from the purpose for which the taxes were levied to other incidental but noneducational purposes. If damages were to be awarded, the diversion of the funds required to pay them would be detrimental to the performance of the legal functions of the board. If the damages adjudged were sufficiently large, such an award would result in the closing of the public schools until it was paid. It has been held that it would not be in the public interest to hold a school district liable for damages caused by the mistakes made by the school board or its employees.

There is, however, some tendency under statutory law toward permitting suits against school boards and awarding damages in case torts have been committed. Under statutory law, school boards are sometimes held liable for negligence, trespass, or the maintenance of nuisances, resulting in damages to adjacent or other property not belonging to the school district. In such cases, taxes would have to be levied and collected for payment of the adjudged claim. A few examples of the opinions expressed by courts may be cited as follows:

It has been adjudged by courts that a board of education cannot be held for damages resulting from the erection of a school building for the purpose of performing the duties imposed on the board by statute;[15] that a board of school commissioners in Maryland is not liable for damages either in common law or by statute, has no power to raise money for such purposes, and is not permitted to divert its funds from the purposes for which they are appropriated to damage payment;[16] that the school districts act as representatives of the state in discharging their functions of providing, at public expense, school buildings for conducting public schools therein and are exempt from corporate liability for the improper construction or lack of repair of buildings and for the "wrongs of the servants employed;" [17] and that moneys collected for the state's function of establishing and maintaining a system of public education cannot be diverted to any other use or purpose. If that could be done, "the public would suffer incalculable injury." No action can be maintained against the school district for injuries suffered due to faulty construction of a school building or poor maintenance of grounds because the law provides no funds to meet such claims.[18]

Personal Liability of School Board Members

School board members may be held personally liable for the acts of the board if it intentionally exceeds its authority and the action is not in good faith. They may be held personally liable for such misuse of school funds as: the payment of salary

[15] Kinnare v. Chicago, 171 Ill. 332; 49 N. E. 536.
[16] Weddle v. School Commissioners, 94 Md. 342.
[17] Clark v. City of Nicholasville et al., 27 Ky. 947.
[18] Ernst v. City of West Covington, 116 Ky. 850.

to a teacher not holding the required legal certificate; misappropriation of funds; expenditures of public moneys for goods or services prohibited or not authorized by law; loss of school funds in unsecured loans; selling school bonds at less than the highest bid; purchasing property at an excessive price; misrepresenting to a contractor the authority delegated to a member by the board; and many other similar actions. Board members are sometimes held to be personally liable for the board's inadequate performance of a ministerial duty requiring no exercise of judgment. However, liability may hinge on the nature of the neglected duty, the extent and nature of injury suffered, and other features of a particular case.

As a rule, the several members of a school board cannot be held personally liable for actions of the school board that are required of it by law. Usually, they are not personally liable for injuries caused if, while acting within their jurisdiction, they exceed their legal authority by mstake or use unintentional poor judgment in making decisions. This is particularly true because the members of school boards generally serve without compensation. Usually, the members are not personally liable for injuries suffered by teachers or pupils at school due to negligence or to wrong use of school equipment. As a rule, the members of school boards are not liable for failure of the school board to perform its legal obligations, since no one member can make decisions for the board. Members of a school board are usually not personally liable for the fulfilling of legal contracts made by the board. The liability, if any, is that of the school district.

Opinions expressed by courts on the personal liability of school board members in two particular cases may be cited as follows:

> No statutory duty is imposed upon the members of this board individually. . . . They had no power and were charged with no duty except to act together in a quasi-corporate capacity. The negligence which all the defendants are charged with involved malfeasance and nonfeasance in their governmental duties connected with the construction and maintenance of this school house. We are impressed that if the board as such is not liable,

its individual members are not liable; no individual liability is created by statute.[19]

It is not seen how a member of a corporate body upon which body a duty rests, can be held individually liable for the neglect of its duty by that body. There is no duty upon him to act individually. His duty is as a corporator, and it is to act in the corporation in the way prescribed for its action and by the use of its powers and means and if there is neglect to exact its powers or all its means, it is the neglect of the body and not of the individuals composing it.[20]

Discretionary Powers of School Boards

Discretionary powers of school boards are those involving the use of judgment in promoting the legal objectives of the board. School boards have discretionary power limited only by the requirements and restrictions of law as such are interpreted by the courts. Many decisions require the exercise of quasi-judicial functions by the board. Probably most of the activities of a school board are discretionary rather than ministerial and are accepted and deemed to be necessary even though not prescribed by law.

As a rule the courts have no jurisdiction over (and do not interfere with) the exercise of judgment by a school board, even though it may appear to be bad judgment, unless it is clear that there has been an abuse of discretionary power and the act is clearly unreasonable or violative of law. The courts have been liberal in their interpretation of the discretionary powers exercised by school boards in the performance of their functions. A school board may make such decisions as it deems best within the limits of its discretionary powers. The courts do not pass upon the wisdom of the decisions made.

The courts tend to accept the adopted rules and regulations of a school board without passing on their advisability or propriety. Unless the board's rules and regulations are not in con-

---

[19] Daniels v. Board of Education of Grand Rapids, 191 Mich. 339.
[20] Bassett v. Fish (1877) 12 Hun. N. Y. 209 (1878); 75 N. Y. 303.

formity with law and unless there is evidence of injustice, unreasonableness, bad faith, fraud, malice, or detriment to the public interest in the exercise and enforcement of their provisions, the adopted rules and regulations of the board have the force of law, subject only to state legal restrictions.

The school board exercises its discretion in determining the kind and number of schools required and to be provided in the school district. It usually issues bonds as voted, selects and purchases sites for new school buildings, and determines the kind of material and the style of such buildings. It is limited by state laws, the rules and regulations of state government departments, and the purpose for which the building construction bonds were issued. It uses its discretion in selecting and purchasing equipment for school buildings. It decides who may use school property and for what purposes it may be used, both school and nonschool, and whether or not rentals shall be charged.

The decision for the location of subdistrict boundary lines and residence areas assigned to each school is at the discretion of the school board. The board decides what standards shall be applied to determine whether or not a pupil living with relatives or friends is a resident of the board district or must pay tuition as a nonresident. The board decides what shall be the charges for tuition unless the law specifies the amount or provides that this function shall be determined by the state department of education.

The school board uses its discretion in deciding the following: whether or not schools shall be closed on special days not designated by law as holidays; the requirement for admission to certain of the schools; for what reasons, such as physical, mental, or moral defects, pupils shall be excluded from school; what shall be the grounds for suspension of pupils by principals or expulsion by the school board; what laboratory or incidental fees, if any, shall be collected from pupils; and the like. It uses its discretion in setting the standards of conduct for pupils and in punishing violators of its adopted rules and regulations. It delegates most of these powers of discretion to its professional staff.

Unless prohibited by law, the school board uses its discretion in prescribing the qualifications of teachers beyond those required by law or public policy, such as refusing to employ married women as new teachers or discharging women teachers who marry. It makes requirements for teachers, such as that they reside within the school district during the time schools are in operation. The board uses its discretion in selecting and employing qualified teachers and fixing their salaries, subject to restrictions of law. It uses its discretion in making duty assignments, transfers, and promotions of teachers and may discharge them subject to the provisions of law. It determines the period of employment of teachers and other employees. The school board uses its discretion in selecting and employing a qualified superintendent of schools, subject to the provisions of law. It determines the term for which he is employed and the salary to be paid him.

The school board, under the provisions of law, exercises its discretion in determining subjects to be taught and textbooks and courses of study to be used. As a rule, it uses its discretion in supplying library books, visual education aids, and other materials of instruction to the schools. Within the requirements of any applicable laws, it determines the number of sick leave days with pay allowed employees and whether or not sick leave shall be cumulative.

Often the law requires that contracts be awarded to the lowest responsible bidder. The board has discretion in determining the responsibility of the bidders, but it usually has no power to award a contract to any except the lowest of such bidders as are responsible. Of course, if the lowest responsible bidder does not fully meet the specification requirements, the board can refuse his bid and accept the next higher one.

These are examples of the exercise of discretionary powers of school boards. A reading of well prepared minutes of meetings of any school board will reveal many more. In fact, other than ministerial duties, adoption of formal resolutions, transactions of business pertaining to the board itself, and the like, most of the work of the school board consists of exercising its discretionary powers in making decisions relating to the schools under its jurisdiction.

CHAPTER 6

The Method of Selection and Term
of School Board Members

Method of Selecting School Board Members

Extent of Use of Different Methods of Selection. In a comprehensive study[1] made of certain matters relating to school boards and their members, it was shown that, in school districts of 1,894 cities of various sizes above 2,500 population, board members were elected in 87 per cent and appointed in 13 per cent. In the cities above 500,000 population, board members were elected in 46 per cent and appointed in 54 per cent of the school districts. In the cities from 100,000 to 500,000 population, they were elected in 75 per cent and appointed in 25 per cent of the school districts. In school districts below 100,000 population the percentage of elected school boards was much higher. In some cases boards of both elected and appointed membership had one or sometimes more *ex officio* members such as the mayor, a councilman, the city treasurer, the city manager, a judge, the city auditor, or some other official.

Nomination and Popular Election of Members. Nomination of candidates for the position of school board member may be made by petition, at a primary election, by announcement of the candidate, at a political party caucus, at an open meeting, or by more than one of these methods. The most common and probably the best method is nomination by petition.

---

[1] National Education Association, Research Division. "Fiscal Authority of City School Boards." In *Research Bulletin.* April 1950.

As a rule not many signatures are required on a petition to place a name on the ballot. The number usually ranges from 50 to 500 in different states. Sometimes it comprises a percentage of the electors voting in the last school election. For example, the method used a few years ago in Portland, Oregon, involved either (1) filing with the county clerk, 30 days before the date of the election, a certificate of nomination signed by 2 per cent of the qualified electors voting for school directors at the last election (but not less than 200 such signers) or (2) payment of a $25 fee to the clerk and the filing of a certificate of nomination signed by 500 qualified electors of the school district.

Nomination by petition indicates that there is a desire by a part of the public to have the candidate run for the office and insures his having given some consideration to the question of his availability. The duty of circulating the petition falls on him or his supporters.

Nomination at a primary election is a satisfactory method if such an election must be held for city or state officials at the same time. Otherwise it would entail additional expense for a separate primary election which would draw very few people to the polls. Nomination at a political party caucus is the poorest possible method of nominating candidates to run for the office of school board member.

Sometimes both a petition and a nomination at a primary election are required. For example, at Woburn, Massachusetts, candidates are qualified by petition, nominated by primary election on a nonpartisan ticket, and elected on a nonpartisan ballot. Thus, each member owes his allegiance to all of the people of the city and not to any party or community group.

As was shown, election is the most commonly used method of selecting school board members, except in the few large cities above 500,000 population, and it is used in nearly half of those cities. People generally have more confidence in a board whose members have been elected. They pay for the support of the schools, and they are the school system's patrons. Election by the people is deemed to be more democratic than appointment, even by an executive or legislative body which is itself elected.

Appointment of Members. Of the relatively small percentage of school boards consisting of appointed members: 65 per cent have members appointed by the city council or similar legislative body; 26 per cent have members appointed by the mayor; and the other 9 per cent have members appointed, variously, by county boards (such as county commissioners) or by judges, the governor of the state, the state legislature, or other government authority. Although the usual method of selecting school board members in rural school districts is by popular election, in places where appointment is the method used, the county superintendent of schools is sometimes the appointing authority.

In Maryland the governor of the state appoints the county school board members, but the people in some of the counties are, at present, trying to secure for their counties the right to elect their own members. In North Carolina some of the local school board members are elected by the state legislature. In Tennessee the county court appoints county school board members. All of these methods remove from the people the direct control of their schools.

Virginia, where many of the elements of our democratic system originated, has, perhaps, the most undemocratic system of selecting school board members for its school divisions. Three resident qualified voters, not officers, are appointed by the circuit court of the county to serve as an electoral board to select division school trustees. This does not mean that poor selections are usually made, but control is far removed from the people who financially support the schools and who depend on the schools for the education of their children. It is a method that does not tend to free the school system of political control. Under such a method of selecting school board members the people are ignored. Recently, Arlington County, peopled largely by employees of the Federal Government from all states, has secured the right to elect the members of its board of education after much organized effort.

The District of Columbia's public school system is governed

by a board of nine members, appointed by the justices of the District Court of the United States for the District of Columbia who are themselves appointed by the president of the United States and need not be residents of the District. The members of the board of education, however, must be residents. In this case the people have no control of the government of their schools. There has been and still is a good deal of agitation for the election of the school board members of the District of Columbia.

Usually educators tend to favor the election of school board members by popular vote. However, there have been instances where such has not been the case. In Boston, the school committee members were elected by the people at large, but as a political body. In a survey of the public school system of that city,[2] some years ago, it was recommended that the mayor appoint the school committee members from lists of nominees proposed by a nominating committee consisting of nine members: the chief justice of the supreme court of Massachusetts; the president of the Boston Chamber of Commerce; the president of the Home and School Association; the president of the Boston Federation of Labor; the president of the Boston League of Women Voters; the president of Boston College; the president of Boston University; the president of Harvard University; and the president of Simmons College. The plan provided that the mayor should make appointments for two years after which the voters would vote for or against continuing the appointees in office for four more years. If any were rejected by the voters, the mayor would fill the vacancies from a new list of nominees. This proposal has not been adopted.

A few years ago the mayor of Chicago appointed a committee of the presidents of several universities and colleges and the president of the North Central Association of Colleges and Secondary Schools to make recommendations for the improvement

[2] Finance Commission of the City of Boston. George D. Strayer, Director of Survey. *Report of a Survey of the Public Schools of Boston, Massachusetts.* Boston: Finance Commission 1944.

of school board control of the public schools of Chicago. This committee recommended that "a politically independent board of education be provided for." With reference to the method of selecting school board members, the committee stated:

> The committee has given careful consideration to the relative merits of an appointive board of education versus a board elected by the people. Many large cities employ the latter procedure, but this practice is by no means universal. There exists no convincing body of experimental or other evidence that either method of selection is inherently superior to the other, nor is expert opinion ranged solidly on either side of the question.
>
> The committee is not convinced that an elective board of education would function more effectively in Chicago than would an appointive board selected under the type of procedure proposed below. The committee believes that well qualified individuals are more likely to serve if appointed pursuant to the recommended procedure than if they must seek election at the polls.

The committee recommended that the mayor create a commission on school nominations to consist of a workable number of Chicago organizations reflecting the social interests of the city. The organizations would select their own representatives. They would represent business, education, the home, labor, the professions, and welfare. The commission as recommended would be city-wide in scope and nonpartisan, nonracial, nonethnic, and nonreligious in character. The commission, not to exceed 15 members, would include: the Chicago Association of Commerce; the Chicago Bar Association; the Chicago Congress of Industrial Organizations; the Chicago Federation of Labor; the Chicago Medical Society; the Chicago Technical Societies Council; the Civic Federation of Chicago; the Parent-Teacher Associations; and others not specified. This required no change in the laws but could be adopted by the mayor at any time since he is responsible for making the appointments. This commission would supply the mayor, each year, a list of citizens eligible for appointment to the board of education. It was suggested that twice as many persons be nominated as there are yearly vacancies to be filled.

In Evanston, Illinois, a member from each of certain civic, nonsectarian, nonpolitical, and nonschool employee groups, appointed by their respective organizations, forms a committee to nominate and endorse persons for board membership. The organizations consist of the following: the American Legion, Boy Scouts, Girl Scouts, Business and Professional Women's Clubs of Evanston, the five parent-teacher associations, the Council for Democratic Action, the Evanston Chamber of Commerce, the Evanston Dental Association, the Evanston Medical Association, the Evanston Real Estate Board, the Evanston Women's Club, the Daughters of the American Revolution, the Kiwanis Club, the Lions Club, the Optimist Club, the Rotary Club, the Young Men's Christian Association, the Young Women's Christian Association, and the Zonta Club.

Ex Officio Designation of Members. Fortunately there are few, if any, school boards consisting entirely of *ex officio* members. The few school boards having, in part, *ex officio* membership seldom have more than one such member. *Ex officio* members of school boards are usually the mayor of the city included in the school district, a councilman, the city treasurer, or some other official. Sometimes the *ex officio* member is an educator, such as the county superintendent of schools for county boards.

It has been observed that *ex officio* members seldom make good school board members from the standpoint of providing effective legislative and policy-making control for the public schools. They are often not deeply interested in the schools and have their other official duties to perform. A city official may unduly emphasize economy as opposed to effectiveness in school operation. He may also try to use his position for political purposes in the selection and appointment of teachers and custodians. He may not realize it, but such use is especially pernicious when applied to the public schools. If an educator, such as the county superintendent of schools, he may tend to interfere with the school executive officer's functions. It is better to have no *ex officio* members on the school board.

Case for Elective Boards. The following arguments are sometimes advanced in favor of an elective school board:

1. People take more interest in their schools and in local
educational issues when the issues are popularized as the result
of an election campaign. Under an appointive board the solution of school problems seems far removed from the people,
and voters feel frustrated in securing changes in school policies
and school administration.

2. Election of school board members is more democratic
than appointment. Where elected, members are directly responsible to the people for their actions in maintaining the kind of
schools the people want at a cost they are willing to pay.

3. School boards consisting of elective members are more
free than are boards consisting of appointive members to act
independently for what they deem to be the best interests of
the schools and the people who elected them. Appointive boards
may feel themselves bound to act in accordance with the desires
of the authority that appointed them. In fact, one of the stated
arguments for appointment by a mayor is that it will make
the mayor responsible for the schools as well as for the city
government. Since the mayor or other appointing authority is
responsible, a school board consisting of appointed members
is either directly or indirectly responsible to an official who is
elected upon local municipal issues and not necessarily upon
school issues. A board, to the extent it is responsible to such
authority, is not free to act independently and in the best interests of the schools when issues cause a clash of opinion. School
board members should owe allegiance to no person or political
party but only to the whole public.

4. An elective board is more responsive to the will of the
people than is an appointive board because the members are
elected to represent the people in determining policies for the
schools. An elective board can be held responsible by the people
for its actions, whereas an appointive board is only indirectly
responsible to the people of the school district, through the
mayor or some other official or body.

5. Election, more often than appointment, protects the schools from local politics. If appointed, members are sometimes selected for the purpose of using the schools for patronage or for the award of purchase contracts to supporters of local politicians. The use of schools for patronage purposes results in the selection of teachers and other employees for political reasons and not on the basis of their qualifications. Such selection results in less efficient teachers than would be secured if qualifications alone were the criterion of choice. Furthermore, the use of the schools for political purposes results in the misuse of school funds to the disadvantage of both the schools and the taxpayers. Any sense of obligation to a municipal authority by the members of a school board may result in the use of the schools to help to maintain the political power of the existing municipal authorities. Such misuse of the public schools demoralizes a school system.

6. In making its decisions, a school board has the benefit of the advice of its specialists in education, in theory and usually in practice. These are the superintendent of schools and the various officers of administration working under his general direction. Boards whose members are appointed, if subject to direction by the mayor or city council, do not have the advantage of acting freely on professional advice on large matters in which the city authority may be interested. As a consequence, costly and educationally unsound actions may be taken to the detriment of the public schools. Control by a city authority is not professional and that authority does not come in close enough contact with the board's administrative officers to obtain the professional viewpoint. No authority from above should be permitted to come between the school board and the executive officer it has employed to make effective its policies and to advise it on what policies are needed.

7. A final argument for elective school boards is that this method is generally preferred to the appointive method. First, it is the most commonly used method. Second, only a few changes in method have been made in recent years, but those

have been from the appointive to the elective method. Third, although authorities in school administration are not unanimous, the great weight of their opinion favors the election of board members.

Case for Appointive Boards. The people of a school district have no inherent right to elect school board members. The legislature has the right to prescribe the method of selection. Those who maintain that the appointive method of selecting school board members is superior to the elective method base their opinions on the following contentions:

1. It is often possible to secure better school board members by appointment than by election. Many of the foremost citizens in any city, who are well qualified as laymen for membership on a school board, will accept the position by appointment. Such persons often refuse to become candidates for membership by election. Many professional and business people, such as physicians, bankers, manufacturers, and merchants, shrink from subjecting their names and reputations to the misrepresentations that sometimes are made in a political campaign. This may be the case even if the ballot is nonpartisan. Many persons who would become good school board members are not used to the acceptance of defeat, and, desiring to avoid the necessity for spending a great deal of time and sometimes money in a campaign for election, they refuse to run. Appointment seems to be considered more of an honor, and such people are more likely to accept the office on that basis as a civic responsibility. Having accepted, they will devote much time and effort to work for which no remuneration is paid.

2. If school board members are appointed, the appointing authority can be held fully responsible to the people for the actions of the school board, for the integrity of the members appointed, and for any misuse of the schools by the appointing authority or by the school board for its members' political or selfish purposes. In case the mayor is the appointing authority, it is logical to hold him responsible, as the chief executive officer of the city, for all government in the city including that of the

public schools.[3] In the case of an elective board, it is sometimes argued that a mayor who has a firm control over the politics in a city may be able to control the election of school board members without the assumption of any responsibility for their actions. In appointing school board members he cannot avoid responsibility.

3. Appointment for long, overlapping terms of persons deeply interested in the welfare of the public schools, from nominees selected by representatives of civic and other organizations of the city, will secure members who are less politically inclined than would be persons competing for school board membership in a popular election.

4. It is desirable that the length of service of school board members be fairly long. The average length of service on the board is usually greater under the appointive than under the elective method of selection. Fairly long service by board members is usually advantageous because it results in more consistent actions by the board and because the experience of members is valuable in the work of passing sound school board legislation and adopting wise policies.

5. When individual school board members are elected on particular issues, they often feel they have a mandate from the people to make those issues good in the school system. The issues may be those the new member has himself raised without fully understanding their relation to sound educational theory and practice. The desire to make changes, by newly elected members, is likely to result in three pernicious practices or conditions. First, the school board may be led to assume certain administrative functions that should be performed by the superintendent of schools and his staff. Second, with frequent changes in school board personnel, the superintendent of schools may find it difficult to work with new board members and be forced out, resulting in too frequent changes in the chief executive

[3] This argument assumes that the public schools are a city agency, performing a city function, which is not conceded by school boards, as a rule, and is in opposition to many expressed court opinions, but it is held to be good governmental theory by many political scientists.

school official. Third, with too frequent changes in board membership, educational policies and practices may be kept in a state of flux, and consistent development of the school system may be retarded.

Joint or Separate School Elections

Opinion is divided with regard to the desirability of holding school elections jointly with general elections. The National Education Association[4] found that school board members were elected at general elections in 38.6 per cent, in special elections in 59.3 per cent, and in both general and special elections in 2.1 per cent of the school districts studied.

Where possible and practicable it is probably better to hold the school election jointly with other elections. Most of the advantages claimed for separate elections can be obtained if the school board members are elected on separate, nonpolitical ballots at general elections. The holding of separate elections, at different times of the year or even in different years from those in which the general elections are held is an expense for which there are few compensatory returns. The main objection, however, is that few people will take the time to vote at a special school election. Usually, a special school election draws only a very few persons interested in particular candidates or the issues for which each stands. The results of a special school election are often determined by a relatively small group, sometimes working quietly and agreeing among themselves to vote for their selected candidate. Such results in no sense represent community opinion. The elected members may not represent the will of the public but only of a minority group. Manipulation of a school election is more difficult when a general election draws more persons to the polls, particularly if separate, nonpolitical ballots are used for school board candidates.

[4] American Association of School Administrators. *School Boards in Action.* Washington: National Education Association, 1946.

Political Party Representation

A study made in 1950 by the National Education Association, to which reference has already been made, shows that 82 per cent of elective school board members are elected on nonpartisan ballots and 18 per cent are elected as members of political parties. It is generally held by persons interested in public education that school boards should be nonpartisan rather than partisan or bipartisan. The schools have their own peculiar problems which are not in any sense related to the issues defined as Republican or Democratic. Political considerations should have no weight in the selection of members of school boards. The schools are maintained for the education of children whose parents are of all political affiliations. Whether a person is a Republican or a Democrat has not the slightest bearing on his ability to be a good member of a school board. Political considerations should not enter into its decisions.

Many excellent professional and business men are unwilling to make a campaign for office on a political party ticket because they have patients, clients, or customers in all parties. If board members are elected as members of political parties, pressure is sometimes brought to bear upon them to use the schools for party purposes, such as the rewarding of loyal party workers with positions. In any case, there is usually considerable rivalry between members of parties if they are nearly evenly divided. In a large city a few years ago, the board of education was divided by political parties, four to five members. On important matters the board usually voted by political affiliation, and this arrangement extended even to the selection of a site for a high school building; there were both Republican and Democratic sites.

Sometimes there is an attempt to equalize the effect by having a bipartisan board. At the time of a survey of its school system, Kansas City, Missouri, had such a board, consisting of six members. Two were elected every two years for six-year terms. At each election, the Democratic party named a candidate and the

Republican party named another and each party endorsed the other's nominee. Anyone else who was qualified could have run if nominated, but none did. The city thus maintained a bipartisan board consisting of three members of each political party.

This system, although superior to political party competition for membership on a board that should have nothing to do with political party issues, is not satisfactory; it greatly restricts the number of possible candidates. The nonpartisan ticket is to be preferred. No board member, in his official actions, should be obligated or predisposed to the support of or owe allegiance to the platform or policies of any political party. Educational issues are not and should not be made political issues. The allegiance of the school board member should be to the whole community and the requirements of the state.

Ward Representation

When separate city school districts began to consolidate, there was at first a confederation of the school boards for the management of matters that were common to all of them, such as the employment of a superintendent or a singing or sewing teacher. The central body gradually took over more and more functions but was so large that it had difficulty in performing them. The number of members on the central board was reduced by the use of representatives of the boards of the several districts, which were often identical with the city wards or precincts. Finally, the ward boards were eliminated and control of the schools of the city was vested in the central board. Now ward representation has largely disappeared, and school board members are elected or appointed to represent the people of the whole city in the management of all the schools of the city.

It is reported [5] that the members of 85.7 per cent of elective school boards are elected at large, 10.7 per cent by precincts or

[5] American Association of School Administrators. *School Boards in Action.* Washington: National Education Association, 1946.

wards, and 3.6 per cent in part by each method. The cities have largely discontinued division representation, but representation by divisions persists in some of the county school systems of the southern and border states. It is also used in some consolidated high school districts in which the high school board is made up of representatives of the boards of the elementary school districts that comprise the high school district. In a few states, candidates are nominated by subdistricts and are elected at large.

Selection of school board members as representatives of precincts, wards, magisterial districts, or other subdivisions of the school district, is generally condemned as a method of selecting members of school boards. Election or appointment at large is generally approved. It is difficult to find any valid reasons for the representation of separate subdivisions of a school district. Some of the reasons against selection by subdivisions are as follows:

1. The entire school district is a unit for taxation, administration, and supervision. Members should be elected by and to represent the entire school district so that legislative control will be unified.

2. If members represent wards or other subdivisions, they may be interested in the development of their schools only, to the neglect of the schools of the other divisions of the city or county school district. Differences in the quality of teachers, school buildings, and school equipment may develop in the various subdivisions, depending on the power of their representatives on the board.

3. Representation by subdivisions of a school district tends to perpetuate political control of the schools, logrolling, bickering and dickering for the benefits of the several subdivisions, and competition among them for securing funds for expenditure from the common pool.

4. The less favored subdivisions of a city or county may send less capable representatives than the more favored ones—persons who could not be elected on a city-wide or county-wide basis.

5. Election by subdivisions sometimes leads to the appointment of friends or relatives of members as teachers and sometimes to the assessment of teachers for campaign funds and to other corrupt practices.

Occupational and Other Group Representation

A few educators and sociologists have recommended that school board members be elected to represent occupational and other community groups. They point to the fact that the number of members from professional and business groups predominates and that the relatively large number of skilled and unskilled laborers furnish very few of the members of school boards. It would probably be well for the people of the school district to elect more school board members from the skilled and unskilled labor groups, but it would probably also be a great mistake to elect members as representatives of any occupational groups, be they labor, professional, or business. Each school board member should represent all groups of the community; there should be no professional representatives, no labor representatives, no farmer representatives, and no homemaker representatives; there should be persons from different occupations only if they are elected when they run for membership. Good members can be elected from any group without being elected by groups or to represent groups.

What is true with respect to the undesirability of selecting school board members as representatives of occupational groups is likewise true of selecting them as representatives of religious, civic, or other community groups. There should be manufacturers on the board, but not representatives of manufacturers; laborers, but not representatives of laborers; women, but not representatives of women; Baptists, but not representatives of Baptists; persons of various racial or national origins, but not representatives of races or nationalities; members from poor wards and wealthy wards, but not representatives of those wards. The only allegiance of a school board member should be to the whole people of the school district. Even if it were desirable to have all principal occupational and other groups represented, the board would have to be so large that a plan for representation by interest groups would be impracticable.

Length of Term of School Board Members

When school boards were originally designated to administer the schools, the members were usually elected or appointed for one or two years. Terms of office were later increased. One study[6] showed that the average term of school board members in cities from 30,000 to 100,000 population was 4.0 years and in cities over 100,000 population was 4.3 years. Other studies indicate that 3 years is the average term in small city, town, and rural school systems.

Terms of 4, 5, or 6 years give members more time to learn from other members, from the superintendent of schools, and from their own observation and study so that they are better able to perform their functions in the best interests of their communities.

Even with the intention of acting in the interests of the people of the school district, new school board members have difficulty in discovering what problems of the schools need to be solved, what ones have been solved, and what ones are developing. In considering problems and possible solutions they are likely to ignore some relevant considerations because they do not have the necessary background of intimate experience with the schools and their problems from a governing point of view. New members may, unwittingly, act on superficial considerations unless they listen to and are guided by the opinions of members of longer standing and the superintendent of schools. Such might be the case until they have had time to learn enough about the schools to judge wisely on the basis of their own experiences.

[6] Deffenbaugh, W. S. "Practices and Concepts Relating to City Boards of Education." In *Biennial Survey of Education in the United States, 1938–1940.* Vol. I, Ch. VII. 1941.

A school board member's usefulness increases with his years of membership. Hence, terms should be relatively long and members frequently re-elected. In some school systems, in which terms are short and members are seldom re-elected, new members never learn how to perform their functions well. Often the better residents will refuse to accept office for a short term. Under such conditions of frequently changing board personnel the schools are sometimes in turmoil due to frequent policy changes made by new members who do not have the necessary background for passing wisely on such matters. Actions of the board are often inconsistent with past actions, and teachers and others lose confidence in the school board's ability to govern the schools.

Although terms of office should be longer in many school districts, it would be well if school board members were more generally re-elected, particularly if their terms are for only 2 or 3 years. The purpose in selecting school board members should not be to give a large number of persons experience as members, but rather to secure wise decisions, consistency of actions, and continuity of policy. It may be very costly, both educationally and financially, for school districts to change the personnel of their boards too frequently. Many such examples have been observed by the author.

Importance of Overlapping Terms

The desirability of electing or appointing school board members for overlapping terms of service is generally recognized in nearly all states by provisions of law for the election or appointment of some members each year or every alternate year. On a 7 member board, for example, the plan might be to elect 2 members at each of two biennial elections and 3 at the third election, each member for a six-year term.

The overlapping of terms is important in preserving the continuity of the board by providing that normally not all members will be changed the same year. It is even important that a majority of the members always be experienced if unfinished projects and plans for new projects are to be completed.

A brief example may be given of how well-considered actions and plans may be disrupted by a change in the majority of board members in one year. A few years ago the author made a study of a county school system recommending the consolidation of eight rather small and inefficient high schools with a ninth and much larger one at the county seat. All but one of the high schools were overcrowded. The provision of a central senior high school in a new building would free sufficient facilities in each of the eight small town or rural centers for the remodeling necessary to provide for the rapidly increasing elementary and junior high school population, already being served at the same 8 centers by means of a fleet of 35 busses. The school board adopted the plan unanimously. It immediately purchased 25 centrally located acres for the new high school. The new site adjoined the county seat city near the center of the county, and highways radiated from it in all directions and past the eight schools. The board employed an architect to prepare plans and specifications for the building and prepared the bonds for sale.

However, there was a school election in the summer, and 3 of the 5 members on the board were displaced. The new majority on the board stopped the bond sale, sold the land that had been purchased for a site, and constructed cheap and inadequate additions for high school purposes at three of the existing school buildings. The people of the five towns and rural regions not selected for the three high schools were disappointed that the board did not locate one of the high schools in their community, as each expected would be done. Their high school children had to be transported across the county on undeveloped roads, usually at greater distance than to the proposed central location, to schools that were still very inferior in quality. If a majority of the board members had not been changed by that election, the well-considered plans of the board would not have been disrupted by inexperienced new members who had not studied and did not comprehend the problems. A majority of the members should not be elected in any one year except when it is necessary to fill vacancies caused by death or resignation.

Some patterns for overlapping terms of office that provide for the election or appointment of less than a majority of members at any one time are presented as follows:

Number of Members	Length of Terms	Span of Elections (Years)	Number of Members at Each Election
5	3	1	2-2-1
5	4	1	2-1-1-1
5	5	1	1-1-1-1-1
5	6	2	2-2-1
7	3	1	3-2-2
7	4	1	2-2-2-1
7	5	1	2-2-1-1-1
7	6	1	2-1-1-1-1-1
7	6	2	3-2-2
7	8	2	2-2-2-1

Other plans can be devised and are often used, but it is important that a majority of members be experienced at all times. In the above plans, a majority of regular vacancies would not be filled at any one election. Of course, in case of vacancies caused by death or resignation there might be additional members to be elected or appointed for short terms, and, in such an instance, a majority might be selected at one time. On the other hand, some members might be re-elected, in which case there would be fewer new members than those indicated in the table.

Filling of Interim Vacancies in School Board Membership

Sometimes vacancies occur in school board membership due to death, resignation, removal from the school district, loss of physical or mental health, or disqualification by a court for malfeasance, misfeasance, or neglect of duty. In at least one state members may even disqualify themselves by absence from three or more consecutive meetings, and their position will be declared vacated unless they are specifically reinstated by the board.

A common method of filling interim vacancies, due to any cause, is by action of the remaining members of the board. This method makes unnecessary the calling of a special election. In case of an appointive board, the vacancies are usually filled by the appointing authority, such as the mayor or city council. Sometimes vacancies on elective boards are filled at a special election. In some of the cities of Massachusetts, vacancies are filled by joint vote of the members of the school committee and the city council. In some of the towns there is similar action by the members of the school committee and the selectmen.

Often the filling of a vacancy is for the unexpired term, but sometimes it is for the period until the next election. If the term has not then expired, the vacancy will be filled for the unexpired term by election. In one state, if a board of education fails to fill a vacancy within a period of 90 days, the state board of education does so for the unexpired term by the appointment of someone residing within the school district.

Conclusion as to the Selection and Tenure of School Board Members

Members can be secured by either election or appointment who are interested in the public schools and the welfare of the community. Either method sometimes produces members who will use their position for political, business, or personal advantage. Regardless of the method of selection used, it is important in securing the best quality of personnel for a school board that: (1) terms be reasonably long, such as for six years; (2) there be re-election or reappointment of members when such is deserved; (3) terms be overlapping to secure continuity and consistency of action; (4) members be either elected or appointed to represent the whole school district and not as representatives of divisions of cities or counties; and (5) members be elected or appointed without reference to political, religious, occupational, or other affiliations.

CHAPTER 7

Qualities Required for School
Board Membership

Qualifications for School Board Membership

Legal Requirements. As a rule, there are relatively few legal requirements to be met by candidates for the office of school board member in the school districts of any one state. Among some of the more usual requirements for eligibility are citizenship, residence in the school district for a specified number of years, ownership of property in the district, taxpayer in the district, and the like. Frequently it is required that a member shall have attained a minimum age, such as 21 or 30 years. Sometimes it is required that he be "literate" or "able to read and write the English language" or that he shall have "completed the eighth grade." Sometimes it is specifically required that the candidate be of "good moral character." Occasionally, he is required to be a patron of a school in the district. In one state it is required that a board member be not related to another board member "within the third degree of affinity or consanguinity." Usually not more than three or four requirements, such as have been mentioned, apply in any one state.

In Kentucky, to be eligible for school board membership a person must have completed the eighth grade or have had equivalent education. In case his educational qualification is questioned, it must be proved by reference to school records, affidavit of the teacher under whom he completed the eighth grade, or passing of an examination given by direction of the state board of education. In a few instances, members of school boards in Kentucky have been removed from office because they did not meet the education requirement. However, an education requirement for eligibility for school board membership is unusual.

The qualifications for school board membership in Chicago are that a person must be a citizen of the United States, shall have been a resident of the school district for the five years next preceding his appointment to the office, shall be 30 years of age, and shall hold no other federal, state, or local office. The requirement in Kansas City is that a person shall be 30 years of age, a resident of the state for one year prior to his election, and a taxpayer of the school district. The requirement in Portland, Oregon, is that a person shall be a citizen of the United States and a resident of the school district for one year immediately preceding his election.

There seems to be little rhyme or reason in such requirements. Why should a person be required to have attained the age of 30 years in one school district and not in another? Why is a state librarian or the postmaster or mail carrier eligible for local school board membership in some states and not in others? There seems to be no sound reason for the differences in requirements. Anyway, the lawful requirements miss most of those qualities of a person that are important to his successful participation as a member of a school board.

Qualities That Voters Should Seek. A list of the qualities voters should seek in the candidates from whom they select board members, must include those that constitute a good citizen, and a good person. Such a list can be little else since school board members are expected to be laymen and not professional educators. There are, of course, no perfect school board members as there are no perfect persons. It will have to be sufficient to select the candidate who most nearly meets the requirements the voter or appointing officer has in his mind. Some qualities are more important than others for membership on a board which is to govern a public school system successfully, or they may become more important when a particular school system faces a peculiar combination of problems for solution. A list of some of the more important qualities required for membership on a school board is presented herewith. It is not held that the list is complete, but it is believed that a member who meets most of them is likely to be a fairly good school board member. A school board member should:

Be interested in the development of children and have a strong belief in the importance of their education in the public schools.

Act with sincerity and without prejudice in the interests of the people of the school district and be willing to subordinate personal, political, and religious interests to the good of the larger group.

Be well balanced and not biased toward or against any particular kind of education—classical or vocational, fundamental or progressive—or toward or against any particular subject or activity of the schools.

Be progressive in improving the public schools but conservative in adopting changes of unproven merit except for the purpose of well-considered experimentation.

Be foresighted and farsighted in helping to plan public education for the future.

Be mature enough to exercise sound judgment and young enough to be interested in the future; age in years is not the criterion of maturity or youth.

Be successful in his profession, business, or trade and be willing and ready to act on expert advice on educational matters when he deems such advice to be sound in general principle.

Be accustomed to making decisions promptly and with dispatch.

Persevere in securing desirable board action and insist on corresponding zeal by the superintendent and his staff in making all adopted actions effective.

Be willing and able to devote time and energy to the work of the school board.

Have a strong loyalty to democratic processes and subordinate personal opinions and desires to the will of the majority.

Be agreeable, courteous, good natured, and tolerant in dealing with persons whose opinions oppose his own.

Be courteous and co-operative and work as a member of a team.

Be capable of withstanding pressure from without in supporting a policy that has been adopted after thorough consideration by the board.

Be courageous and not susceptible to being intimidated nor influenced except by reasons that seem to him to be sound.

Act in a logical and judicious, rather than emotional, manner.

Be open to conviction and subject to change when proved wrong, even after a stand has been taken.

Be decisive, not vacillating.

Have a feeling of loyalty to the board, its several members, and the staff and pupils of the schools.

Be able to face criticism without flinching even if unjust and be willing to stand back of sound principles regardless of the source of opposition.

Be ready to accept responsibility for mistakes made by himself or the board.

Be frank and straightforward, not secretive and devious.

Exercise leadership in the larger community.

Be public spirited and active in promoting the interests of the public.

Be well poised, secure in the respect and esteem of the people of the larger community.

Be discreet and tactful with respect to the school's public relations.

Have a reputation in the community for integrity and good judgment and be worthy of his reputation.

In general, members of school boards are usually given credit for having superior qualities of character, education, and intelligence. Although the public should re-elect good school board members, because they have been initiated, have learned the work required, and are less likely to make the mistakes that even a well-qualified inexperienced member may make, it is important that members who do not act in the interests of the people and their schools be not re-elected. Some school districts seldom have good school boards and others seldom have poor ones. However, most school districts undoubtedly have some good and some poor members, usually a greater number of the former, it is believed.

Qualities That Voters Should Avoid. In considering the merits of candidates for school board membership, voters will have to weigh good qualities against bad ones and select those candidates who most nearly approximate the high standards needed for the office. In general, the voters should look with disfavor on the opposites of qualities listed under the preceding heading as good. Candidates should usually be denied school board membership who:

Lack sufficient intelligence to enable them to secure the elements of an education, but a highly intelligent, self-educated person may become a good member.

Are unsuccessful in their occupations and other endeavors.

Are not interested in public education.

Are unable or unwilling to devote time to the work of the board.

Are primarily running for the office as representatives of special groups or organizations and not as the representatives of all the people of the school district, such as representatives of a political party, the taxpayers' association, a religious group, the teachers, and the like, so that they are not free to act for the best interests of the people of the whole school district.

Lack balance and are known to be "cranks," or persons desiring to use the schools to promote some social reform or purpose other than public education.

Are prejudiced for or against certain community groups or certain school policies.

Are merely glib talkers, adept at making excuses.

Have made pre-election pledges to work for specific reforms, such as to reduce taxes, to establish a city teachers college, and the like, regardless of needs or consequences, when they have not had an opportunity to learn the needs.

Propose to "reform" the schools but do not have a background of understanding or experience of what reforms are needed.

Desire the office so they can grant to others or secure for themselves special favors not extended to all persons of the school district.

Qualities Considered by Voters. An investigation was made by Shannon[1] to determine what characteristics of candidates are

[1] Shannon, J. R. "What 1,000 Terre Haute Citizens Look for in Voting for School Board Members." In *The American School Board Journal.* Feb. 1947.

prominent in the minds of voters for school board members. A total of 1,330 reasons were given by voters of Terre Haute, Indiana for voting as they did. It was found that:

Personal qualities were given as the reason by 259 voters, including character (120), honesty (61), intelligence (28), progressiveness (13), broad-mindedness (12), common sense (2), and the like.

General qualifications were given by 177 voters, such as education (81), capability and efficiency (45), parent of children (32), suitable age (17), and the like.

Interest in the community and the schools was given as the reason by 149 voters.

Business experience was considered important by 124 voters.

In 99 cases the voters were influenced by their family, relatives, or friends.

Among other influences mentioned were politics, religion, sex of candidates, the part of the city in which the candidate resides, promise of lower taxes, neighborhood gossip, etc.

Terre Haute is a city of medium size (under 100,000 population) having a large state teachers college and a polytechnic institute that grants degrees. The school system is good, and the people are probably more enlightened than average. Still, few or none of the voters mentioned many important factors as their reasons for voting as they did.

Motives for Accepting School Board Membership

Service on a school board is different from most other public services rendered at the local level, except service on other boards, such as library or hospital boards. Salaries or other forms of compensation are usually paid to members of city councils, but school board members give of their time and energy, and sometimes take more abuse than do other public servants, usually without remuneration. Sometimes they are reimbursed for expenses or are paid very nominal honorariums, but they are seldom paid enough to prompt persons to accept the responsibilities and duties involved. In Tennessee, for example, certain school board members are paid $4 per day while boards are in session. In Massachusetts it is illegal for members to be paid any compensation for either their time or expenses in attending school board meetings.

The usual and traditional practice of providing no compensation for the services of school board members, but of expecting them to give of their time and effort unselfishly, is generally approved throughout the United States. This is a tradition worthy of preserving. Generally, men and women who will accept the responsibilities of the office and who are often targets of public criticism, all without compensation, are at least likely to have good intentions, whether or not they know exactly how best to serve their communities. If the members were to be paid full salaries, or even fairly large lump amounts, a board might feel impelled to earn them by managing the schools directly. School administration is a profession which laymen cannot well perform. It would not be wise to substitute administrative acts of a board that exists for making official decisions only when in session for the administrative actions of the superintendent of schools. Without compensation it is usually possible to secure the services of some of the more public spirited citizens in the community.

School board membership, like membership on other local boards, is usually accepted as an opportunity to render service to one's community. Good men and women seek or accept membership on a school board because they secure personal satisfaction from rendering the service and they deem it a personal honor to be elected to its membership. Of the many school board members the author has known during his years of service as an educational consultant, it is believed that a very large majority of them were motivated wholly or largely by the desire to render service to their community and its schools.

There are, of course, other motives that may cause a person to accept membership on a school board. Members who desire to improve their status or influence in their communities may be sincere and become excellent school board members as they learn about the schools. There are, however, some wholly unworthy motives, such as the use of the office to secure personal publicity by "playing to the gallery" through keeping the schools in turmoil and creating dissension in the board or as a springboard to political advancement by keeping the member's name before the public. A person may seek the office as a means of exercising his spite against someone, possibly the superintendent or a principal. The author once knew of a principal who was induced to resign by the superintendent under threat of presenting a charge of insubordination before the school board if he should refuse. The principal went into business, was elected a member of the school board, and devoted his energy to making life miserable for the superintendent.

Another unworthy motive is a desire to use the schools for developing political power through the use of influence in the process of selecting teachers, clerks, and custodians for employment. Other motives, worthy or unworthy, are a desire to secure some particular change, such as more (or less) discipline in the schools, to promote (or de-emphasize) athletics, to reduce expenditures, and the like, before the member has come to understand the problems and needs.

There can be no doubt that most school board members have assumed the duties of their office because of a sincere desire to render an important public service. Whether the motive be civic interest, a desire to give the community the benefit of their business experience, or any other worthy purpose, most school board members have a firm belief in the importance of public education for the children of the school district, to be attained with the least possible waste of public funds.

CHAPTER 8

School Board Organization

Requirements for Legal School Board Actions

A school board, being a body corporate, can act officially only in a duly authorized and legally held school board meeting. It acts on formal motion, usually passed by a majority vote of the members present. Any action taken on the basis of consent of members given individually, other than in a legal meeting of the board, would not be a legal action. To be legal there must be action by the board on a formal motion, normally after opportunity has been presented for discussion of the issue or by unanimous consent. Of course, an action taken by a member or group of members will be legal if it has been previously authorized by the board or if it is subsequently ratified by it, but it will not be valid as the board's action unless the board previously or subsequently takes action. Duties required of or permitted to the officers of the board by law or by board regulation are legal under the general provision without specific action for authorization.

Authority to act to bind a school board or to act in its name is vested only in the board, not in the persons of its members. An individual member of the board has no more authority to act for the board on his own volition than has any other person in or out of the school district. He has power to act for the board only as such authority has been delegated to him previously, expressly, and specifically. Such is also the case if his action is a part of or made necessary by power that has been delegated to him by the board. Any unauthorized action of a member of the board is not binding on the board until it has been ratified.

Delegation of authority to the president, a committee, or any member to act for the board is unwise where any considerable discretion is required. Action in routine matters is required for making the board's expressed will effective. Such actions as the signing of documents for the board by officers or designated members are necessary after board authorization. However, actions requiring basic decisions should be taken by the board and not by a member, a committee, or the board's executive officer.

Organization Meeting

Usually one meeting a year is designated by law or board regulation as the organization meeting. Sometimes the organization meeting is held biennially if the board elections are held biennially. The organization meeting is likely to be required soon after the election or appointment of new members, or it may be held soon after the beginning of the board's fiscal year. Sometimes it is an extra thirteenth or twenty-fifth meeting required by law, where only organizational business is transacted. In other cases the organization meeting is one of the regular monthly or semimonthly meetings, and organization is only a part of the business transacted.

One of the principal purposes of the organization meeting is to induct new members. In many of the states this requires an administration of the oath of office prescribed for state, county, and city officers. The oath, specifically worded by law, usually requires members to swear that they will support the Federal and state constitutions and laws and faithfully perform the duties of the office of school board member. The wording varies from state to state.

The school board officers are elected in the organization meeting. The members of standing committees, if any, are usually appointed at that meeting. Other business classified as organization of the board may be transacted. The following may be enacted at an extra meeting: selection of a treasurer and a depository; determination of the day, hour, and place of holding meetings; and the adoption of board rules of procedure. These are usually done in case the board is considered to be a "new" one. However, a school board is never actually new. Even if all of its members should be changed at one time, it is a continuing corporation that is bound by actions of the board in previous years. This continues until the actions are changed. A board simply cannot wash the slate clean and start as a new board. Still, there is some precedent for considering the board to be a new one, even though it is not actually new. The board is a legislative body. Other legislative bodies, such as state legislatures and the Federal Congress, are considered to be new bodies after organization, even if bound by acts of the previous bodies. The "new" legislature or congress is given a different number from the preceding one. In 1953 this question was raised in connection with the organization of the Federal Senate. Some senators, desiring a rule to limit discussion by majority vote, maintained that new rules needed to be adopted for the organization of the "new" congress. This was not done.

At the organization meeting, the board usually elects a chairman and vice chairman or president and vice president, from among its members. "Chairman" is sometimes considered to be a better title than "president" for the presiding officer, since the latter often connotes executive duties. No chairman should have such duties, other than the management of the board. The appointed superintendent of schools or a principal or head teacher, if there is no superintendent, should perform the executive and managerial duties required. Other officers, usually elected by the board but sometimes specified for the office by the popular ballot electing them, are a secretary and a treasurer. Sometimes the board appoints a nonmember as the board's attorney to furnish legal advice and service.

Voting for officers of the board should be by secret ballot, rather than by voice vote or show of hands. This guarantees full expression of each member's choice.

Chairman of the Board

Method of Selection of the Chairman. Election of a chairman from among the members of the board is the practice in most city school districts. This procedure may be accepted as standard practice. In a few cases the mayor is an *ex officio* member of the board and is designated as chairman by city charter. In such cases he is seldom an active participant, and board meetings are usually conducted by the vice chairman. Without the understanding of educational problems derived from regular attendance and participation as a board member, such an *ex officio* chairman may use the prestige of his office of chairman, his position of mayor, and his influence with the city council to induce the board to act against its better judgment. This is a serious defect, for the board is then made responsible for actions not in accordance with its considered judgment. In an unusual case known to the author, the mayor was *ex officio* chairman of the board, but not a member. In this case, he seldom conducted any meeting except the one concerning the budget. In that meeting he usually exerted the full force of his power and prestige.

Rotation of Chairmanship. In Portland, Oregon, and Laramie, Wyoming, the board uses a plan of rotation of chairmanship among school board members. In Portland, the law provides that the director who has served the longest "under an election" shall act as chairman of the board's meetings. The provision would exclude the time served by an interim appointee. If there are several members who have served equal time (the method of election in Portland makes this normally the case), the board applies the following rule:

> When there is no one director who has served longer than another, the senior members who are eligible for the office of chairman shall decide the question of the chairmanship. In the event the senior members fail to select a chairman, the board shall elect a chairman from the senior members who are eligible for such office.

With regard to the length of term of the chairman, the board's rules and regulations provide that

> The term of office of the chairman shall be determined by dividing the two-year period by the number of senior members who are eligible for the chairmanship.

Applied, this means that when four members are eligible, the term of each as chairman is six months; when three are eligible, the term of each is eight months.

The rotation of chairman has the merit of keeping all members interested in and responsible for the work of the board. It is democratic in the extreme. It limits the work of the chairman to presiding at meetings and performing the necessary routine duties in the name of the board; it prevents him from acting as an executive or administrative officer for very long; it is based on the assumption that the chairman is merely a board member with an extra temporary function; it clarifies the fact that no one member wields all the power; and it shows that the board can act only as a corporate unit.

Some school board members and superintendents object to rotation of the presidency because not all members have the ability to conduct school board meetings with dispatch and in accordance with parliamentary procedure. It is argued that some are not good discussion leaders and that much valuable time can be wasted in prolonged and indecisive discussion. These arguments seem to have a sound basis, but the members are likely to try to help the chairman, knowing that their term is coming. From observation of a board in action under chairmen selected on a rotation basis, the author is inclined to believe that the advantages of the plan outweigh the disadvantages.

Duties of the Chairman. The chairman or president of a school board has duties concerning meetings of the board, routine acts as directed by the laws of the state or the official actions of the board, and representation of the board for non-official actions. It is true that a board chairman sometimes acts as a top executive officer (above the superintendent of schools), but such is not a proper function of the presiding officer of the board. The following is a list of some of the more important duties of the chairman or president of a school board:

Presiding at board meetings. This principal duty includes a large number of component duties.

Calling special meetings of the board when he deems them to be necessary or, as required by law or board regulations, at the request of other members.

Appointing members of school board committees if such are required by the board organization. It is not advisable for the chairman to be a member of all or any of the committees, either with or without a vote.

Signing the minutes as having been approved after their approval by the board.

Signing contracts and other documents in the name of the school board.

Countersigning warrants or checks in payment of claims against the school district, or authorizing use of his signature.

Representing the school district in legal and business matters.

Referring persons who appeal to him on matters relating to the conduct of the schools to the superintendent for his action or acting as a channel to the board.

Keeping foremost the aims and objectives of the schools in dealing with school personnel and in the school system's relations with community groups or local government agencies.

Seeking expressions of opinion by community groups on controversial matters as a guide to board deliberations and actions.

Issuing, in the name of the board, statements of policies and actions as officially expressed by the board.

Representing the school board at official, community, and school functions.

A few other duties of similar character might be added, or some of these could be separated into components. The main point is that the list should neither include any duties of an executive or administrative nature, which belong to the superintendent of schools, nor any duties concerning the determination of policy, which belong to the whole board.

In a few instances, certain long term presidents have built up executive offices of considerable power and come to rule the board and the schools with an iron hand. An example is the control built up by the president of the board of education in a very large city prior to the district's school administrative reorganization. The president had held the office for a considerable number of years. He maintained a suite of rooms for his office and a staff responsible only to him. His was a super-executive agency for certain matters, including political patronage for certain school positions, public relations, and some other functions that had political significance. He also acted for the board in so-called "emergency" matters, reporting his actions for ratification at the next regular meeting of the board. Reorganization of school administration for the district found an elaborate and surplus president's office, with no place provided for it in the new organization. Most of its functions were transferred to agencies under the general superintendent's direction or were discontinued. A board of education consisting largely of new members had no use for the old organization. The modification of the functions of the president resulted in less political use of the schools, improved the selection of personnel, and vastly bettered public relations.

Requirements as a Presiding Officer. One of the most important requirements for the chairman of a school board is that he be an efficient presiding officer at school board meetings. Meetings of the board should be conducted with dignity and decorum. It is desirable that he be able to conduct meetings according to accepted procedure. He should be familiar with the board's rules and regulations. If the board has separate by-laws, he should know them, all of their implications, and the reasons for each. He should: have knowledge of accepted parliamentary procedure; be well poised and preside with ease; be able to present delegations to the board for hearings with a minimum of resulting friction; be good-natured and courteous but able to conduct deliberations without permitting discussion to diverge from the question at issue; keep in mind the motion before the

house and properly recognize members who desire to speak on
the issues of that motion; not take a vote on a motion until there
has been full consideration; and, although being fair to every-
one, not permit the use of time for endless repetition and irrelevant discussion.

Vice-Chairman

The duties of a vice-chairman (or vice-president) are to preside at board meetings, to sign documents, and to perform other
duties of the chairman in his absence or at his request. Since the
vice-chairman may be required to act as chairman, he should
have the same qualifications and should be selected in the same
manner as the chairman.

Secretary of the Board

Method of Selection and Person Selected as Secretary. It is
the general practice in cities above 30,000 population for the
school board to elect a part or full time secretary other than the
superintendent of schools or a board member. A board member
is elected as secretary in a considerable number of the smaller
cities. The superintendent serves as secretary in a growing number of cities.

In some school districts the secretary, often called "clerk,"
is elected by the board either from among its members or from
outside. Sometimes the clerk has not only secretarial duties but
also performs some of the functions of business management,
including bookkeeping and purchasing. In some cities the business manager of the school system serves as secretary of the
board. Usually the positions of business manager and secretary
of the board are separate in the larger school systems. They
should not be held by one person, since some of their duties are
incompatible, even though others are complimentary. It is not
good policy to entrust the duty of keeping the records of board
expenditure authorizations (in the minutes) to the person who

keeps the financial records and draws the checks for expenditures.

In some of the states having county school districts, such as Florida and Tennessee, the superintendent of schools is designated by law as secretary of the board. In many cities and towns throughout the United States, the superintendent serves as secretary of the board because the board elects him to the position or because he holds the position *ex officio* by statute or by the adopted rules and regulations of the board. In other cities and towns the position of secretary is filled part time by some employee in the school system or by some one from outside. In many of the larger school systems a full time secretary is employed, and in very large city school districts, such as Chicago, the secretary may have a considerable staff.

In school districts not large enough to warrant the employment of a full time secretary, but large enough for a superintendent of schools, there are advantages in assigning the position of secretary of the board to the superintendent. The position is appropriate to the work of the executive officer of the board. It obviates the necessity of drawing a line between the duties of the executive officer and the secretary in functions relating to agenda, minutes, the calling of meetings, and correspondence for the board. If either the superintendent or a board member is secretary, he should have a stenographer to take shorthand notes on important proceedings and to transcribe them for reference in making the permanent record of minutes. Ordinarily, the secretary of the superintendent performs the duties for him. Stenographic notes and their transcription insure greater accuracy and make it unnecessary for the superintendent or board member to take notes when he needs his time for other matters. The stenographer's notes also often serve as a safeguard against errors in the records.

Duties of the Secretary. Some of the more important duties of a secretary of the board are as follows:

Keeping a calendar of business to come before the board at specific dates.

Preparing agenda for school board meetings. This duty can often better be performed by the superintendent of schools, as the board's executive officer, whether or not he is also the secretary.

Sending copies of materials to board members, such as communications calling special meetings, minutes to be presented to the board for approval, agenda of meetings, relevant letters, and documents relating to agenda items.

Attending all regular and special school board meetings.

Taking stenographic notes on procedures at board meetings, or having notes taken for use in preparing the minutes to be presented to the board for approval.

Preparing a correct record of the minutes of all regular and other meetings of the board. Sometimes the secretary also keeps minutes of committee meetings if the board has committees, but committees usually keep no records of their meetings or else they appoint a committee member to keep them.

Conducting correspondence for and in the name of the board, as authorized by the board.

Keeping supplementary records from past years available for ready reference on short notice. Some of these are: coal and fuel oil records; prices of certain goods and names of firms from whom goods were purchased or who bid on contracts; use of electricity; cafeteria patronage; travel by employees; pupil transportation; school enrollment by rooms and schools; and other similar records that are likely to be needed frequently for reference.

Preparing reports for the board, under the direction or with the help of the superintendent of schools.

Signing certain official documents with the chairman of the board, for and in the name of the board.

Signing orders on the treasurer when authorized by the board.

Safeguarding the old and current minute books of the board.

Safeguarding official documents belonging to the school district, such as deeds and abstracts, insurance policies, and contracts.

Treasurer

Method of Selection of the Treasurer. In some school districts a member of the school board is elected by the board to serve as treasurer of the district or is so designated on the ballot that elects him as a board member. In some states the law provides that the county treasurer shall serve as treasurer of the county school district. In others, he may be treasurer for all of the school districts in the county. In city school districts, the city treasurer is sometimes designated by charter or by vote of the school board to serve as treasurer of the school district funds.

In many city and town school districts, the school board selects a nonmember treasurer who serves as an officer under direction of the school board. The board also selects a depository or several depositories for its moneys. It is the practice in some school districts to appoint an officer from a depository to serve as treasurer. In any case, the treasurer is usually required to furnish a fidelity bond. Also, the depository is sometimes required to furnish collateral security for funds.

It is the author's opinion that the city or county treasurer can best serve as treasurer of the school district's funds. This need not require that the school district become involved in city or county politics since a treasurer has no policy-making or administrative functions. It merely means that the city or county performs a service function for the school district similar to those often performed by the police, fire, recreation, or other departments. In states where a school district treasurer must be selected by the board, it is well to select an official of the school district's depository.

Duties of the Treasurer. The treasurer has few duties and none that cannot be performed by a city or county treasurer or an officer of the depository. Some of the treasurer's more important duties are as follows:

Receiving and depositing all moneys belonging to the school district, including those for current expenses, capital outlays, sinking funds, and trust funds.
Keeping funds of the school district in the designated depository or depositories.
Keeping cash accounts, by funds, of receipts and disbursements.
Disbursing moneys in payment of salaries and claims as ordered by and on warrant of the board.

Preparing and presenting to the school board monthly statements of cash received and disbursed by sources of receipts and by funds.

Opening books and records for independent audit as ordered by the board or for audit by state officials.

Investing the money of any sinking or trust funds as directed by the board or subject to the board's approval.

Safeguarding school district securities.

Standing Committees

Development and Decline of the Standing Committee System. Some of the facts concerning the development and decline of the standing committee system were presented in Chapter 2. These should be recalled at this point. There were standing committees of school boards before there were superintendents of schools. Their purpose was mainly to divide the administrative duties among the members of the board because of the amount of such work involved. Committees produced the curriculum, selected textbooks and library books, examined and employed teachers, purchased supplies, visited classrooms, and performed other administrative and supervisory functions. The standing committee system persisted and seemed to be necessary in city school districts when they were consolidated. The number of board members increased to the point where the boards were so unwieldy that their functions could be better performed by committees. However, the committee system developed to a point at which the board had few functions remaining other than to approve the actions of a ridiculously large number of committees. During the present century, with the decline in the number of school board members, committees of the board have become generally recognized as obsolete. The number of standing committees of boards has declined to the point where there are very few, if any.

Extent of Use of Committees. School boards are now small enough so that standing committees are no longer needed in view of the employment of administrative staffs. However, tradition is a powerful deterrent to change, and many boards still have one or more standing committees. The study made by the National Education Association in 1946 shows that although few boards in rural and county school districts have any standing committees, they are still used in more than half of the districts of the larger cities. The trend is still toward elimination of standing committees. Forty-eight per cent of the school boards in cities of more than 100,000 population and 41 per cent in cities from 30,000 to 100,000 population have no standing committees. In county school districts only 12 per cent, in rural districts only 1 per cent, and in town districts 19 per cent have standing committees.

Kinds of Standing Committees. Probably the most common current standing committee is that on finance. In fact, it is the only standing committee some boards have. Other frequently retained standing committees are an executive committee and those on rules and regulations, teachers, and school buildings and grounds. Some other standing committees still to be found are those on such matters as: legislation; complaints and appeals; public relations; publications; subdistricts; audits; salaries; school supplies; equipment; repairs; community use of school buildings; custodial service; insurance; library; designated special subjects; athletics; curriculum and instruction; textbooks; cafeterias; transportation of pupils; school activities; and health and medical service. Any one school board is likely to have only one or a few of these standing committees. Most of them have none.

Duties of Committees. It is difficult to describe the work of standing committees because their functions are poorly defined. Often they are rather harmless but useless and confine their meetings to about 15 or 20 minutes immediately preceding school board meetings. If they must make important decisions for the board, they sometimes meet at other times and places or even hold hearings on matters such as teachers' salaries or the budget.

Committee titles usually define their supposed or real activities. One might wonder just what contribution a committee on textbooks can make toward their selection and adoption. Selection is a professional matter. It requires analysis and rating of the different textbooks in each subject of each grade by committees of teachers who will use the books as teaching instruments. Adoption of the books is a matter for action of the whole board on recommendation of the superintendent. What is the committee's function? Other than giving careful consideration to the recommendations made and possibly checking the books for subversive material, there is no function for such a committee to perform. Even these are functions of the executive officer or persons appointed by him. Similarly, what contribution can a committee on teachers make toward the selection of teachers? The selection of teachers is also a professional matter for the performance of the superintendent and his professional staff. It involves the evaluation of the qualifications of applicants.

A study of the rules and regulations of boards indicates that the duties of standing committees are largely administrative and advisory. School committees should not be expected to perform administrative duties; such duties are the province of the superintendent and his staff, who have been trained for the work and are experienced in it. Legislative and larger policy-making functions can be performed only by the board itself. A committee's work appears to be limited to the preliminary consideration of matters of policy for board action. Its recommendations would be useful only in case the board does not have confidence in the superintendent's professionally considered recommendations. If that condition obtains, it is time for the board to secure a superintendent in whose judgment it has confidence.

There is little more to be said concerning the duties of standing committees of the board. It appears that there are no real functions for such committees to perform that are not the board's legislative and policy-making functions or the superintendent's administrative and advisory functions. The weight of professional education opinion is against the use of standing committees. They were necessary for the performance of administrative duties before there were superintendents, and they were needed to expedite the board's business in the days of the 100-member city school boards. However, it seems to be a little absurd for a board of seven members to divide itself into committees.

Disadvantages of the Committee System. There are few real advantages in the committee system of transacting school board business. For this reason there is nothing worthwhile to present here under a heading, "Advantages of the Committee System." However, there are serious disadvantages in the use of standing committees, some of which may be presented.

A committee system divides the school board into a number of smaller ones which make recommendations to the full board. The board may act in one of two ways on the recommendations. First, it may "rubber-stamp" a recommendation, adopting it without consideration. In this case the real decision has been made by the part of the board composing the committee only. Second, it may give consideration to the arguments pro and con the question at issue. If this is done, the members of the board are required to repeat the committee's procedure. In either case the services of the committee have not been useful; the committee's time has been wasted. Some school boards nearly always adopt committee reports unanimously, without discussion. In one school system, no committee report had been rejected for nine years and there had been no vote against a committee recommendation for four years. Use of committees is a poor method of determining school policies.

The school board, itself, should not be an administrative agency. It is legally responsible for the execution of its policies, but the enforcement and administration should be under the direction of the superintendent. It is impractical for a board to administer the schools because it can act only when in session. For the same reason, neither can standing committees successfully administer the schools. The board's functions of determining policies, authorizing procedures, and adopting or rejecting recommendations of the superintendent cannot be performed by committees. There simply are no distinct functions for committees to perform. Lacking real function, committees are sometimes tempted to assume either the board's legislative functions or the superintendent's executive functions to justify their existence. Confusion is caused in the execution of board policies to the extent that committees assume the functions of the superintendent. The board also relinquishes its right to hold the superintendent responsible for results. Such responsibility is necessary to insure effective administration.

The demarcation between the functions of different standing committees is seldom clear even though rules and regulations attempt to define the functions of the committees. The difficulty arises from the fact that few problems present themselves in a single field. Matters relating to teachers, building repairs, and the like often involve finances, and one committee cannot give complete consideration to the problem without entering another committee's field. A problem may deal with both teachers and the curriculum or with the curriculum and school buildings. Overlapping functions may cause friction among committees.

More serious difficulties arising from overlapping of functions result in inconsistent actions by the different standing committees. These may result in unco-ordinated board legislation by adoption of committee reports. Any one committee will not know what other committees are doing until their recommendations are presented and then may not know the reasons for them. It is true that the whole board should be expected to iron out any inconsistencies and co-ordinate the separate recommendations of committees, and it sometimes does. However, that requires full board deliberation on each question, in which case the committee's work has not relieved the board in any way.

Some standing committees conceive their functions to be investigation preliminary to board action. This is not sound. Research in a professional field is better accomplished by a professional staff. It is the function of the superintendent and his staff to make "reports" on special subjects as required by the board. These should consist of facts gathered by the superin-

tendent or his assistants. They ought to be professionally interpreted to help the board members understand their significance
and presented by the superintendent to the full board, usually
in written form. This is the superintendent's "report" on an
assigned subject. The board should refer problems to the superintendent rather than to standing committees for report and
recommendation.

The referral of matters to standing committees postpones
action by the board until the report of the committee has been
prepared and received. The sometimes superficial consideration
given matters by standing committees and the often uncritical
acceptance of the report result in poorer legislation than would
be secured without the services of the committees. A plurality of
committees means that the school system may be controlled by
several sub-boards whose actions are not co-ordinated. It means
that a minority of the members decides what policies are to be
adopted. This tends to cause irresponsibility in the members.
The delays and inconsistencies impair the effectiveness of the
board's work. The actions of the committees make it difficult
or impossible for the superintendent to perform his work effectively. To some extent, they substitute nonprofessional administrative control for professional administration.

The standing committee system of conducting board business
provides that lay members shall perform professional education
functions. To the extent that committees function, the board
ignores the fact that the superintendent and his assistants have
devoted years to the study of the problems of managing a school
system, have a background of knowledge of the relationships
among the parts of the local school system, and have had experience in solving similar and related problems. It is no more logical
to have committees of laymen dealing with technical education
matters, such as promotion and grading, courses of study, curriculum, school supplies, and school buildings than it would be
for a hospital board to have committees of laymen dealing with
technical medical matters, such as skin and heart diseases, gyne-
cology, pediatrics, and operations.

If anyone should maintain that standing committees are necessary to conduct school board business, whatever arguments he advances can be met by the fact that nearly half of the city school boards have no committees and a large majority of county and smaller district boards have none. Weight of opinion has approved the elimination of or a decrease in the number of committees.

Committee of the Whole

Instead of standing committees, a board of from 3 to 9 members can advantageously organize itself as a committee of the whole for the informal consideration of issues. In a committee of the whole, a board can deliberate freely and make recommendations for action, but it cannot take official action as a board. To act officially it must meet again as a school board when it is ready to adopt a motion. A meeting of a committee of the whole is not usually open to the public. This makes it possible for the board members to exercise somewhat more freedom in their discussion than is practicable in an open and formal board meeting.

Sometimes the board meets in executive session. An executive session is like a meeting of the committee of the whole in that the public is excluded, but it is an official meeting at which business can be transacted unless the law provides that all business shall be transacted in open meeting.

The rules and regulations of the board of education of the Chicago school district include a provision adopted in 1946 for a "general" committee, as follows:

> There shall be a general committee of the board. This committee shall consist of the president, who shall be chairman, and all other members of the board of education. Any matters pertaining to school affairs may be referred to this committee.
>
> The general committee shall meet at 1:30 P.M. on the day of the regular Board of Education meeting and at such other times as the committee may determine.

Special Committees

Much of what has been presented here concerning standing committees does not apply to special committees. A special committee is one appointed for a special purpose. Standing committees are permanent and continuing; special committees are discharged with the board's acceptance of their report. Usually the problems they are to study or the duties they are assigned are nonrecurring. They may be appointed to study or act and report to the board on such matters as: legislation to modify the plan for securing special school aid; visitation of a new school building in another district; debt limitation; school building insurance; school transportation routes; need for revision of the teachers' salary schedule; collection of delinquent school taxes; heating problems in a particular school; cost of fencing school grounds; and cost of surfacing the athletic field. More than half of the school boards in cities above 30,000 population have occasional special committees, whether or not they have standing committees.

When a special committee is required, it should be appointed to report by a particular date on the specified matter. It should be discharged if its report is accepted or, if not accepted, discharged or continued to an extended date. The purpose should be unusual and nonrecurring after its mission has been accomplished. Its report should consist of findings and recommendations, usually presented in written form. Each special committee should leave all decisions to board action unless the board has found it advisable to form the committee "with power to act." A special committee should not be appointed to secure and interpret data that are more applicable to the capabilities of the superintendent of schools and his staff.

Legal Counsel

School boards need legal services in the form of advice on the following: interpretation and significance of particular school laws; the drafting of contracts and their approval from a legal standpoint; representation of the board in civil suits on the fulfilling of contract requirements either in defense of the board or in prosecution of the contractor; prosecution of claims of the board for damages to property; and the study of abstracts and approval of titles of land before purchase. In some states school boards can secure advice concerning the interpretation and enforcement of school laws from the legal staff of the state department of education. The attorney general's office will furnish rulings as to the meaning of laws, the service varying in different states. In some states the board is entitled to such services, though they seldom extend to the approval of contracts and the devising of legal forms.

Many school boards employ legal services irregularly, as needed. School boards of the larger cities usually employ a part or full time attorney, and a staff of attorneys may be employed in very large cities. In 1947, the board of education of Chicago employed a staff of 15 or more persons in its legal office, several of whom were lawyers and the others clerical workers. Even then, its legal office employed additional outside assistance.

One may wonder why it is necessary to employ legal service when there are often lawyers on the board. The author has known boards that depended on their lawyer members for free service which was rendered willingly. But it is an imposition upon lawyer members to obtain free service from them. Much study and time are required to render sound legal opinions or to approve contracts. Attorneys should no more be expected to furnish free services to the board than physicians should be expected to furnish free medical service to school children or merchants free supplies to the schools. However, lawyer members and others may wish to render small services when they find it convenient. Lawyers should not furnish legal services for pay to a board of which they are members. But legal services should be available when needed. Except in the larger cities, where the volume of legal work may be fairly large, and a special legal staff is needed, it would seem to be satisfactory and more economical for the school board to secure such legal services as are available from the city or county legal office and to supplement them with outside services as required.

If a part or full time lawyer or larger legal staff is required, the duties will usually be performed directly for the board. For this reason the board sometimes requires the attendance of its attorney at board meetings. The attorney is usually considered to be a staff employee of the board much like its appointed secretary. The work is not administrative, and it would seem that the logical place in the organization is as a staff member directly responsible to the board, rendering advisory service to the members and to the superintendent and his administrative assistants on legal matters pertaining to the schools.

Executive Officer

The superintendent of schools is an important officer of the board, elected by the board and responsible directly to it. His duties should be to manage the school system as the board requires according to adopted policies and in accordance with his own best judgment where no such policies apply. He should also act as executive officer of the board in making its policies effective in the school system and in enforcing the state laws relating to public schools. In some states the statutes specifically provide that the superintendent shall be the board's executive officer, though no provision is made for a superintendent of schools in the laws of many other states. The Massachusetts laws provide that the superintendent "shall be the executive officer of the committee, and under its general direction shall have the administration and supervision of the public schools, shall assist in keeping its records and accounts and in making such reports as are required by law, and shall recommend to the committee, teachers, textbooks, and courses of study."

As executive officer, the superintendent should prepare the agenda for board meetings and attend those meetings so that he will be available to furnish information concerning the school system and make recommendations concerning proposed actions. If the board's policies are poorly executed, the board should secure an executive who can and will make the board's expressed wishes effective. Full responsibility should be placed on the chief executive officer for effectuating the expressed will of the board. It is necessary that there be mutual trust between the board and the superintendent and that the superintendent be well qualified for his work so that he will not unwittingly give the board poor advice.

Administrative Organization

Patterns of Top Organization. There are several ways in which an administrative staff may be organized on a functional basis. Each is different from the others in lines of authority and responsibility to the school board and has differences in merit regarding soundness of organization. The following patterns for large school systems are presented as samples. They include only the principal administrative offices.

In Type A, the principal functions may be combined or divided depending upon the number of assistant superintendents. For example the functions of assistant superintendent in charge of instruction may be performed by three assistant superintendents in charge of high schools, elementary schools, and vocational schools. There may be still another for special schools and classes. The functions of the assistant superintendent in charge of physical plant may be performed by two assistant superintendents, one in charge of plant operation and maintenance and the other in charge of building construction. The others could be divided similarly. On the other hand, the functions could be combined to provide fewer assistant superintendents. For example, one assistant superintendent could have charge of both employed and pupil personnel or of both business and physical plant. Instead of too many assistant superintendents, it probably would be better to have directors in charge of the subfunctions who would be responsible to the assistant superintendents.

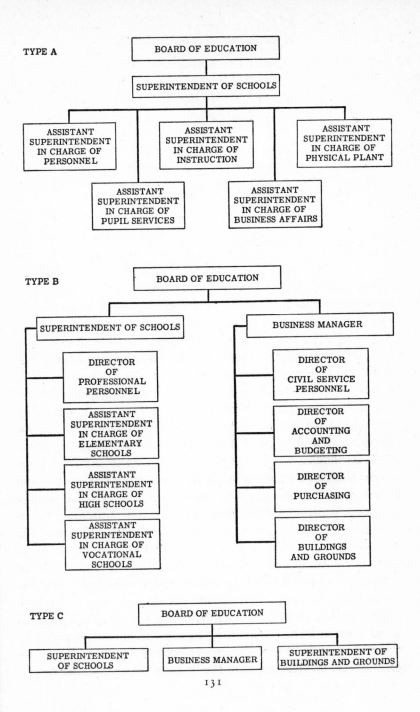

TYPE A

BOARD OF EDUCATION

SUPERINTENDENT OF SCHOOLS

ASSISTANT SUPERINTENDENT IN CHARGE OF PERSONNEL

ASSISTANT SUPERINTENDENT IN CHARGE OF INSTRUCTION

ASSISTANT SUPERINTENDENT IN CHARGE OF PHYSICAL PLANT

ASSISTANT SUPERINTENDENT IN CHARGE OF PUPIL SERVICES

ASSISTANT SUPERINTENDENT IN CHARGE OF BUSINESS AFFAIRS

TYPE B

BOARD OF EDUCATION

SUPERINTENDENT OF SCHOOLS

BUSINESS MANAGER

DIRECTOR OF PROFESSIONAL PERSONNEL

DIRECTOR OF CIVIL SERVICE PERSONNEL

ASSISTANT SUPERINTENDENT IN CHARGE OF ELEMENTARY SCHOOLS

DIRECTOR OF ACCOUNTING AND BUDGETING

ASSISTANT SUPERINTENDENT IN CHARGE OF HIGH SCHOOLS

DIRECTOR OF PURCHASING

ASSISTANT SUPERINTENDENT IN CHARGE OF VOCATIONAL SCHOOLS

DIRECTOR OF BUILDINGS AND GROUNDS

TYPE C

BOARD OF EDUCATION

SUPERINTENDENT OF SCHOOLS

BUSINESS MANAGER

SUPERINTENDENT OF BUILDINGS AND GROUNDS

The Type B form of organization is defective because it provides that administrative authority shall be divided between instruction and business. There is no co-ordinating head in this form of organization, and therefore the policy making or legislative body is required to co-ordinate the activities of the two executives. It cannot do this satisfactorily in its monthly or semi-monthly meetings. A great deal of friction between the two heads or their staffs will usually be engendered. Such problems cannot be resolved except by the board.

There are three executive officers directly responsible to the board in the Type C organization form. Each has assistants or directors under him. This was the form of organization in Louisville, Kentucky, some years ago. Some of the titles were not the same as those used here, but they represented the same three principal functions. It was also the form of organization used in Kansas City, Missouri, before that school system was reorganized, except that the city librarian constituted a fourth executive head under the board of school directors. The plan is very defective because it makes it necessary (as was the case in Type B) for the board to co-ordinate the executive activities of the several departments, each of which is distinct from the other two. This gives the board the executive as well as the legislative functions. A board cannot serve in an executive capacity advantageously because: it is not always available; it is not a single person that can act immediately but a deliberative body; and the members are not prepared by education or experience for administering a professional education enterprise. It is difficult for a board to decide problems when it is advised differently by several of its head departmental executive officers, all of equal authority and rank.

Certain school officers perform auxiliary or staff functions. They are not shown in the charts because they are not administrative officers. Still, they must be at the top level of organization. They are extensions of the superintendent of schools, and their functions are to help him with his overhead duties. If charted, these agencies would be out of the direct line of authority, but would function directly under the superintendent in an organization such as Type A. They could not function properly in the other two forms of organization. These agencies are public relations, research, and office services. They must necessarily be at the top level of organization as staff agencies because they must represent the authority of the executive head and be able to reach into any or all departments and divisions of the school system. If there is unit organization (Type A), these staff agencies would be responsible directly to the superintendent of schools; if there is a multiple form of organization, they would have to be directly responsible to the board in order to have access to all of the line organizations. A board could not effectively direct these functions.

The plan adopted for top administrative organization of the Chicago public school system, as changed from the multiple system, may be shown in outline form. Positions on the same vertical line, under the next superior position, are equally subordinate to that position. The Chicago plan of organization follows:

Board of education
  General superintendent of schools
    Secretary of the general superintendent
    Assistant to the general superintendent
      Director of the bureau of research and statistics
      Director of the bureau of public relations
      Director of the bureau of office services

    First assistant superintendent in charge of instruction
      Director of the bureau of instruction materials
      Director of the bureau of subject supervision
      Director of the bureau of education extension

    Assistant superintendent in charge of personnel
      Director of the bureau of teacher personnel
      Director of the bureau of administration and office personnel
      Director of the bureau of operation, maintenance, and lunchroom personnel
      Director of the bureau of civil service records

Assistant superintendent in charge of elementary education
  9 district superintendents
  President of Chicago Teachers College

Assistant superintendent in charge of secondary education
  5 district superintendents
  3 presidents of branches of Chicago City Junior College

Assistant superintendent in charge of vocational education
  Director of the bureau of technical subjects
  Director of the bureau of special services
  Director of the bureau of veterans training
  Director of the bureau of distributive education

Assistant superintendent in charge of special education
  Director of the bureau of exceptional children
  Director of the bureau of special classes
  Director of the bureau of child study
  Director of the bureau of guidance and counseling
  Director of the bureau of school attendance

Controller (in charge of the department of finance)
  Director of the bureau of the budget
  Chief accountant (in charge of the bureau of accounting)
  Assistant auditor (in charge of the bureau of audits)
  Paymaster (in charge of the bureau of payrolls)

Director of purchases (in charge of the department of purchases)
  Assistant purchases agent
  Buying staff
  Printer (in charge of printing plant)

Architect (in charge of the department of architecture and building repair)
  Assistant architect (in charge of the bureau of architecture)
  Assistant superintendent of repairs (in charge of the bureau of general maintenance and repair)
  Supervising engineer (in charge of the bureau of electrical and mechanical repairs)

Director of plant engineering and lunchrooms (in charge of the department of plant engineering and lunchrooms)

Chief engineer (in charge of the bureau of plant engineering)
Director of the bureau of lunchrooms
Secretary of the board
Director of the law department

The above outline presents only the positions in the top organization for a very large city school system. Functions that may seem to have been omitted are subordinate to some of the positions shown and do not appear in the outline of principal administrative positions. Under the bureaus or equivalent organization units there are usually divisions, each with its head. In a few cases, the divisions are further separated into sections.

Preferred Form of Organization. The main point at issue in determining the best form of top organization is whether the administrative organization shall be a unit form or a multiple form. Form A, the organization adopted by the board of the Chicago school district, is an example of the unit form, in which all operating employees are responsible directly or indirectly to the superintendent of schools. The board's secretary, attorney, and treasurer, if under the board, are the only exceptions to this subordination. The superintendent is the only executive officer. The others are multiple forms of organization.

There is almost universal acceptance of the principle of the unit form of organization by students of organization structure for any government or industrial organization. If there is no single administrative head, difficulties arise between executives of equal rank. This might occur between the superintendent of schools and the business manager, the superintendent of schools and the superintendent of buildings and grounds, or the business manager and the superintendent of buildings and grounds. In such cases, the board has to become the chief executive officer, for there is no other agency to compose the differences arising among executive officers of equal rank. A lay board is unfitted to serve as chief executive in professional educational matters and unable to do so properly because it is not in continuous session and is not available to act when problems arise. Therefore, it is desirable to have a single executive head of a school system. This head should be the superintendent of schools, who by training and experience is better able to understand the objectives and work of the school system than are the others. A single executive heads the organizations used in 67 per cent of the larger city school systems and nearly 100 per cent of the small city, town, and county school districts that have executive officers.

It is very important that the board be able to hold its executive officer responsible for the management of the schools. The superintendent cannot be held responsible for the work of the schools if there are other executives of equal rank. The Chicago public school district was changed from a three-headed to a one-headed system because of the inefficiency and waste that had developed. If the policies of the board are to be executed satisfactorily, there can be no more than one pilot for the ship— one director of the whole system.

Some authorities have maintained that instruction, business, and building functions are separate and that the superintendent is not qualified to perform the business and building functions. This is a wholly wrong conception of his qualifications. First, the functions are not separate. The sole purpose of the schools as to educate children. Effective education depends on the auxiliary business functions of budgeting, accounting, purchasing, property control, the furnishing of adequate building and equipment facilities for learning, and the maintenance and operation of school buildings. Second, under the unit plan of organization there will still be specialists in school business and buildings, but they will be under the general direction of the superintendent of schools instead of immediately under the direction of the board. This will help the board to perform its functions, and to keep in mind that the only purpose of the schools is to educate children. If every president of an industrial corporation were required to know more about procurement, production, sales, accounting, labor relations, and public relations than heads of those departments, there would be a dearth of persons qualified to fill the positions of president.

The arguments for a unit form of organization structure in a school district with a single top executive are the following: it is generally accepted as the most desirable form; it is the plan in use by large industrial and army organizations the world over; it is recommended by practically all students of administrative organization structure for all government organizations, including the school district; it helps to eliminate friction in administration by removing its principal cause, undefined authority; it makes possible the co-ordination of the work of different branches of the service; it locates administrative authority in a single executive and administrative head who can be held responsible for results; and finally, it places all employees under one head, a far more economical method than multiple control because it results in wiser expenditure of school funds.

Whatever the form of organization structure, the lines of authority and responsibility should be clearly defined. Every employee should know his place in the organization. The function of each part should be related to, but separated from, the functions of all other parts. The relations can be clarified by including all of the elements in a chart of the complete organization structure. As a basis for the chart, there should be a complete analysis of the functions of each position and the duties of the position's incumbent. When necessary, the separate duties can be shifted from their present location to a more logical place in the organization, so that related parts will be placed together.

An organizational outline might be prepared in addition to the chart. Such an outline would show the lines of authority and responsibility from the board of education to the smallest administrative unit. It would show the inconsistencies in the existing plan of organization. The limits and authority of each administrative position should then be clearly defined by the board.

CHAPTER 9

The Functions, Powers, and
Responsibilities of School Boards

Nature and Classification of School Board Activities

It is impossible to list or classify precisely all of the functions, powers, and responsibilities of school boards. They vary according to state and the several kinds of school districts in each state. Legally, some activities are mandatory; some are permissive at the discretion of the board; and some are implied in the general legal provisions for the maintenance of public schools. Certain activities in which school boards might be tempted to engage are sometimes prohibited by law. A school board's work must be performed subject to numerous legal controls that require, permit, restrict, or prohibit specified activities. What is required of local school boards in one state may be a function of the state department of education in another, e.g., furnishing free textbooks or supplies; what is discretionary in one state may be either prohibited or required in others, e.g., the oral reading of passages from the Bible in elementary schools. The nature of school board activities was stated by a superintendent to new board members as follows:

> The board of education is a specialized legislative body acting as the agent of the state and of the community it specifically represents. This legislative body is empowered to make the state educational plan effective in its own locality. Since only a small part of this plan is mandatory, the actual development and

execution of a complete educational plan for most communities must be conditioned not only in the interpretation of community needs but also by the development of a community consciousness of these needs.[1]

In general, the activities of school boards may be classified under the following seven headings:

1. Complying—which includes those activities of boards necessary to effectuate the laws of the state and the regulations of state educational or other authorities. These controls relate to such matters as school elections, taxation, budgeting, purchasing, contracting debt, constructing school buildings, transporting pupils, school attendance, pupil health, length of school terms, teacher qualifications, teacher salaries, employment and dismissal of teachers, the curriculum and instruction, athletics, and scores of others.

2. Policy making—which includes board actions establishing basic formal rules and regulations and the directives and authorizations addressed to teachers, pupils, and others. These are not contrary to the provisions of state laws and the rules, regulations, and directives of state authorities, but extensions or applications of them.

3. Executing—which is the work of the superintendent of schools and his administrative staff. The board is made legally responsible to the state for this work, and its members are morally responsible to the community that selects them.

4. Operating—which includes the work accomplished by teachers, supervisors, custodians, and others, performed in accordance with the adopted policies of the board.

5. Observing and evaluating the condition of the schools— which includes their activities relating to the curriculum and instruction, special services, pupil enterprises to determine their effectiveness and needs, and the inspection of buildings and equipment. This is done as a basis for future educational planning.

6. Interpreting—or the activities of the board with regard

[1] M. L. McCoy, Superintendent of Wayne, Michigan, Public Schools.

to reporting its stewardship to the public and planning and maintaining good public relations.

7. Judging—or the activities requiring the adjudication of disputes between executives of equal rank under the board, where such form of organization exists; or appeals of a subordinate or of the public over the head of the superintendent; or hearing the appeal of an employee on the board's decision.

Limitations on School Board Authority

School boards are limited in the exercise of their powers within school districts. They are restricted by the following: state laws as interpreted by courts, rules and regulations of state boards of education, and sometimes city charters; requirements of efficiency and expediency in performing functions that are professional in character; and public policy and practices that are acceptable in the community.

The courts hold that a school district is a public corporation with limited authority and that its board may exercise only such powers as are conferred on it by law, expressly or by implication. The board cannot act beyond such powers. It is not legally circumscribed by limitations other than those provided directly or indirectly by the laws of the state.

The powers and duties of school boards are defined in varying detail in the laws of the states. Powers are stated as general authorizations for many actions, and boards may exercise discretion as to the extent of their compliance with them. Even restrictions imposed by a state board of education or county or city officials must be based on laws granting such officials authority over certain specific functions of school control.

The charters of some cities require that the mayor, the council, or some other agency approve school budgets. In some cases, such outside agency is empowered to change the school district's budget or some parts of it. Other powers sometimes granted by law to city authorities are for the purchase of school supplies, the purchase of school sites and the construction of buildings, the repair of school buildings, the furnishing of accounting services, and the furnishing of medical inspection and control. Such provisions are sometimes serious restrictions on the authority and power of a school board, regardless of possible advantages. However, they do not generally prevail; most boards are independent of control by officers of the city or county. Where outside authorities exercise such powers to control school board policies and actions, the board is so restricted that it cannot be held fully responsible for the conduct of the schools.

The school board may do many things but it is restricted to public education purposes. Within legal restrictions it may do such things as borrow money, issue bonds, and furnish free pupil transportation to school, but it can do them only for the purpose of public education. The board is also properly limited by the functions assigned to agencies of the city or county. For example, the making of a driveway on the school grounds might be considered a school board function, but the building of a road necessary for a part of a school bus route would not be so considered since that would be a function of the county or state. A school board is prohibited from performing functions belonging to another government agency even though they may be needed for public education purposes.

School boards usually have the right of eminent domain with their power to provide school buildings and the necessity of securing suitable sites for them. However, a school board seldom has the right to condemn other public property such as a public park or library. A court may take into account the relative importance of the proposed use of public property and might condemn unused public land for the site of a school building or unused school land for use by a city, but public property cannot usually be condemned for school use. In some states condemnation proceedings for the purchase of school sites are rare. In others, the method of acquiring land by condemnation is common. Some boards would not acquire sites by any other method because the court action relieves the board from the responsibility of determining the monetary value of the land.

Examples of legal restrictions are the requirements that the school board: employ only certificated teachers; pay a minimum salary of some specified amount; do not discriminate between men and women in salaries paid for the same duties; make purchases above a certain amount only on bids; and require all children to repeat the oath of allegiance to the flag. The interpretation of restrictive as well as of other laws rests with the courts of the respective states.

Other than legal restrictions are those imposed by the desire to maintain an efficient public school system. If a school system is to be operated effectively, the board must not perform the administrative functions, though it usually has the legal right to do so and is legally responsible for the effective administration of the schools. The board, itself, is restricted by its inability to administer or operate the schools. This includes such professional activities as selecting textbooks and library books, rating the competency of teachers, selecting and promoting teachers, and operating school buildings.

School boards have the power to enter into such contracts as are permitted by express or implied law, but a contract will often be void or voidable: if it is made by a board with one of its own members; if it deals with a matter prohibited to the board; if it is opposed to public policy; if it exceeds the authority of the board; if it is oral when the law requires it to be written; or if it is not let to the lowest responsible bidder when he meets the specifications fully.

Discretionary Powers

Many of the powers and actions of school boards are permissive by law and discretionary on the part of the board. It is usually within the discretion of the board to determine whether or not to furnish preschool, junior college, adult, vocational, or other kinds of education; to repair an old school building; to have French, Spanish, Polish, or any other language taught in high school; to require physically normal pupils to take physical education; to offer agriculture, music, or home economics courses; to accept tuition pupils; to employ teachers within the legal requirements for certification and salary payments; and to make hundreds of other decisions within the provisions of law and the requirements of the state board of education.

State laws usually grant general powers to school boards by providing that they shall have power to conduct schools subject to legal requirements. Sometimes the laws provide that the boards shall have authority to adopt such policies as they deem necessary to conduct schools effectively or to adopt such rules and regulations as they deem fit, subject to the provisions of the laws of the state and the rules and regulations of the state board of education. Some laws prescribe minimum requirements and permit the board to exceed them. An example would be the certification of teachers.

School boards are generally upheld by the courts in the exercise of discretionary powers. However, the court may hold that a board abuses its discretionary power if, in the court's judgment, its decisions have been caused by temper, passion, stubbornness, prejudice, partiality, or discrimination. A court will not hold a board responsible for making infallible decisions if they have been made in good faith. If a board uses discretionary power, a court will be likely to uphold an honest decision of the board regardless of how disastrous may have been the consequences.

Planning for the Schools

An efficient school board, with the aid of its superintendent, makes plans for the future of its schools and does not permit their operation on a day-to-day basis or even on a year-to-year basis. The board's plans may need modification in case of war or economic depression. Such modification may merely involve the postponement of plans or may require re-evaluation of the importance of improvements needed and corresponding changes in priorities. Whatever plans are made require dating if they are to be realized and not merely idle dreams. No other course has meaning for systematic improvement of the schools.

The annual school budget is the short term financial plan. It is also the most important part of the short term educational plan expressed in financial terms, since most activities planned for a school system will cost money and provision must be made in the budget for their effectuation. Of course, improvements can sometimes be made by reassignment of duties or by replacing unimportant functions with important ones. In such cases there may be no increase in cost, but most plans for the year have to be reflected in the budget. If reallocation of amounts is allowed in the budget, there is planning for less than a year.

Planning should be long range as well as for the immediate future. Long range planning should deal with the physical plant among other matters. The number and size of elementary and high school buildings required at various times in the future should be based on carefully computed estimates of future elementary and high school populations. Such planning should also include plans for the replacement of outmoded school buildings. The replacement of obsolete desks, seats, and other equipment with a type better suited to modern methods of socialized and activity instruction should be considered as well. It should include a repair program for painting, plumbing, electrical work, roofing, grounds improvement, and other forms of maintenance.

Long range planning should not be limited to the physical plant. It should also include the following: maintenance of good public relations; improvement of school procedures; improvement of the teaching staff by more careful selection and better provision for inservice training; curriculum development; securing materials of instruction; establishment of needed educational services, such as kindergartens or vocational education; expansion of the testing program; development of guidance and counseling; development of visual education; improvement of special services to pupils, including school health and dental services, psychological and psychiatric services, lunchroom services, and pupil activities of various kinds; and other matters concerning the effective and economical operation of the schools.

Planning will help school boards to make decisions when some community group demands that something be done. For example, a group might demand that: a new trade course be offered; a new elementary school building be constructed to replace an old one in a section of the city that is being abandoned; a supervisor of penmanship be employed; or more time be devoted to the teaching of some subject, such as spelling or arithmetic. Unless there is planning, decisions are likely to be made without adequate consideration and may prove to be educationally unsound. Without the guidance of a carefully considered and formally adopted plan, the board may be led to mount the hobby horses of community blocs and ride off in all directions, extending the schools in so many ways that they will be able to do nothing well.

Policy Determination

In the interest of the public, it is a school board's duty to determine what policies are basic to the operation of the public schools. Determination of policies may be defined as the agreement of the members of the board on certain principles for use as guides to actions of the board, the employees, and the patrons of the schools, and their formulation and adoption by board action. The basic principles adopted should be incorporated into a set of principles or rules and regulations. Circumstances are seldom identical, but a policy should be capable of being applied equitably in all circumstances to which it refers. If a board finds that it must modify an adopted policy for a particular case, it is an indication that the policy is not adequate. The board should amend this policy for the future and not allow it to stand while acting in a different manner.

A board's policies must be consistent with the provisions of state law. Any policies the superintendent announces in the form of administrative directives must be consistent with both state law and the school board's policies and must implement them in his administration of the school system. Even beyond the superintendent's directives, much policy determination is still left to each school and even each classroom in supplementation of the general policies of the board and the administrative policies of the superintendent.

The school board of any city, town, or county school district should employ a superintendent of schools, but it must retain for itself the control of the public schools through the adoption of policies and the approval of executive actions. It is the board (not the superintendent or any board member) that should determine, after considering the advice of the superintendent, such matters as: when textbook titles are to be changed; whether or not a plan of release of classroom teachers for curriculum construction is to be adopted; whether or not teachers shall be exchanged with other countries or school districts of other states; whether or not new positions are to be established; whether or not home economics and industrial arts are to be taught in the upper elementary school grades and open to both boys and girls; and what shall be the teachers' salary schedule. After consultation with his staff, the superintendent should advise the board on specific policies under consideration. It is he who will be held responsible for making such policies as are adopted effective in the school system.

Many school boards adopt no general, fundamental policies but act separately on specific cases as they arise. This is a very bad practice because it results in inconsistent action. Members of the board cannot remember all past actions and often consider cases with too little regard for precedents. In any event, as board members are changed, the new ones know but little of past actions of the board and may act contrary to former actions. A study of the minutes of any such school board will frequently show this to be the case. Furthermore, consideration of individual cases consumes a great deal of time in meetings. On the other hand, a policy once adopted can be applied fairly in all cases. If a policy is not adequate for a particular case, it should be amended for that case and future ones instead of making the case an exception and continuing the inadequate policy as before.

Action taken on individual cases—every teacher employed, every salary fixed, every application for use of a school building, or every group desiring to solicit contributions from pupils and teachers—is wasteful of time. If a board attempts to act separately on cases, it will find itself overburdened with work. Conservation of time requires that policies be adopted to cover the requirements of specific cases and that the superintendent administer the schools in accordance with these policies. Boards that are overworked might well consider whether the cause is not their acting on individual cases instead of adopting policies to be applied by the superintendent.

A school board, through its superintendent, should follow up the result of the application of adopted policies to determine (1) whether or not they are being applied as intended and (2) if so applied, whether or not the results are as anticipated. From the results, the board must decide whether to continue, modify, or repeal each policy.

Legislation on Specific Cases

Kinds of Legislative Actions. Legislative activities include policy-making actions but not all legislative actions are policy making. Legislative functions may be effectuating and approval in character. Adopting a budget, approving the appointment of a teacher, declaring a special holiday, approving a claim, and others are legislative but not directly policy-making, though they may have indirect effects as precedents for similar future actions. Although approving the appointment of a teacher would not be a policy-making action, determining the qualification standards for eligibility for a particular class of teaching positions would be a policy-making, legislative action. Similarly, passing a motion to permit the boy scouts to use a room of a particular school building every Wednesday evening free of charge would not be adoption of a policy. However, determining the conditions under which school buildings may be used, the kinds of organizations that may or may not use them, which organizations shall pay fees, and the amounts to be charged for using various parts of buildings, would be policy-making legislation.

Establishment of Policies by Precedent. Some policies may be established by precedent from specific actions. For example, a teacher may request an excuse from classroom duties to attend a national meeting of high school classroom teachers. Permission may be granted by the board for the particular case without formal adoption of a policy covering such leaves of absence. Later, another teacher may make a similar request for time off to attend a meeting of another organization. Action in the first case may predispose the board to similar action in the second and in those following. In this way a precedent may establish a loosely defined regulation. On the other hand, there may be differences in the cases that will lead the board to make different decisions. The second request may come from an elementary instead of a high school teacher, and there may be a dearth of substitute elementary school teachers available at the time. Or, the second may be a request to attend a state instead of a national meeting, or vice versa. Perhaps one teacher may be an officer in the national organization and the other only a member. If the board should decide differently in the two cases it might be subject to a charge of inconsistency or favoritism by those not cognizant of the considerations leading to the opposite decisions. The application of published regulations will protect a board from becoming hopelessly involved in inconsistencies or seeming ones to its own embarrassment. Of course, the policy should provide for all present or future contingencies the board deems to be relevant.

Nonpolicy-Making Legislation. The following is an example of a situation that may be the source of many problems that require legislation but not necessarily the adoption of policies for their solution, since they may never or seldom recur:

The situation—The school buildings are crowded with pupils. The high school building is 50 years old and inadequate for instruction in the sciences, music, physical education, industrial arts, and homemaking. The increase in the enrollment of primary pupils and in births indicates that there will be an increase in school population for the next eight years, followed by a leveling off on a higher plateau. The probable number of pupils by grades has been estimated for the next twelve years. Facts concerning the location of the homes of elementary, high school, and preschool children, and declining and developing areas of the city are known.

The possible problems—The conditions may require the solution of many problems, a few of which are: Shall new elementary school facilities and an addition to the high school building be constructed, or shall a central junior high school be established for grades 7 to 9 to relieve both elementary and high schools? If the former, shall there be one large or two small elementary school buildings? If the latter, shall the old senior high school building be remodeled for the junior high school and a new senior high school building constructed with more adequate facilities for instruction in sciences, fine arts, practical arts, and physical education, or shall a new junior high school building be constructed? Where shall the new building be located? How large shall be the site? Shall the building be one or two stories? What shall be the size of classrooms? How shall the construction be financed? After consideration of the professional advice of regular employees or special consultants, these and many other problems must be solved and legislative action taken by the board.

Appraisal and Approval Actions. Probably the most common functions of school boards are those of appraisal and approval. The superintendent recommends specific actions such as the following: adoption of a proposed budget; making of certain physical plant repairs or improvements; appointment of the teachers he nominates; adoption of textbooks; establishment of special classes; provision of new bus routes; or approval of new high school subjects. It is the function of the board to appraise the value and importance of each recommendation and to act on the proposal. Other actions, not forbidden by law or the rules and regulations of the board, are performed by the superintendent and reported to the board for approval. These are approved by motion or by consent. If any appear unwise to the board, the policy covering them is changed or a new policy is adopted and the future actions of the superintendent are modified accordingly.

It is also necessary that the board continually appraise the schools, the staff, and the quality of the work being performed. Nothing less than a high degree of efficiency should satisfy a board. No half-hearted time-serving work of an employee can be tolerated. But action cannot be taken unless there is a prior appraisal of the school system or its parts. The members of the board are qualified only in the most general way to make such appraisals. The board must make its appraisals on the basis of the professional opinions of the superintendent and his staff. It can only evaluate the superintendent's opinions and recommendations in terms of its members' knowledge of the general principles of organization, procedures, personnel administration, and materiel management as such principles apply to all enterprises.

Since a board must rely so completely on the superintendent, it is essential that the members have full confidence in the soundness of his judgment, his professional competence, and his integrity. As boards change in membership, the members sometimes lose confidence in the ability and good intentions of the superintendent. If board members are convinced that the superintendent exercises poor judgment or is otherwise unworthy of their confidence, it is necessary for the board to employ a different superintendent—one in whom the members will have complete confidence. For this reason the superintendent is in a hazardous situation. However, the board should act slowly in changing its executive officer and should do so only after efforts to secure harmonious relations and mutual confidence have failed. Often, working together will develop good relationships if the members of the board and the superintendent are open minded and frank with one another. Boards should largely accept the recommendations of the superintendent on professional matters if not impracticable, but should require full explanation and hold him responsible for results. The board's authority for appraisal and approval should not be relinquished under any condition.

Authority of the Board to Delegate Its Powers

As a rule, the laws of the states place the executive as well as the legislative authority in the school board. Of course, the board cannot perform administrative acts advantageously because its members are not qualified as school administrators. Also, it is in session only about 3 or 4 hours out of 200 or more working hours in an ordinary superintendent's month. Some person must translate the will of the board into administrative action. The early boards delegated the executive or administrative powers to a principal or the various members. Now, except for very small school systems, the powers are usually delegated to a superintendent of schools or a supervising principal.

There is no question of a board's right to delegate its executive powers, but in no case can a board escape responsibility for the actions of agents to whom it delegates them. Since it has legal responsibility for administrative actions, it is important that the board's executive officer properly effectuate the board's policies. It is unwise to place a superintendent of schools on permanent tenure, but, if that has been done, the board is still responsible for his actions and has the power to remove him for cause in accordance with prescribed legal procedure. The most important duties of a board are the selection of a superintendent of schools and his dismissal if he proves to be incompetent or unreliable in administering the schools in accordance with the board's adopted policies. A competent superintendent should be granted much freedom in managing the schools and should be held responsible by the board for results.

Final action often cannot be delegated to a superintendent or to anyone else. A superintendent cannot make a legally binding, written contract in the name of the board. He can negotiate for the board, state the terms the board will accept, and draw up the instrument, but the contract will be legal only when the board has adopted it by motion and the necessary members or officers have signed it for and in the name of the board. Sometimes the board instructs the superintendent to make appointments of teachers which it later confirms. This is authority delegated to the superintendent, but the contract becomes legal only upon approval by the board. However, the board should not neglect to act for specific approval, and the superintendent should make certain that a record of the approval is made in the board's minutes, so that the persons will have been legally employed and the payment of their salaries by the board will be legal. Many other actions delegated to the superintendent must be confirmed by the board.

Executive Responsibilities

Though the superintendent of schools is employed by the school board as its executive officer, the laws of most states either do not provide for the position and leave responsibility for administering the schools with the board or provide only the most meager duties and responsibilities. Almost all executive and administrative duties and responsibilities are charged by law directly to the school board. The superintendent performs them for the board by authority delegated to him. It is the board's duty to make certain that the schools are properly administered, not necessarily to administer them itself. The board must hold the superintendent responsible for the proper and efficient administration of the schools.

Who it is that administers the schools is very important in determining their efficiency. Fully qualified and capable administrators can perform the multitude of executive and administrative actions required far better than can a board whose members are laymen in education. School boards can no more properly administer school systems than hospital boards can administer hospitals, or the board of directors of an industrial corporation can administer that enterprise. However, there must be close co-operation between the school board and its superintendent. Otherwise the legislative and executive functions will be competing and sometimes antagonistic. Legislative and executive functions are complementary, but sometimes the line of demarcation between them may not be distinct. Concessions by the board or the superintendent may be necessary. Usually the concession should be made by the board on purely professional education matters. The superintendent must concede in case the board is convinced he is wrong and that the matter is important, for the board is legally responsible for the management of the schools. It can only delegate the duties, not its responsibility to the state, so it must retain ultimate control.

Judicial Functions

In most states teachers have permanent or continuing tenure if employed after the close of a probationary period, three years for example. Such teachers can be discharged only after a hearing, if it is demanded by the teacher concerned. Usually the hearing must be public. However, at the option of the teacher it may be private, and the teacher has the right to be defended by counsel. The discharge can be only for such specified reasons as immorality, insubordination, or inefficiency. The causes and terminology vary among the states. The burden of proof for disqualification rests on the board. A teacher has the right of appeal to a court over a board's decision. In New York, review and decision may be secured on appeal to the state commissioner of education. When appealed to a court, the procedures are reviewed, but courts are usually reluctant to change a board's decision.

School boards usually try to avoid the necessity for public hearings on the discharge of teachers. They do not fear lack of support from a higher authority, but such hearings often seriously disturb a community. Any established teacher is likely to have friends who will put his welfare above that of the schools. This may be the case even though the teacher may be insubordinate, inefficient, or otherwise unqualified to retain his position. Emotions are sometimes aroused in school patrons, pupils, or other teachers. Merchant members of the board may lose some of their customers; physician members, some of their patients; and others may lose business. Former friends of members may become their critics or enemies. Such possibilities result in the retention of teachers who should be discharged and replaced, and the children pay the penalty year after year because of the board's inaction.

The board is sometimes "made the goat" in public hearings and is ridiculed by the defendant's counsel. The causes for dismissal are often cumulative and the result of gradual deterioration; a counsel can maintain that the teacher must have been satisfactory the previous year because he was employed then. It is difficult for the board or the superintendent to explain why the teacher has become suddenly inefficient and was not inefficient enough to be discharged the year before. A skillful lawyer can sometimes make the board or superintendent appear ridiculous. One might say that sometimes the board and the superintendent are on trial instead of the teacher they deem to be inefficient.

In spite of the emotions aroused and the possible discomfiture of members of the school board, it is often necessary to hold hearings on the discharge of teachers, though every honorable means should be used to discharge incompetent teachers without necessity for hearings. Only members with fortitude will place the board in a position requiring a public hearing on dismissal of a teacher, but when that is the desirable course the board should act. If the board is right, it will generally have the passive support of the local teachers' associations or unions, for teachers are usually interested in removing inefficient ones from their ranks.

The school board must serve a quasi-judicial function when

it acts on appeals made by teachers, other employees, parents, or pupils on decisions made by the superintendent of schools. Persons should be referred to the superintendent for rulings on matters dealing with the management or conduct of the schools, but, in case his decision is unsatisfactory, they have the right to appeal directly to the board. In professional matters the board should usually uphold the decision of the superintendent. If it is convinced that his decision was wrong from an ethical or policy standpoint, it should act to overrule it.

Board action on an appeal from the superintendent's decision should not be made at the same meeting as presented. There should be time for reflection and deliberation by the board. The matter ought to be shelved for a month unless immediate action is required, in which case a special meeting may be called for its consideration. Postponed action will allow board members time to confer with the superintendent concerning his decision, so that the board can support him if convinced that his decision was right. If the matter is merely trivial or the board is satisfied with the decision of the superintendent, it can be settled immediately by motion to support the decision. In any case, the board's procedure should be dignified and judicial in character.

Specific Functions and Duties

School boards have many functions, duties, powers, and responsibilities. Some are large and important, others minor and trivial; some are policy-making, legislative, and approval in character, others executive and delegated to the board's executive officer and his staff; some apply in certain states but not in others; some are performed locally in some states, but by the state department of education in others. The following list is incomplete in spite of its length, though many of the items are stated in general terms and could be rearranged as a greater number of detailed items. Among the functions, duties, powers, and responsibilities of school boards may be listed the following:

Relating to School Board Activities and Procedures:

Holding an annual organization meeting of the board, selecting officers, and fixing their terms of office.

Appointing a secretary of the board.

Adopting by-laws to guide the board's procedure in meetings.

Adopting a procedural form for meetings.

Setting dates for regular board meetings.

Meeting in regular and special sessions when necessary.

Deliberating and acting on proposals made by the superintendent or some member of the board.

Accepting petitions, holding hearings, and acting on these in accordance with the expressed judgment of the members.

Determining matters of administrative and operative policy.

Accepting or refusing donations to the schools.

Approving the minutes of school board meetings.

Adopting rules and regulations for the government of the school system.

Providing for the enforcement of the state laws relating to public schools in the district, the applicable rules and regulations of the state board of education, and directives of the state department of education.

Approving the annual statistical and financial school report to the state department of education as prepared by (or under the direction of) the superintendent of schools.

Providing for the holding of school elections.

Ordering the preparation of a comprehensive study of the school system or of some element of it.

Suing or defending itself in suits at law.

Relating to the Superintendent of Schools:

Selecting and appointing a superintendent of schools.

Investing the superintendent of schools with the power to act for the board and designating him as the board's chief executive officer.

Delegating administrative duties to the superintendent and granting him authority to act commensurate with his responsibility for the delegated duties.

Requiring the superintendent to furnish special reports with regard to matters on which the board desires information.

Conferring with the superintendent on policies and actions contemplated by the board and counseling with him on matters dealing with the administration of the schools.

Approving means for effectuating the board's adopted policies.

Approving, disapproving, or modifying and adopting recommendations made by the superintendent.

Making school employees subordinate in authority and responsibility to the superintendent and refusing to deal with individuals except through the superintendent or directly in case of their appeal from his decision.

Referring complainants about school matters to the superintendent as the channel to the board, except in case of appeal from his decision.

Referring applicants for positions to the superintendent.

Holding the superintendent responsible for the efficient administration of the schools.

Accepting responsibility before the public for the execution of the board's policies.

Relating to Staff Employment and Organization:

Adopting salary schedules for teachers and other employees.

Determining the number of teachers and other employees and establishing teaching and other positions.

Employing only legally qualified teachers and other personnel.

Fixing qualification standards at or above the state requirements for various classes of teachers.

Appointing school personnel on the recommendation of the superintendent.

Determining the form of school organization.

Approving personnel duty assignments, transfers, and promotions or demotions.

Acting on recommendations of the superintendent for the dismissal of employees.

Providing means for the supervision and inservice training of personnel.

Determining policies relating to the employment of substitute teachers and other substitute employees.

Determining policies relating to leaves of absence.

Accepting employee resignations.

Relating to the Curriculum and Instruction:

Fixing the number of months in the school year at or above the minimum requirements of law, the times of opening and closing schools, and the hours of daily sessions.

Determining subjects of instruction within the requirements of law.

Providing materials of instruction, including textbooks, school supplies, and audiovisual materials for school use.

Adopting textbooks recommended by the superintendent as selected by committees of instruction employees after careful consideration.

Having the flag of the United States displayed on school buildings or grounds.

Awarding diplomas of graduation.

Making special provision for the instruction of children having various kinds of physical, mental, or social defects.

Deciding whether or not the public schools shall provide the means for adult education.

Deciding whether or not the schools shall be extended downward into preschool years, and, in some states, upward into the college years.

Relating to Evaluation, Appraisal, and Judicial Functions:

Having board members visit the schools and classrooms.

Appraising in terms of general principles the effectiveness of administration, supervision, and instruction.

Holding hearings on appeals from decisions of the superintendent of schools.

Acting as an appeals body for the settling of disputes or disagreements between members of the staff or public and the superintendent.

Holding public or private hearings and making decisions relating to the dismissal of employees.

Relating to Policies Concerning Attendance of Pupils:

Determining the age of admission of pupils to school.

Providing for a continuing school census or for annual child enumerations.

Requiring the enrollment and regular school attendance of pupils.

Expelling pupils from the public schools for specified causes.

Providing for the transportation of pupils to school.

Arranging for the attendance of children at schools outside the school district and for the payment of their tuition from school funds.

Relating to Pupil Service Activities:

Authorizing the purchase of foodstuffs, the sale of school lunches, and the operation of lunchrooms in school buildings.

Determining policies relating to the furnishing of busses and drivers for pupil transportation and the establishment of routes.

Providing for the furnishing of school supplies and textbooks free to children of indigent parents or providing them for all pupils.

Requiring immunization and vaccination of pupils.

Providing medical and dental service to certain pupils.

Establishing the positions of school physician, school nurse, and school dentist.

Providing guidance and counseling, psychological, and psychiatric services to pupils.

Co-operating with civic authorities in maintaining recreation facilities.

Controlling athletics and other forms of extracurricular activities.

Relating to the School Physical Plant:

Providing an adequate physical plant, according to the board's standards of adequacy, for operation of the school district's public schools.

Selecting school sites and determining whether or not they should be purchased in anticipation of future need.

Acquiring and selling real estate and personal property for and in the name of the school district corporation.

Exercising the power of eminent domain when the board deems such to be desirable or necessary.

Determining the number, size, and location of school buildings.

Closing school buildings not currently needed and disposing of obsolete or surplus buildings.

Contracting for school building construction, improvement, or repair.

Adopting an architect's plans for school buildings after approval by education authorities.

Authorizing the purchase and installation of educational equipment.

Insuring school property.

Controlling the normal use of school property.

Providing for the operation and care of the physical plant of the school district.

Recovering for damages to school property.

Determining the conditions under which outside agencies will be permitted to use school buildings.

Relating to Business Policies and Practices:

Determining the means of financing the public schools.

Authorizing the preparation of the school budget and adopting it in its final form.

Determining the amount of money required from tax sources for school support after estimating probable income from other sources.

Borrowing money in anticipation of tax or other income.

Requiring fidelity bonds from certain business employees.

Providing for an adequate set of financial and auxiliary records.

Approving the expenditure of moneys.

Awarding contracts for goods or services.

Approving claims for purchases made after proper audit of invoices and bills by the business staff.

Providing for efficient purchasing and storage of goods.

Providing for the custody of documents.

Determining the means of financing capital outlays.

Issuing and selling bonds for school building construction or improvement in accordance with the provisions of law.

Relating to Public Relations:

Keeping the public informed of the work and accomplishments of the schools.

Keeping the local community apprised of the needs of the schools.

Having the annual report of the schools printed and distributed to the interested residents of the school district.

Evaluating the work of the schools in terms of the desires of the people of the school district.

As a board and as individual members, having no selfish interests to serve, taking the initiative and accepting the responsibility for leadership of the community in promoting adequate moral and financial support for the public schools.

Olsen[2] devoted 142 pages of his book to an analysis of the problems and duties of school boards as compiled from the minutes of school board meetings. It is estimated that he discovered well over 2,000 separate responsibilities and duties. A list compiled from the minutes of board meetings would not be complete, for many duties are performed by the superintendent and his staff and do not require action by the school board, yet it is responsible for them.

Responsibility of the Board to the State

It has been shown elsewhere that a school board is a state rather than local agency. Its functions, duties, powers, and responsibilities have been defined by the legislature. It is the board's function to effectuate the state's education program within the school district for which it is responsible. In order to serve well as the state's agent, the members of the board should be familiar with the state laws relating to public schools. The

[2] Olsen, Hans C. *The Work of Boards of Education and How It Should Be Done.* New York: Bureau of Publications, Teachers College, Columbia University, 1926.

state department of education usually publishes a compilation of laws relating to the control, administration, and operation of the public schools, together with the interpretation of the laws by court decisions within the state, and the opinions of attorneys general of the present and past. Each member of a school board should have a copy of the most recent publication of the school laws and all supplements containing new school laws and recent amendments to older laws.

Not only the laws but also the rules and regulations of the state board of education and the directives of the chief state school official, in the spheres assigned to them by law, must be observed by the school board. There are often so many of these that it is too much to expect board members to become familiar with the details of all of them, but the superintendent should be familiar with most of them and copies should be available for the use of board members. They should also be aware of the board's corporate powers. They should know: the board's rights and responsibilities with respect to its real and personal property; whether or not it has discretion in accepting or rejecting donations and bequests; what are its powers to sue or to defend itself in case of suit; what power it has to condemn real property for educational purposes and by what procedure; what are its entitlements to a share of state funds and how apportionments are made; how the boundaries of the school district can be changed; the provisions of school election laws; and many other similar matters.

Responsibility of the Board to the Local Community

Though the school board is a state agency, the members are elected or appointed from electors of the school district and are subject to the requirements and limitations of state law. It is the board's duty to serve the school district's welfare and the wishes of the people to the extent it can determine them. It should report to the local public concerning the conditions, activities, needs, and accomplishments of the schools of the district, and the plans of the board for their improvement. In some states the voters of the school district are entitled to give specific instructions on some matters at the polls or in town meetings. Within legal limitations, the board is required to make the electors' will effective if thus expressed. In the absence of such provisions, a board should be on guard against the temptation to interpret the expressions of minorities as being the voice of the people.

CHAPTER 10

School Boards as Legislative Bodies

School Board Responsibility for School District Legislation

A school board is a deliberative body with legislative and other powers delegated to it by the laws of the state. The members are charged with the duty of maintaining public schools in accordance with the requirements of law. All the school boards of a state are responsible to the legislature and the people of the state for effectuating the state's plan for public school education. As their representative the board is responsible to the people of the school district for providing the kind of schools the community desires and is willing to finance for its children. It is responsible to the people for the executive functions, but it delegates them to a superintendent whom it selects. Only the board can perform its principal legislative functions.

Many legislative actions should involve the making of policies. Policies are principles or rules established by the board as guides for its own decisions as well as for the administrative and operative decisions of its employees. A case involving the granting of sick leave with pay is one example among hundreds of problems requiring board decision. The board may make its decision to consider the particular case at hand, or it may establish a policy to be applied to all cases in the future. Its policy might be to grant to any teacher needing sick leave 10 days each year, with full pay, accumulative of unused leave to a total of 30 days; it might allow a different number of days per year or a different number of days of accumulation for unused sick leave; it might or might not require proof of sickness; or it might or might not allow sick leave to include any absences due to sickness or death in the teacher's immediate family. Once adopted, the policy would be applicable to all classes of employees specified, and all would have equal rights under its provisions. Fairness requires the adoption of policies on many matters. Without policies, a board's actions may be inconsistent. Board members, employees, and patrons must assume that unless the board has adopted guiding principles its actions will be capricious and undependable.

School boards are responsible for adopting innumerable policies on such matters as the following: the selection of a superintendent; the management of the schools; the discontinuance of unneeded schools or the opening of new ones; the length of the school term; the curriculum; textbooks; special classes; expenditures; salary schedules; repair of school buildings; sanitation; community use of school buildings; school attendance; food service; pupil health; pupil transportation; and many more. In each case, the school board should adopt policies and refer administrative problems to the superintendent of schools for settlement in accordance with the terms of the adopted policies.

Many controversial issues, some temporary and others of a permanent or recurring nature, should be settled by school board policy action, such as: Shall collections from pupils and teachers be permitted in the schools for "worthy" causes? If so, which causes are worthy? Shall sex education be taught? Shall salary increases or decreases be granted, and, if so, shall they be temporary or permanent and shall they be a fixed cost of living amount or a percentage salary change? Shall teachers be permitted to hold outside positions in addition to their school positions? Shall teachers be required to reside within the boundaries of the school district? Hundreds of other problems might be added. Often guidance can be secured from groups in the community if the board is not afraid to ask their advice.

Establishment of Bylaws for the Board's Organization, Meetings, and Procedures

Some school boards adopt bylaws as a guide to their own organization, procedure, and deliberations. Probably most boards that have adopted rules and regulations devote a chapter or article to these bylaws, thus making one instead of two documents.

Some topics that need to be covered in such bylaws are the following:

Organization:
Name of board
Boundaries of the school district
Selection of officers and committees
Duties of the chairman
Duties of the vice chairman
Duties of the secretary
Duties of the treasurer
Duties of the attorney
Duties of standing committees
Committee meetings
Committee reports
Duties of special committees
Meetings of the committee of the whole
Filling of vacancies on the board

Board Meetings:
Time of regular meetings
Place of meetings
Organization meeting
Adjourned meetings
Special meetings
Executive sessions
Requirement for attendance of members at meetings

Board Procedure:
Quorum
Minutes of meetings

Order of business
Polling the board
Parliamentary procedure
Rules of order
Amendments to bylaws

Not all of these items will be required for headings by every school board, and in some cases additional headings may be required. A particular board may not select a treasurer or an attorney or have any standing committees. Or it may not need or desire to compel the attendance of its members at meetings.

Bylaws should be brief and clearly stated. Duties of board officers should be stated in broad rather than detailed terms so that all duties will be covered and frequent additions and amendments to the bylaws will not be needed.

Rules and Regulations

Legal Requirements. In all states school boards are permitted (and required in some) to make rules and regulations for the control of the public schools. The provision of the law of Kentucky is as follows:

> Each board shall make and adopt, and may amend or repeal rules, regulations, and bylaws for its meetings and proceedings for the government, regulation, and management of the public schools and school property of the district, for the transaction of its business, and for the qualification and employment of teachers and the conduct of pupils. The rules, regulations, and bylaws heretofore made by any governing body of a school district, or hereafter made by a board of education, shall be binding on the board of education and parties dealing with it until amended or repealed by an affirmative vote of three members of the board. The rules, regulations, and bylaws shall be spread on the minutes of the board and be open to the public. (Kentucky Revised Statutes. Sec. 160.290)

Need for Rules and Regulations. The need for rules and regulations for school systems becomes more pressing as the schools develop in complexity and scope of educational services, as the states extend their central financial assistance and controls, and as influences of pressure groups in the community and among school personnel increase. Though sometimes galling to individuals, rules and regulations are necessary to orderliness in the school system. Formally adopted, codified rules and regulations are important to the smooth and efficient operation of a school system.

A school board's policies are definitely stated in a well-constructed set of rules and regulations; without these, board policies would often be in doubt. If policies are to be found only in the minutes of meetings, those that are less frequently used will be forgotten as board members and superintendents are changed. If policies have been forgotten, the board is likely to adopt new and different ones without repeal or amendment of earlier ones. A part of an old policy may remain valid but unenforced. Conflicting rules and regulations lead only to confusion.

In searching the minutes of one Massachusetts school committee, nine changes, over a period of twelve years, were discovered in the policy regarding the employment of married women teachers. There may have been others that were overlooked, for the minutes had not been indexed. None of the previous regulations had been specifically repealed. The provisions ranged from the employment of married women without restriction, through various modifications concerning differences in salaries paid; types of positions open to them; temporary employment at daily wages; employment for three years with the lapse of a year before re-employment to avoid granting them permanent tenure; employment as intermittent substitutes only; and requirement of resignation at time of marriage of employed teachers; to a restriction against the employment of married women teachers at any time for any position. It is certain that so many changes in policy would cause confusion in the minds of many persons unless the latest adopted policy is included in the rules and regulations.

Adopted rules and regulations reduce the number of times school board action is required by substituting administrative for legislative action. It would require an enormous amount of time for a board to deal separately with every complaint against a teacher, to act on every transfer of a teacher, to determine the school every pupil shall attend, to pass on every separate request for use of a school building, and to perform scores of other duties separately. In a large city a board could not perform all such functions if it were in continuous session. Therefore, it is necessary to establish board policies by which administrators can perform such actions. Policies are most easily used if they are compiled into a code of rules and regulations. In general, most of the work of school boards should be done by applying adopted policies to all applicable cases, and the board should hold the superintendent responsible for making the policies effective.

Thousands of school boards are very unbusinesslike in that they legislate for each separate case as it arises, causing unnecessarily long board meetings and ineffective and inconsistent actions. Such boards are often in difficulty with a part of their public. Their actions cause so much resentment among school employees that they cannot do their work properly, and the schools suffer as a consequence. It is unfair to deal with cases separately. Boards that do so are frequently defending their actions against charges of inconsistency.

Boards often take action on such individual cases as the following: granting leaves of absence; suspending a rule concerning deduction from salaries when sick leave has expired; determining hours of work of particular employees; determining bus routes; granting permission to particular teachers to attend a teachers' convention; establishing new positions; awarding contracts; assigning and transferring particular teachers or janitors; and granting permission to use a school building. Individual actions would seldom be needed if the board would adopt general policies for application to specific cases by the superintendents. Rules and regulations are needed to preserve the consistency of the actions of both the board and its chief executive officer.

If school employees have copies of the rules and regulations, many problems that arise from ignorance of the requirements will not occur. There is no way to inform large groups of employees of the current policies of a school board except by the codification, publication, and distribution of copies to them.

A compiled set of rules and regulations will save much time, since employees and parents will read them instead of asking questions. Administrators would otherwise have to search through old minutes of the board to discover which policies are effective according to date of adoption. A code of rules and regulations is necessary in order that teachers and other employees can learn what procedures are acceptable to or required by the board.

With a code of rules and regulations as a guide, there will be better mutual understanding among employees as to definition of authority and responsibility, their work will be expedited, and much potential friction will be eliminated. It will inform employees of their duties, to whom they are immediately responsible, and which persons are immediately responsible to each of them. Published rules and regulations will serve as a source of information to new employees concerning their authority, duties, and responsibilities. They will help the school board and superintendent to fix responsibility for inefficiency and to give credit where credit is due because the place of each employee in the organization will be defined.

Published rules and regulations provide legal protection to the board and the school district. Contracts can be so drawn as to refer to the board's authority in the rules and regulations, by the number of the appropriate provision.

Characteristics of Rules and Regulations. If properly constructed, a set of rules and regulations will constitute the basic and fundamental principles for the control, management, and operation of the public schools. They should usually be general in character and prepared in such manner that they can be used conveniently. They should include all of the policies adopted by the board that are not merely temporary. Even the salary schedule for teachers is a statement of policy that permits the superintendent to determine automatically the salaries to be paid.

Salary schedules might well be included in the published rules and regulations.

Rules and regulations of school boards, if within their discretionary authority and legal jurisdiction, have the force of law. Courts assume that board rules and regulations are reasonable and legally permissible unless there is evidence to the contrary. When published and distributed, the rules and regulations should provide employees with the basic information for their duties in school administration and operation.

Inadequacies of Compiled Rules and Regulations. Often school boards have very incomplete and inadequate compilations of their rules and regulations. The subject matter is often poorly selected; the rules and regulations may not express the ideas they are expected to convey; they may not include important and necessary items; the list may be badly organized; and the items may include unnecessary detail that might better have been left for the superintendent to incorporate into administrative directives. Examples of detailed regulations are "Teachers shall be in their classrooms for thirty minutes after the dismissal of school," or in another school system, "Teachers shall vacate rooms ten minutes after the dismissal of school," or still elsewhere, "Custodians shall sweep classroom floors daily." Most of the faults mentioned are to be found even in some large cities where the board maintains a legal department to prepare its rules and regulations. Perhaps this is to be expected, for one could demonstrate with considerable success that the same faults exist in considerable measure in the school laws of many states.

Often rules and regulations have become largely out of date; nobody has taken the initiative in having them revised. Periodic revision is better than none, but rules and regulations should be revised on the official copy or copies immediately after each board meeting in which changes have been made. A guide that is out of date is unsuitable for use.

Sometimes school boards adopt a rule to meet a temporary situation that proves to be unwise in meeting other similar situations as they occur. For example, during the depression years of the thirties many school boards tried to improve the economic situation in the local school district by requiring that all teachers reside within the district during the school year. Since the late war this regulation has had to be repealed or disregarded in many school districts due to housing shortages. During the depression, when many teachers were unemployed, some boards adopted regulations favoring the employment of local teachers. Postwar scarcities of teachers have caused this regulation to be ignored. Repeal of obsolete rules and regulations is to be preferred to their remaining in force and being disregarded.

School board legislation should be directed at the matter at fault, not at some element in its setting. For example, a teacher may act indiscreetly at a social function, and a board may adopt a rule against attendance of teachers at such functions. Such legislation would usually be ill-advised because it is not directed at the indiscretion but against the circumstances in which it occurred. Perhaps similar circumstances have not before and may not again have the same result. It ignores the many other instances at which teachers have acted discreetly. Such a regulation would be analogous to the act of a teacher who takes away the recess period of an entire class because he cannot determine who broke a window. He reasons that the unknown culprit is certain to be punished if he punishes the entire class. The teacher expects the resentment of the class to be directed against the guilty pupil for causing the loss of recess, but it is more likely that most of the resentment will be directed against the teacher.

Sometimes rules and regulations are retained long after the need for them has expired; sometimes they are written in detailed rather than general form. The following, from the rules and regulations of a large city, is an example of both of these faults: "The confinement of pupils in a closet or wardrobe, and the use on the part of a teacher of sarcastic or discourteous language is forbidden." Aside from the fact that there is no connection between the two acts of the teacher, though they are both included in the same sentence, the rule deals with detailed acts rather than general policy. Administrative matters should be included in administrative directives. Also, the first part deals with a matter that probably occurred only once many years ago.

Another detailed rule which is more suitable for inclusion in administrative directives than in the fundamental rules and regulations of the school board follows:

> On sweeping days classrooms shall be vacated in accordance with a schedule regulating the vacating of classrooms approved by the respective principals or teachers in charge; custodians shall be permitted to begin sweeping the first room not later than five minutes after the close of the day session in the day elementary and day intermediate schools; and not later than 3:30 o'clock P.M. in the . . . day high schools. Notice of the time at which such rooms shall be vacated shall be given by custodian by placing a card in said room not later than 2:00 o'clock P.M.

However, there are excellent sets of rules and regulations in a few school districts that deal with basic legislation and are founded on the assumption that the superintendent and his staff will be able to administer the details under the adopted general policies. It cannot be said that many whole sets of rules and regulations would rate very highly in this respect, but many have excellent qualities in some of their parts.

Principles of Formulation and Construction. Some of the more important principles of the formulation and construction of rules and regulations for school systems may be summarized and presented here for the benefit of boards that have no codified set or whose rules and regulations need revision. Rules and regulations should:

1. Be not violative of provisions of state law and regulations of state agencies, and make these effective in the school district in accordance with local requirements.

2. Be not merely a compendium of all school board policy actions of the past but omit repealed actions and add provisions necessary to round out or complete the plan for a systematic school district code.

3. Include regulations on board organization, procedures, and members' duties and responsibilities relating to their membership unless a separate set of bylaws to include matters relating to the board has been adopted.

4. Describe, present in outline form, or present in chart form the desired organization structure of the school system, indicating clearly the lines of authority and responsibility of all officers and classes of employees of the school district so that each will know his place in the organization.

5. State in general terms, but sufficiently completely for clear demarcation, the duties and responsibilities of all officers and classes of employees.

6. Be statements of adopted policies and not merely of duties and restrictions.

7. Be stated as principles to guide employees and not merely as instructions to them or an enumeration of the details of administrative and operative procedures.

8. Be formulated so as to guide action in specific cases and be binding in all cases to which applicable until the board shall repeal or amend any particular regulation or set it aside temporarily.

9. Recognize the fact that most members of the staff are professional people and allow for their being guided by professional attitudes, including honesty in rendering service to the schools.

10. Allow leeway for the exercise of initiative, permit freedom of action to the greatest extent practicable, and not be unduly restrictive on individuals.

11. Include provisions for the amendment or repeal of parts of the adopted rules and regulations.

12. Be consistent among the different parts; when a new regulation is adopted conflicting provisions should be modified or repealed so that the validity of older regulations will not be in doubt.

13. Be kept up to date by the addition of new or amended rules and regulations as needed, properly designated in accordance with the adopted numbering system and by the repeal and removal of rules and regulations that have been discarded or are no longer enforced.

Preparation Staff. Although every school board should adopt a set of rules and regulations as the basic code for its governance of the school district, it does not necessarily follow that a member or a committee of the board should personally construct these fundamental and basic policies. Board members are usually busy people and accustomed to performing duties in a hurried manner. If board members prepare the rules and regulations, the results are likely to be poor unless the person assigned the work should chance to be one whose training and experience is that of writing and organizing the results of research.

A method that has met with some favor is that of constructing the rules and regulations as a co-operative project under the general direction of the superintendent of schools. Board members, administrative and supervisory personnel, teachers, custodians, and even parents and pupils may contribute to the co-operative effort. Employees should be given an opportunity to make suggestions on matters for inclusion in the proposed rules and regulations. A co-ordinating committee should organize and rewrite the material into a systematic draft for submission to the board, possible modification, and adoption. The co-ordinators should use only such suggestions as are suitable and meet the standards set by the committee for the code. With a co-ordinating committee, this method should produce good results.

Often the better prepared rules and regulations have been constructed by well-qualified and experienced educational consultants, who can devote their full time to the project for a few months. If done properly, the work requires considerable study and research. Even a specialist should secure suggestions from board members and employees. Of course, whatever is produced by a specialist should be submitted to the board for consideration, modification, rephrasing if desired, and adoption or rejection by parts.

Scope of Coverage. Rules and regulations should define the larger relationships among employees and the functions of positions without stating the minor and specific duties of each employee minutely. The functions of each class of position should be stated in general terms, sometimes with specific examples of duties for clarity. Some of these are superintendent, supervisor, principal, teacher, and custodian. The rules and regulations should also deal with basic policies relating to personnel administration on such matters as: selection and appointment; duty assignment; transfer; resignation; dismissal; trials and appeals; inservice training; leaves of absence; sick leave with pay; substitutes; and salary schedules, for the different classes of employees. They should deal similarly with basic policies for pupil administration, physical plant administration, business administration, and the management of auxiliary enterprises. The person responsible for the final preparation of the codified rules and regulations should keep in mind the distinction between policies of the board and the details of management and avoid including the latter in the coded set presented to the board for its consideration and action.

The rules and regulations should differentiate the lines of authority and responsibility among positions and define the functions of the classes of positions that the board has established. They should include the fundamental policies relating to curriculum and instruction and provisions for the control of pupil activities, policies relating to public relations responsibilities and activities, policies relating to pupil transportation, food service, pupil health, and many other similar matters. They should be inclusive of matters concerned with definition, organization, functions, administration, operation, and procedures. An excellent outline for the differentiation of authorizations, responsibilities, functions, duties, and restrictions on the board and the professional personnel is presented on pages 21 to 37 of a publication by Carpenter, Capps, and Townsend, entitled *Suggestions for Procedure for Missouri Boards of Education.*

Sources of Material. To determine what should be included in the rules and regulations of a particular school system, one should first study the minutes of the board for a number of years in the past and compile all adopted policies and rulings still in force. The board should give these consideration and eliminate or repeal all policies it deems undesirable or unnecessary. Also, general policies should be formulated from the board's past legislation on particular cases, and these should be combed for desirability. The surviving regulations included in the draft should be submitted to the board for consideration.

Suggestions from board members, employees, and other interested persons are another source of material for rules and regulations. Of course, such suggestions will have to be rewritten in the form desired to avoid duplication, but they will be valuable from the standpoint of ideas furnished. Many will have to be discarded as dealing with the details of management, but some of them will suggest general policies that are needed.

Ideas for important rules and regulations can be appropriated from codes used in other school systems, but, again, many of these may deal with administrative details and others will not fit the conditions required. However, many existing codes have some very good features, and some school systems have adopted rules and regulations in recent years that are excellent school district "laws" from some standpoints. Not many parts are likely to be applicable without modification or complete rewriting, but at least the reading of many different codes by the compiler will be a fertile source of ideas and may prevent his overlooking important matters.

It will not suffice for a board or its agent to copy a code of rules and regulations from some other school district. It must be tailor-made or it will not fit. For example, rules relating to the kindergarten or a trade school in one school district would be useless in another school district that has no kindergarten or trade school. It has been said that a certain inland state without even a navigable river in it adopted certain laws of New York State *verbatim*. It was a surprised legislature that discovered, after adopting the code, that the stenographer had included certain requirements and restrictions on ships coming into port and the operation of lighthouses. Scissors and paste pot methods of producing rules and regulations are not satisfactory, but a reading of the rules and regulations of different school systems indicates that many of them have been constructed in that manner, with but little adaptation to the requirements of the local school system or consideration of their appropriateness to the needs of the local schools. Needs for a particular school district may differ from those of another due to differences in state laws, geographical location, area, size of population, wealth of the people, industries, occupations of the people, school services rendered, and many other respects.

Writing and Editing. Rules and regulations should be prepared in clear, concise, precise, and nonlegal language. The aim should be to avoid misunderstanding or lack of understanding of the meaning and intent of each provision. Generally, the items should be stated in positive rather than negative terms. Tentative rules and regulations should be carefully edited to secure reasonable freedom from grammatical errors, proper sentence structure, and correct paragraphing.

Organization and Codification. Rules and regulations should not be a mere collection of jumbled guides, but systematically arranged school district "laws." A hit or miss compilation, such as one arranged by the order of adoption indicated by the dates of board minutes, would be difficult to use. They should be logically organized and codified according to a scheme for the orderly consolidation of the items into divisions or parts dealing with the same or related subjects. Such a scheme usually involves the organization of the items into chapters, articles, and sections, each with an appropriate title, the titles of subordinate items being included under the larger divisions of which they are a part.

The codifier might devise a functional plan of main headings such as legislative, administrative, supervisory, instructional, plant management, business management, research, auxiliary services, and other activities for the various chapters. There might be subordinate articles with subordinate sections, or the chapters may be headed with the general classes of employees. Other classifications might be devised. The functional scheme would have advantages but might not be sufficiently inclusive for all desirable regulations, including all that are definitive, organizational, and regulative. They might not relate strictly to functions, so that other headings might be required.

Rules and regulations should not only be organized and codified in a systematic scheme under logical headings, but a numbering system should be used to indicate the relation among parts and to serve for convenient reference. Only a good plan of organization and codification is adequate to make the rules and regulations meet the tests of good correlation, co-ordination, and consistency necessary to avoid conflicting interpretations in their application by different persons. For convenience, a code of rules and regulations should have a table of contents, provide brief but expressive marginal notations, and have a reasonably complete index when prepared for publication.

Contents. It would be impracticable to present a model outline of a code of rules and regulations. First, the fact that school systems vary in size, in organization structure, and in the services they render means that no plan would fit all of them. Second, no one plan of organization can be defended as being better than others, provided they are equally systematic and logically arranged. Third, to prescribe a complete outline would require more pages than can be devoted to that purpose in this chapter.

Rules and regulations should include: board organization and procedures unless that is done separately in bylaws; administrative organization, indicating lines of authority and responsibility, possibly by the inclusion of an organization outline or chart; a variety of matters relating to personnel; curriculum and instruction matters; matters dealing with auxiliary services and school activities; business matters; and policies relating to the physical plant and its operation. There should be articles under chapter headings, and, where further division is necessary, sections under articles. Sometimes subsections may be needed.

Copies of the rules and regulations of a number of school systems are at hand. The schemes of organization vary considerably. A list of items, most of which can be subdivided into many subitems, will be presented here as an aid, so that anyone constructing a code of rules and regulations may check to determine whether or not he considers it necessary to include regulations on matters he may have omitted. The list, not complete, follows:

Absences of employees; sick leave, extended leave, excused absences, etc.
Accounting
Administrative organization
Advertising in the schools
Amendments to rules and regulations
Appeals to board over decisions of superintendent
Assistant principals
Athletics: coaches, fields, financing, accidents, insurance, etc.
Attendance: of pupils, of teachers
Attorney of the board
Auditing: of accounts, of invoices and bills
Board of education: organization, procedures, meetings, order of business, etc.
Bonds, fidelity
Bonds, issuance and sale of
Borrowing for current expenses
Budgetary control
Budget: preparation, adoption, allotments, etc.
Buildings and grounds: construction, lease, alteration, maintenance, operation, community use of, etc.
Business management
Census, continuing
Class size and teacher-pupil ratios
Clerical employees
Collection of school district moneys
Committees, special
Committees: standing, organization, functions, meetings, reports, etc.
Conduct of employees
Contracts: for goods, for services
Curricula and courses of study: development, principles, contents, etc.
Custodial employees
Custody of documents
Custody of school moneys

Depositories
Discipline, pupil
Dismissal of employees
Duties of officers and employees
Duties of the board
Elementary schools
Employees
Evening schools
Extracurricular activities
Financial statements
Financing the school district
Fine arts education
Flag, display of
Fraternities and sororities
Grievances, presentation of, to board
Guidance and counseling
Handicapped pupils' education
Health of pupils: preventive measures, contagions, co-operation with
    city health department, medical service, dental service, etc.
Health of teachers
Hearings by board
High schools
Holidays
Industrial arts education
Insurance: physical plant, vehicles, athletes, etc.
Junior colleges
Junior high schools
Kindergartens
Leaves of absence
Libraries
Lunchrooms
Maintenance of physical plant
Marking system
Medical examination of pupils; of teachers
Methods of teaching
Objectives of the school system
Officers
Operation of the physical plant
Payment of claims

Payrolls
Personnel administration
Personnel: professional and nonprofessional, certification qualifications, assignment, transfer, retirement, etc.
Petitions to board
Physical plant: management, operation
Powers of the board
Preschool children
President of the board
Principals of schools
Promotions
Property loss and damage
Public relations
Pupils: reports to parents, office records, admission, expulsion or suspension, discipline, examinations, etc.
Pupil trust funds
Purchasing: specifications, bids, orders, etc.
Qualifications for positions
Real estate, acquisition of
Records and reports of school system
Research
Revolving funds
Safety
Salary schedules
Secretary of the board
School collections
School elections
School organizations
School terms
Special schools and classes
Special teachers
Substitute teachers
Superintendent of schools: duties, responsibilities, reports, etc.
Supervision and supervisors
Supplies and equipment
Suspension of the rules and regulations
Teachers
Textbooks
Tradesmen, employment and management of

Traffic regulations at schools
Transportation, pupil: safety, eligibility for, insurance, etc.
Treasurer of the school district
Tuition of pupils
Use of school buildings
Vacancies: on board, in school positions
Vacations
Vice chairman
Visual education
Vocational education

An outline for a sample code of rules and regulations is provided by Carpenter, Capps, and Townsend in their publication, *Suggestions for Procedure for Missouri Boards of Education*, pages 40 to 75. A sample code of school board rules and regulations is included as Chapter IV of Sears' book, *City School Administrative Controls*. This cannot be said to be a perfect code, but it has been constructed largely as a scheme that will serve as a working model. It will be useful in constructing a set of rules and regulations for a particular school system.

Adoption. After rules and regulations have been prepared and material organized by a specialist, by the superintendent and his staff, or as a part of these processes, the superintendent should present the product to the school board for study, discussion, modification, and action. The superintendent should be prepared to give the reasons for and against items that are questioned and to suggest means for their modification if desired. The board should give careful consideration to each proposal, viewing it from all angles. Then it should formally adopt, modify, or reject it. When all parts are satisfactory as indicated by majority vote, the board should adopt the whole production as the code of rules and regulations of the school system.

Publication. Rules and regulations should be published either in printed or otherwise duplicated form for placement in the hands of board members, administrative and supervisory employees, operative employees, and interested persons of the community. They may be printed on looseleaf pages for insertion in a binder. Supplementary pages may be prepared to replace those containing rules and regulations that have been repealed, amended, or supplemented with additional sections. Replacement pages can be published once or twice a year. For example, in place of page 29 another largely blank page also numbered 29 may be inserted if parts on the old page have been repealed or replaced by briefer parts. If additions have been made, sheets numbered 29a, 29b, etc., may be inserted in place of the original page 29. Some school systems merely publish an insert slip with a glued edge, to be pasted in the published booklet at the appropriate place in the numbered sections of the rules and regulations. In any case, the secretary of the board should keep an accurate list of the persons holding official copies so that the insert sheets or slips can be furnished them.

Many boards publish their rules and regulations in bound booklet form. This may be unwise if no means are furnished for keeping them up to date. After a few years such publications may be misleading in many places unless holders of the copies have been informed of changes and directed to write them in the margins of their copies.

Amendment and Revision. Since a school board is a continuing body with changing membership, old rules and regulations are continued in force until they have been repealed or modified, even though the entire membership of the board may be changed. The rules and regulations should be amended or repealed whenever the board decides amendment or repeal is necessary or desirable. Confusion is caused if any regulation remains valid after it has become obsolete or ineffective by neglect. Although the board should retain its right to set aside any rule or regulation temporarily, it should seldom do so; the provision should be changed if it is not applicable to all cases that appear.

In one case that came under the observation of the author, a rule was set aside that provided for the deduction of pay in case of absence for any other reason than sickness. A certain teacher was absent for a few days prior to the death of her mother. She had but few absences in her record of 25 years of service. The rule was that death in the immediate family would not be allowed to count as sick leave. The rule probably should have been repealed. If it was desired to retain it, modification should have been made to apply to this teacher's situation and all other similar situations. The board's rule is a law, made by a legally constituted legislative body for its school system and should not be set aside for one person while being applied to others.

Boards that are aware of the importance of their rules and regulations in preventing problems from arising and in reducing the number of situations causing embarrassment to the board, continually alter, amend, repeal, and adopt new rules and regulations. If modification of rules and regulations has been neglected in previous years, it would be well to have a complete revision or remodeling of them every ten years. Such reconstruction should be based on a thorough study of the board's policy actions over the intervening years.

Before a new policy is adopted or an old one modified, careful consideration should be given to the effect of the proposed change on other rules and regulations and whether or not any of them will have to be amended or repealed to make them consistent with the new or modified section or sections. Rules and regulations should always be subject to revision or repeal when changed conditions indicate they are no longer needed or their observance has become harmful. Enforcing them as long as they are valid will force the reconsideration of useless or harmful rules and regulations and lead the board to repeal or modify them. Keeping the code of rules and regulations up to date with the changing needs of the school system is an important legislative function.

It should be expected that changes will be made in rules and regulations and possible to propose amendments or repealers in writing at any regular meeting of the board. The board should be able to make desired changes by a majority vote after the proposal has been laid on the table for a month.

Use of Rules and Regulations

A code of rules and regulations is useful to many people for various purposes. Some of these appear in the following paragraphs.

School board members need a code of rules and regulations as a reference booklet for use in and out of board meetings to determine what are the school district "laws." They need such a code to guide the board's deliberations and to help secure consistency in actions adopted at different times, often by partially or completely different board personnel. Rules and regulations make a board's work lighter by automatically solving many of the problems that arise. Campbell[1] found that over a period of ten years the Spokane board of education dealt with the renting or granting of permission to use school buildings 161 times. In Salt Lake City, where policies had been adopted according to which the superintendent's staff could administer the use of school buildings by outside agencies, the board dealt with these matters only four times in the same period.

Each new board member needs a personal copy of the board's rules and regulations as well as a personal copy of the state school laws. He needs the code to orient himself in his unfamiliar duties and to furnish a point of departure in playing his part in carrying on the work of the board. A code of rules and regulations is especially needed in school districts in which there is rapid change in school board membership, and these are the school districts most likely to have no such code.

The superintendent of schools and his staff of administrative and supervisory officers need individual copies of the code of rules and regulations to determine the scope of the functions for which each is responsible and the place of each in the organization of line and staff personnel. They must be able to distinguish their several and different functions in the organization. They

---

[1] Campbell, Roald F. *Handbook for Utah School Board Members*. Salt Lake City: Utah School Board Association, 1946.

cannot serve as the board's executive staff if the board does not furnish them with information as to what school district "laws" are to be enforced.

Teachers and principals need to consult the rules and regulations. Often serious problems would be avoided if they were furnished with information regarding what is expected of them and outlining their rights and privileges. Copies of the rules and regulations are particularly needed by new teachers in their adjustment to the ways of the school system.

Physical plant employees need copies of the rules and regulations so they will know their powers, duties, and responsibilities. There should be no question of to whom they are responsible—whether directly to the principal of the building or to the superintendent of buildings and grounds for the school district. Divided responsibility is bad, but, if such is the case, the employees should know precisely for what they are responsible to whom.

Parents and other citizens often need to know the board's rules and regulations on many matters. These include pupil absences, failures and promotions, admission requirements, health services and requirements, pupil transportation requirements, use of school buildings by outside agencies, and many others. In some instances it has been found to be practicable to publish a brief booklet or mimeographed sheets separate from the loose-leaf sheets, containing the rules and regulations that will be of interest to parents and other citizens.

For all persons connected with the school system, a code of rules and regulations helps to avoid misunderstandings and to secure a well-adjusted machine for operation. It lightens the work of the board and administrative officers and helps to keep employees better contented.

Administrative Code

In order to make unnecessary the inclusion of matters of administrative detail in the adopted rules and regulations, the school board should authorize the superintendent of schools to issue directives to various groups of employees. These should be prepared in sets for supervisors, principals, teachers, business employees, custodians, mechanics, lunchroom employees, and other groups. They can deal with management, operation, and procedures in the minute detail required. They might deal with such matters as instructions for fire drills, how the fire department shall be summoned, how fire extinguishers shall be used, or how pupils shall be evacuated. They can deal with such matters as the frequency and method of window cleaning or with many other janitorial, engineering, and custodial functions.

The directives, of course, will have to be consistent with both the state laws and other state requirements and with the school board's rules and regulations. If desired, all of the directives can be compiled into a single administrative code or into separate codes for the different groups of employees. The administrative code should be prepared by the superintendent in collaboration with the particular administrative assistants most closely concerned with the employees working under their direction.

The advantages of using an administrative code rather than board rules and regulations for directions pertaining to details of administration, operation, and procedures are that: it is the function of the superintendent and his administrative staff to administer the schools, and the board should allow the staff enough freedom so that it can hold the superintendent responsible for the results obtained; the directives are less permanent than basic board legislation and can be modified quickly by the superintendent to meet special conditions at any school in the district; and administrative directives are more likely than rules and regulations to be changed when it is practicable to change them and less likely to be continued and disregarded when they are no longer useful.

CHAPTER 11

School Board Meetings and Procedures

Characteristics of School Board Meetings

A school board has the legal right to transact business only in board meetings. It is important that high standards for the conduct of meetings be maintained, and that they be conducted legally, expeditiously, and in accordance with correct parliamentary practices. This chapter on meetings and procedures may be introduced by presenting a few hypothetical, contrasting illustrations as follows:

School District X	*School District Y*
Time of meeting: 4:00 P.M.	Time of meeting: 7:30 P.M.
Place: Office of the president of the Noisy Boiler Factory.	Place: Administration building, office of the board of education, adjoining the office of the superintendent.
Board meetings, on the average, three hours in length.	Board meetings, on the average, three hours in length.
Present at meetings: Usually 4 or 5 of the 7 members and the member clerk's personal secretary, a nonschool employee who takes the minutes. The superintendent attends only on invitation, and seldom is invited.	Present at meetings: Usually all of the 7 members, the superintendent, who is also secretary, and his secretary, who makes a record of the proceedings, taking some notes in shorthand from which the minutes will be prepared.
Meetings closed to visitors.	One or two delegations sometimes appear to present petitions. Present at meetings, as a rule, are representatives of the press, the P.T.A. council, the teachers association, and the taxpayers association.

School District X

No agenda for meetings.

No formal order of business.

Informal discussion on various subjects; some school gossip is interchanged, unrelated to the business at hand. Little discussion of issues. Business transacted by informal agreement.

Following a curriculum committee report, in a particular meeting, much argument ensues on whether or not more time should be used for teaching spelling. After discussion and without motion, the chairman of the board appoints George, who is chairman of the committee on teachers, to tell the elementary school teachers to add 10 minutes a day to the time devoted to spelling.

Board committees are expected to manage certain phases of school administration.

A board committee assigns and transfers teachers and custodians and informs them of their duties.

The board members secure information concerning the schools directly from teachers and other employees and seldom clear their actions, based on such information, with the superintendent.

The board hires all teachers

School District Y

Agenda are presented to the board 24 or more hours before the meeting.

A regular order of business is followed.

Discussion and transaction of business follow rules of parliamentary procedure.

Matters of policy are discussed and action is taken in order as listed on the agenda. A minimum of time is devoted to routine matters. A member thinks more time should be devoted to the teaching of spelling. The superintendent suggests that the need may be for improved methods of teaching rather than for more time. The board instructs the superintendent to make a report at the next regular meeting on the time allotments, methods of teaching, and effectiveness of teaching spelling.

There are no standing committees. The board delegates its authority to manage the schools to its selected executive officer, the superintendent of schools.

The superintendent is authorized to make duty assignments and transfers of teachers and other employees.

The board requests the superintendent to furnish it with certain information concerning the schools and to advise it on professional matters. Requests for reports from him are frequently made.

The superintendent actively en-

School District X

directly, from data submitted by the applicants and a photograph or personal interview, without professional investigation of qualifications by the superintendent.

No teachers' salary schedule has been adopted; bargaining is the method used to determine salaries.

The school budget is carelessly constructed and there is no exercise of budgetary control over expenditures.

There is no planning of school buildings for the future, and, in new sections, buildings are constructed on unsuitable small plots left after the construction of dwellings.

The board has no adopted rules and regulations.

The board pays but little attention to legal requirements on such matters as board quorums, the budget, the curriculum, and many other matters.

School District Y

courages applications from teachers and he and the principals investigate the qualifications of applicants. He selects and nominates those best qualified.

A teachers' salary schedule is used to determine salaries.

The board has a carefully planned budget to reflect its educational plan, developed by the superintendent with the help of his staff, and modified and formally adopted by action of the board. When transfers among items are deemed necessary, the superintendent presents a request to the board for authorization to make them.

The board has a planned school building program and purchases building sites in developing areas of the city ahead of the need for school buildings in such areas.

A code of rules and regulations of the board has been adopted, is kept up to date as to changes by the board, and is placed in the hands of every board member and every employee in the school system.

The board pays strict attention to the requirements of law and tries to make the school laws effective within the school district.

The contrasting conditions and practices might be extended to illustrate other differences that exist among school boards with reference to their methods and procedures, but those presented should be sufficient to furnish a picture of the wide differences in their efficiencies.

Regular Meetings

Regular meetings of school boards are generally held 12 or 24 times a year, depending on whether they are held once or twice a month. If they are suspended for July and August, the number would be 10 or 20 regular meetings a year. If a separate organization meeting is required by law or the rules and regulations of the board, there will be one required meeting in addition to those stated, though it may not be designated as a regular meeting and its business may be limited to organization. In some states a specified number of meetings is required by law. In other states the number of regular meetings is determined by each board, and there are wide variations among the districts in the number determined. Usually a school board adopts a resolution indicating when regular meetings shall be held, as on the first Tuesday of each month or the first and third Fridays of each month. Such a resolution (and sometimes provision for a separate organization meeting) determines the number of regular meetings scheduled for the year.

It is general practice to hold 12 or 24 regular meetings, the median being about 18 in the largest cities (over 100,000 population), and to hold 12 in the smaller cities, the median being about 13.5 (30,000–100,000 population). The median number of special meetings is 6. The number of regular and special meetings varies widely among cities of a given population size. If the meetings are well planned and the procedure is executed in an expeditious manner, monthly meetings would seem to be adequate for most school systems. If the organization meeting is held separately, there would need to be 13 meetings a year, besides possibly a few adjourned and special meetings. Special meetings may be needed when the budget is to be adopted or a school building project is in progress. It is not advisable to discontinue meetings in the summer when annual supplies are being purchased, vacant positions are being filled, and activities for the succeeding year are being planned.

The board should have a calendar prepared to show the dates for all recurring important actions or conditions to be noted. Also, the secretary should send the members notices of regular as well as special meetings, but the sending of dated agenda will serve that purpose.

Special Meetings

Various provisions are made in different states for the calling of special meetings. Usually the chairman may call special meetings on his own initiative and must do so upon request of a specified number of board members. Sometimes the secretary of the board or the superintendent of schools is authorized to call special board meetings. It is sometimes, and should be, required that the object of the special meeting be stated in the call. The business of a special meeting should be limited to the purpose for which it is called. Such meetings should be called well in advance, where possible, so as to give the members an opportunity for planning to attend.

Organization Meeting

The work of organization is sometimes performed at a regular meeting of the board and sometimes at a separate meeting required by law or by the rules and regulations of the board for that purpose. The organization meeting is held at a time near the beginning of the board's fiscal year or at such other time as the newly elected or re-elected members assume office.

Adjourned Meetings

Some school boards adjourn their meetings to the next day, or from day to day, or for several days. Adjourned meetings are usually held at the regular meeting hour on a different day. An adjourned meeting is treated as a continuation of the regular meeting and not as a special or called meeting. Regular or general business is conducted at an adjourned meeting.

Social Meetings

It is not uncommon for a school board to meet for a dinner and informal discussion of problems to be considered later in open meeting. The reasons for the practice are said to be to save time, to shorten regular meetings, and to make it possible to begin meetings earlier and without the necessity of waiting for stragglers. If the meals are served by home economics classes, the board should be certain that the pupils gain valuable experience and are not being exploited in any manner. If the board dines at a club or hotel, the members should pay for the meals, not the school system.

A dinner meeting held at 6:00 or 6:30 P.M. will furnish opportunity for informal prediscussion of issues, will free the members for a meeting at 7:30 or 8:00 o'clock, and all members who expect to attend will be present at the opening of the business meeting.

Place of Meeting

Every school district large enough to be an administrative unit should maintain a board room for the holding of meetings. Preferably the room should adjoin the office of the superintendent of schools where the administrative files will be available if letters, reports of studies, or other materials should be needed unexpectedly. The board room should be fitted with a large table and comfortable chairs for all board members, the superintendent, and secretary. There should be seats for delegates, petitioners, and visitors. There should be a map of the school district on the wall showing the locations of buildings and attendance district lines. Spot maps showing the distribution of high school, elementary, and preschool children by place of residence will be useful. Charts showing pupil enrollments and enrollment trends, expenditures and their trends, and other factual material should be available. There should be a library shelf of books and magazines dealing with school control and management in the board room.

Time of Meeting

The place, date, and time of school board meetings should be generally known and should be announced in the rules and regulations. Meetings are held in the evenings by 82 per cent of school boards, in the afternoons by 10 per cent, in the mornings by 6 per cent, and in the middle of the day by 2 per cent. Evening meetings are usually preferred because they are less likely to interfere with the private business and professional obligations of members. Noon meetings are not satisfactory because they do not provide sufficient time for deliberation. At that time members are anxious to return to their own work and may tend to conduct the board's business in a perfunctory manner.

Board meetings should open as early in the evening as it is possible for the members to be present. Many boards meet at 7:30 P.M. They should be called to order promptly at the time set if there is a quorum. Members should be urged to appear on time, and the hour of meeting should be changed if members persist in being late. It is an imposition on members who arrive on time to postpone the call to order for late arrivals. There is no advantage in late opening and such is not required for courtesy to late comers. The saving of the time of prompt members is far more important than meeting the convenience of tardy ones. The chairman should never hold up the business of a meeting in progress to explain what has transpired to a late arrival. The business of a meeting should proceed without interruption.

The hour set for meetings has little to do with tardiness. Sometimes the cause is simply a desire to steal a few minutes from the preliminary activities at the expense of the prompt members. In one city it was observed that meetings were called to order promptly at 7:15 P.M., the time set. In another city there was seldom a quorum present before 8:30 or 9:00 o'clock, though meetings were set for 8:00 o'clock. The preferable practice is obvious.

Length of Meetings

Meetings of school boards usually require from 2 to 4 hours, the average length being 2 hours and 35 minutes. In some school districts meetings have been known to extend over a period of 6 hours—from 8:00 P.M to 2:00 A.M. The length depends only in part on the amount and character of the business to be transacted. More important in determining the length of meetings are: (1) the adequacy with which meetings are planned; (2) the skill of the chairman in conducting meetings; (3) the promptness of arrival of members so that the meetings can be begun on time; (4) the garrulousness of members; (5) the condition of general agreement among members as to social and educational philosophies, outlook on economy in expenditures, desires of persons who support the individual members, and the like; (6) the formality of procedure maintained; (7) the confinement of discussion to matters before the house; (8) the shortening of such routines as the reading of the minutes and roll call; and (9) acting on recommendations of the superintendent of schools. Board members who complain of the long meetings should see to it that they are not in part responsible.

Long meetings have nothing to commend them. Close application to the problems of a school system by persons not familiar with the backgrounds of the problems requires concentration and may be exhausting at times. Instead of extending meetings over a long period, it is often better to hold an adjourned meeting the next evening. From 2 to 2½ hours of planned, snappy board procedure is long enough for one meeting. When delegations must be heard, meetings must sometimes be a little longer, but the delegations can be scheduled on the agenda and the time allowed each delegation can be limited.

Executive and Open Sessions

The laws of some states, New Jersey for example, require that all business meetings of school boards be open to the public. However, in most states executive meetings of the board are permissible and open or executive meetings are held at the board's discretion. One study[1] showed that 68 per cent of school boards open all meetings to the public, 6 per cent hold only closed or executive meetings, and 26 per cent hold both kinds of meetings. The figures of another study[2] were 65 per cent, 14 per cent, and 21 per cent, respectively.

The requirement that all school board business be conducted in open meetings is probably fully justified because it is the public's business, but to open all meetings to the public some-times may be embarrassing to the board, harmful to employees or pupils, and costly to the school district. Such may be the result when personal matters relating to some member of the administrative or teaching staff or other employee require consideration by the board or when it becomes necessary for a board to adopt policies relating to pupil conduct and discipline in the wake of some case of misconduct. In a matter such as the purchase of a particular school site it is sometimes to the financial interest of the school district to keep the board's intention from being made public until the action has been consummated by someone for the board. This may make purchase of the desired site at its fair value possible.

If occasional executive sessions for the transaction of certain items of official business are not permitted by law or the board's

[1] Hubbard, Frank W., "American School Boards." In *N.E.A. Journal*, Feb. 1946, pp. 72–75.
[2] American Association of School Administrators of the National Education Association. *School Boards in Action.* (Twenty-fourth Yearbook) Published by the National Education Association. Washington, D. C. 1946.

rules and regulations, the board usually finds it necessary to meet as a committee of the whole. As such a committee it deliberates informally on matters that cannot be properly discussed in public, but the vote is taken in public. In some cases, meetings of a committee of the whole become caucuses where nonrecorded and nonlegal decisions are made on practically all matters, and the resultant motions are made in the open session immediately following. This is a misuse of the functions of the committee of the whole. The public desires to hear the discussion. Except when the nature of the business or the interests of the public require that discussion and action be secret, the whole procedure should be conducted in open meeting.

So far as possible, open board meetings should proceed without consciousness by members of the presence of visitors. Board members should refuse to "play to the galleries" and should address their remarks to the other board members, not to the visitors. The purpose of open meetings is not to entertain the people.

If executive meetings or executive sessions within open meetings are permitted, they should be held at the request of a majority of the members present, after passage of a formal motion that the meeting be recessed to meet in executive session. The board should return to the regular open session by the same process. If it does not meet in executive session, where legal actions can be taken, but still needs to meet in session not open to the public, where no action can be taken, the motion may be made to recess for a meeting of the committee of the whole for a period of stated length.

In districts in which few persons attend school board meetings except, perhaps, a reporter, the public may be invited to attend. It may be advantageous to hold one meeting a year in an auditorium to which the general public is especially invited by a notice in the press. Visitors should be welcomed cordially at all open meetings with an expression of appreciation for their interest in the work of the board and with full recognition of their right to be present. Secrecy should be avoided as much as possible since it breeds suspicion.

If a board grants the public the right to attend board meetings, it does not by that act grant permission to individuals or groups to participate in the discussion or to disturb the meeting in any manner. The board must insist that visitors be spectators only. Specific time allotments should be made in the agenda for the hearing of delegations or petitioners who have requested such time, and for persons invited by the board to advise it on particular matters.

Preparation for Meetings

It is the duty of the secretary to prepare agenda for regular school board meetings, to consist of items presented to him from various sources. The superintendent will usually have a record of most of the matters of business for each meeting. Since he is interested in the agenda of board meetings as an executive officer, there is an additional reason that the board should select the superintendent to be its secretary. The agenda should consist of items of business to be brought before the board for consideration and action by it. They should be classified under the appropriate headings in the adopted order of business. The items should be numbered for convenience in referring to them. The purposes of agenda are: to expedite procedure and prevent waste of time by furnishing a plan to be followed; to provide for members an opportunity to give reflective thought to the matters scheduled for action; and to prevent the omission of any matters that should receive attention. From these standpoints, agenda are very important.

Agenda should be sent to all members so they will be received at least 24 hours before the opening of the meeting to which they apply. Copies of minutes to be approved can be mailed at the same time if they have not been sent soon after the meeting to which they apply. In order to prepare agenda and deliver them a full day before the board meeting, a cut-off date must be enforced after which no items will be placed on the agenda. Such a date might be 36 hours before the meeting. Any matter received too late to be entered on the agenda should be included on the agenda for the next regular meeting. Board members, parents, teachers, custodians, athletic clubs, music associations, pupils, and other groups or persons should be required to present their petitions and requests in time for their inclusion on the agenda, and they should not usually be heard unless they have been scheduled to appear.

Whenever advantageous to the members of the board in preparing for the meeting, the agenda should be accompanied by copies of important documents, studies bearing on matters scheduled for action, and copies of resolutions, written petitions, communications, statements, diagrams, and tables. If consideration is to be given to a policy change, certain data on its effectiveness, when it was adopted, its purpose at that time, and how often it has been ignored and the reason therefor may be needed for intelligent decision by the board. Copies of the superintendent's report on the matter if requested by the board at a previous meeting and other material may be sent to members with the agenda. If the superintendent presents arguments for a course of action, he should do so objectively and should not promote particular action nor campaign for support of his recommendation other than by the arguments he presents. He should deal with the board as a unit, not with a few of its members.

Meetings should usually proceed in accordance with the order of items on the agenda, but the board should be free to depart from the order of listing or even to add new items if it sees fit. However, the members should try not to bring up matters at the meeting without warning the others. If that is done, the matters should usually be laid on the table until the next regular meeting and entered as items on the agenda for that meeting. Hasty action, without warning or adequate time for consideration by the members, may lead boards to make unwise decisions that require later revocation of the action taken. This places the board in an embarrassing position, particularly if the action has already gone into effect.

Use of Parliamentary Procedure

The business of a school board should be conducted in accordance with generally accepted principles of parliamentary procedure. If there are any laws applicable to school board procedure, they must be observed. Any applicable rules of the board must then have precedence. After these, authoritative principles of parliamentary procedure should be followed. As a means to this end, the board should adopt a standard manual as a guide. Two of these are *Robert's Rules of Order, Revised,* and *Cushing's Manual of Parliamentary Procedure.*

The use of correct parliamentary procedure helps to keep meetings moving quietly and with dispatch. It helps to prevent divergence from the business at hand and wandering from the question to unrelated and irrelevant matters. The adoption of formal parliamentary procedure has been known to reduce the length of board meetings by as much as a third, largely by the elimination of unnecessary and often unrelated conversation. Meetings should be orderly and formal but not so formal that it is difficult for a member to express his opinions freely. Although small boards have many advantages over the former large ones, the reduction in the number of members has had a detrimental effect on the use of correct parliamentary procedure.

A few of the many principles of parliamentary procedure will be mentioned here. Motions should be made, seconded, and repeated by the chairman or read by the secretary before being opened for discussion, and opportunity should be offered for discussion before a motion is put to a vote. A member should be permitted to withdraw his motion with the consent of the person who seconded it before discussion has commenced, but, after discussion has started, he is not permitted to withdraw his motion except with the unanimous consent of the members. If a motion is lost, it cannot properly be reconsidered at the same meeting without the consent of a majority of the members present. After a decision has been made, the question is closed to further discussion at the same meeting unless it is reopened by board action. A motion for reconsideration can be made and seconded only by a member who voted with the majority on the original motion. Amendments to a motion or to previous amendments must be disposed of before a vote can be taken on the original motion as amended. Once before the board, a motion can be interrupted by a motion to lay it on the table, to act on the previous question, for postponement, for amendment, or to adjourn. These are only a few examples of parliamentary rules.

Board members often violate correct parliamentary procedure in various ways. Members should address the chair and be recognized by it before making a motion or speaking on a question before the body. Recognition by the chair is not required for seconding a motion. Sometimes motions are made, seconded, and voted upon when they are out of order due to the priority of a previous motion upon which action has not been taken. In some cases, motions are made and discussed and put to a vote without a second, but if a motion is not seconded it should be declared dead. An amendment is sometimes passed and the original motion as amended is not put to a vote. This makes the amendment invalid because the motion of which it has become a part was not passed. Sometimes important actions are announced as having been adopted by consent or agreement. All important business should be adopted by vote of the board or its legality may be in doubt, though matters of procedure may be settled by consent. Sometimes the chairman fails to announce the result of a vote taken on a motion. These are only a few examples of faulty parliamentary procedure.

Functions of the Presiding Officer in the Conduct of Board Meetings

A well-conducted school board meeting will proceed smoothly, with a minimum of loss of time, according to a plan, and according to rules of parliamentary procedure. There will be discussion on each question by every member desiring the floor, limited by the board if deemed necessary but adequate to present the various views on the issues raised. The vote of the board will represent the members' independent opinions and not the dominance of any one member. Discussion will concern the question and not irrelevant matters. Such results will require exceptional ability to serve as a presiding officer on the part of the chairman.

In conducting school board meetings, it is or may well be the function and responsibility of a chairman to do the following:

Call meetings to order promptly.

Declare meetings adjourned on affirmative vote of the board for adjournment.

Decide the order of procedure or deviations from procedure indicated by agenda.

Accept the voted results of appeals from the chairman's decision made by any member of the board.

Receive, in the name of the board, delegations and petitioners who are in attendance at board meetings.

Seat new members after ascertaining the authenticity of their claim to membership on the board.

Provide a looseleaf notebook for each member in which he may keep copies of agenda, board minutes, documents, studies, and other notes.

See that actions of the board are authorized or approved at regular meetings of the board only, or at special meetings called for a specific purpose.

Rule on matters such as whether or not particular motions are in order.

Require that members receive recognition before addressing the body.

Direct discussion in board meetings.

Hold discussion to the question at issue.

Limit the time of each person, if so voted, on a controversial question to prevent long oration on matters not germane to the question before the board.

Be certain that persons are given opportunity for expressing any point of view they have.

Stimulate participation of board members in board deliberations and call on individuals to express their ideas if the issue is important and there is inadequate discussion.

Permit no member to monopolize the time of the meeting.

Rule impartially on controversies arising among members.

Protect members from intimidation by other members in the expression of their views.

Keep the discussion open as long as anyone has an opinion to express.

Close discussions that do not concern the immediate issues before the board and prevent thoughtless waste of time by members who use the time for joking, gossiping, or quarreling.

Put the question to a vote without delay when relevant discussion has been completed.

State the results of votes on motions and resolutions.

Save time on routine matters by shortening the processes required for them.

Order of Business

Many boards adopt an official order of business and make it a part of their bylaws or of their rules and regulations. Along with correct parliamentary procedure, an order of business dignifies the board's proceedings by improving courtesy among members. These result in the conservation of time and effort. A few illustrations of orders of business are presented as follows:

Plan A	Plan B
Call to order	Roll call
Roll call	Approval of printed minutes
Approval and signing of the minutes of previous meetings	Letters and communications
Hearing of delegations	Hearings and petitions
Superintendent's reports	Report of superintendent on operations

Plan A

Communications
Unfinished business
New business
Adjournment

Plan B

Report of special committees
Budget control report
Special reports of superintendent
Unfinished business
New business
Adjournment

Plan C

Call to order
Reading, correction, and approval
 of minutes
Communications:
 Oral
 Written
 Petitions
Report of superintendent
Reports of committees
Unfinished business
New business
Claims and accounts
Adjournment

Plan D

Call to order
Approval of the minutes
Report of the superintendent
Report of the business manager
Report of the superintendent of
 buildings and grounds
Reports of committees
Petitions and communications
Unfinished business
New business
Claims and accounts
Adjournment

Plan E

Hearing delegations and petitions
 when presented by the petition-
 ers
Calling of the roll
Reading of the minutes
Communications
Report of director of public librar-
 ies
Report of general superintendent
 of education
Report of secretary
Report of business manager
Report of buildings and grounds
 manager
Report of special committees
Report of standing committees
Unfinished business
New business
Adjournment

Plan F

Call to order
Record of members present and
 absent
Approval of previous regular and
 special meetings
Hearing of delegations and indi-
 viduals
Presentation and disposal of peti-
 tions
Reports of the superintendent:
 Financial
 Purchasing
 Personnel
 Transportation
 Instruction
 Buildings and grounds
 Special
Consideration of policies
Approval and authorization of pay-
 ment of bills
Unfinished business
New business
Adjournment

It is important to have a regular order of business, and the order adopted should be followed. The agenda should be classified under the headings of the order of business. Some items will require little time and others much. For example, there may or may not be items of new business. Although any one plan may be considered to be almost as good as another if it fits the conditions required, certain items in some of the plans are not needed for some school systems, and there are certain arrangements of items that are preferable to other arrangements. For example, the hearing of delegations and individuals should be early in the meeting to avoid the inconvenience of long waits for them, and the action on claims should be late in the meeting so that an unwarranted amount of time will not be consumed to the exclusion of other business.

A recommended order of business is as follows:

1. Call to order
2. Record of members present and absent
3. Establishment of a quorum
4. Approval of minutes
5. Hearing ef delegations
6. Written petitions and communications
7. Special committees' reports
8. Superintendent's reports
9. Unfinished business
10. New business
11. Approval of claims
12. Adjournment

In part, the procedure of a school board meeting would be somewhat as follows:

1. The meeting is called to order by the chairman at the exact time set, or if he is absent, by the vice chairman. He raps on the desk with his gavel and says, "The meeting will come to order."

2. The secretary makes a record of the names of members present and absent and announces the number present. A roll call is unnecessary.

3. The chairman states that there is or is not a quorum.

4. If there is a quorum, the chairman asks if there are any

corrections to the minutes as reproduced and sent to the members. If not, he declares them to be approved. If corrections are proposed, consent for them is asked or a vote on motion to correct them is taken. If passed, the minutes are declared approved by the chairman as corrected. This is done for the last regular and any intervening special or other meetings.

5. Delegations and individuals are welcomed by the chairman and are heard in order of listing on the agenda. Except in case of emergency, the matters presented are laid on the table and may be referred to the superintendent or a special committee for report and recommendation.

6. Written petitions are read and treated similarly; communications are read and filed; resolutions of approval, sympathy, and others are proposed and acted on by the board.

7. Reports of any special committees are heard. There are no standing committees in a properly organized board.

8. The superintendent's reports are heard. No reports are heard from other administrative officers except as the superintendent calls on an assistant, such as the business manager or the superintendent of buildings and grounds, to present a report of the superintendent, or as some one reports by a special request of the board.

9. Items of unfinished business, as scheduled under that heading on the agenda or as requested by members, are taken from the table and disposition is made of each item so removed. The secretary presents one item at a time for action by the board.

10. Items of new business are considered one at a time as listed on the agenda. Parliamentary procedure is followed. For example, if a motion is to be made, the member addresses the chair and is recognized by the chairman. He reads or states his motion; the chairman calls for a second, and, if there is a second, a period of discussion follows. If there is no second, there can be no discussion and the motion dies. Disposition is made of each motion before the chairman entertains another motion, except a substitute motion, a motion to amend, or a motion to

dispose of the previous question in some other manner, such as to withdraw the motion or lay it on the table.

11. Claims can be approved with little difficulty if the bills and invoices have been properly audited, checked for accuracy, and approved by the assistant superintendent in charge of business affairs or other similar officer. Any claim requiring investigation should be withdrawn from the list and approved at a later meeting.

12. A motion is made to adjourn, put to a vote, and if the motion is carried, the chairman declares the meeting to be adjourned.

Attendance and Quorum

The secretary of the board or his stenographer should make a record for the minutes of each member present or absent at the beginning of the meeting. Arriving late, members should not waste the time of the board by explaining the reason therefor.

If enough members are present to constitute a quorum, the chairman should declare that a quorum is present and the meeting will proceed. If not enough members are present to constitute a quorum, he should declare that there is not a quorum and the meeting cannot proceed. Some members may telephone the absent ones and urge them to attend, and the meeting may be opened late, or the members present may leave and the meeting may be omitted. A quorum is usually a majority of the total number of members, such as 3 of 5 members, 4 of 7 members, or 4 of 6 members. If a quorum is lost because members leave before the close of the meeting, the meeting is declared closed for lack of a quorum.

The vote of a majority of the members voting for or against a motion usually constitutes an act of the board unless the law or board's rules require a majority vote of all members present or of the membership. Sometimes such a requirement is made for amending the rules and regulations.

Four members of a 7-member board usually constitute a

quorum, and a majority of these (3 members) can pass a motion. Thus, a minority of the members would be able to bind the board in case of absences and a divided vote. In case there were 9 members on the board, 5 would be a quorum, and if only 5 members were present at a meeting, 3 would be a majority of the members present required to pass a motion. Thus, 3 members may legally bind a board of 9, except where a larger than majority vote is required to pass certain measures.

The law provides in at least one state that a member who is absent from regular meetings a certain number of consecutive times without excuse acceptable to the board shall forfeit his position as a member, and the board shall proceed to select someone to fill the vacancy. The author has known of a board member in another state not having such a law, who attended the first meeting after his election and found himself in opposition to the other 6 members but held his position for 2 years without attendance at any other of the 25 regular and about 14 special meetings held each year.

Making of Motions

Often motions will be made under the stimulus of deliberation in meeting. Such motions may be faulty, not only in English construction, but also in expressing the ideas intended by the maker of the motion. The secretary should draft the motions made carefully, or redraft them, if necessary, when handed to him in written form. The motion as drafted, and later as amended, should be read aloud to determine whether or not the intentions have been correctly expressed. Drafting of motions by the secretary is desirable even if the practice is for members to write their motions before or at the meeting. Drafting or redrafting of all motions by a capable secretary has the advantage of providing a common form and of stating them in more accurate and more expressive English than can be had when they are stated orally or are written by the different members of the board.

Although with some boards it is expected that every member will vote on every motion, it would seem to be better practice to permit a member, who is undecided as to how he should vote and whose opinion on each side of a question is about evenly balanced, to "sit on the fence" and refrain from exercising his right.

Some boards present all motions or resolutions at once, discuss all of them in order, and then vote one after another on all of them after the debate has been closed. This method cannot be recommended. It is wasteful of time because discussions are long and drawn out, the deliberations are not sharply delineated and to the point, there is much jumping from one question to another, and reasons are forgotten or confused at the time votes are taken. It is preferable to dispose of one question at a time before proceeding to the next.

Deliberations

A school board meeting is a deliberative assembly. Each board member must settle in his own mind whether it is better to vote for or against a motion before the house. After a motion has been made and seconded, the members are given an opportunity to discuss the question. Each member should keep his mind open to the arguments presented by his colleagues. It is each member's privilege to present his views, if he has convictions and there are differences of opinion, and to listen to arguments presented for and against the motion. The chairman should not permit irrelevant discussion. If several members are undecided as to how to vote after a period of discussion, the proper action might be for some one to move to lay the motion on the table and to refer the question to the superintendent, or to a special board committee meeting with the superintendent, for study, report, and recommendation at the next or some subsequent meeting.

Often there should be differences of opinion among members. In some school districts, boards, by courtesy, pass all motions unanimously according to majority opinion as shown in a caucus. There are some advantages in this practice because it does give a feeling of unity in the board. However, a motion passed by a majority of the members is still the whole board's decision, and every member is obligated to support the board's action. Although harmony within the board is a laudable objective, the passing or rejecting of all motions by unanimous vote, after a previous majority informal unrecorded vote, is too high a price to pay for it. Members that oppose or favor a particular motion still usually like to have their vote recorded, even though they support the board's decision. They should be entitled to this representation of their true opinions and actions, and the public is entitled to know of their opposition to the majority board opinion. The minority may be right and the public may confirm the minority opinion at the next election. Some boards pass nearly all motions made. Of about 2,000 motions made by one board, only 8 were defeated. Lack of difference of opinion in a board is not always a good sign. It may indicate that members may be uninterested in the schools or that they are not acting independently.

Motions requiring changes in school board policy properly may be discussed when the motion is made, but it is a serious matter to change board policy, and a proposal to make such a change should be laid on the table for a month after it is proposed. This might well be adopted as a rule of the board. During the month, the matter proposed for change should be studied by the superintendent or a special committee of the board and a report with recommendation should be made to the board. If desired, the matter can remain on the table for more than a month before action is taken.

Voting and Board Decisions

After debate has been closed, the chairman calls for a vote on the motion before the house. If a voice vote, the chairman announces the result as appears to him to be correct, but a member may call for a poll of the members. Some boards deem it advisable to poll the members on all important motions on which the vote was not unanimous. If this is done, there will be a record of how each member voted and the public will be informed regarding each member's actions. In case of a poll, the names of members voting for, against, and abstaining should be recorded, as well as the names of the mover and seconder of the motion.

Unless otherwise specified by law or the rules and regulations of the board, a motion is passed or lost by a majority vote of the members voting. It will not necessarily be passed by a majority of the members voting if the requirement for passage or rejection is a majority of the members present or a majority of the members of the board. If there should be such a requirement, members abstaining from voting or absent would count against the motion.

On most boards the presiding officer votes when the board is polled or there is a closely divided difference of opinion, for he is a member as well as chairman. In some cases, the board's rules and regulations require that the chairman abstain from voting except to make or break a tie vote. These occasions may be the only times a chairman's vote would count in any event, but it would seem to be advisable in school board practice for the chairman to have the privilege and responsibility of having his vote recorded in the minutes along with the votes of other members. After all, the chairman is a member.

The board must have accurate facts as a basis for the votes of its members. The office of the superintendent should be the main source and the superintendent's reports the principal means of securing them. Any superintendent who knowingly produces wrong, distorted, or "doctored" facts and figures for a board to use as a basis for its actions has committed an unforgivable breach of confidence, and the board would be entirely justified in discharging him and employing a new superintendent of schools.

Action on Petitions and Requests of Delegations

Petitions should be read in board meetings and requests made by delegations or individuals should be heard respectfully and with courtesy by the board in session. It may be advisable to limit the time allowed for the presentation of the request. In addition, presentation in writing should be required in order to avoid misunderstanding. The actions requested should be given consideration by the members in session, but the board should not be rushed into action and should seldom or never deliberate or act at the meeting at which the matter is proposed. The board should seldom or never commit itself while the delegation or petitioners are present or before time has been allowed to give full consideration to the matter because of the possibility that their presence may influence the decision. The matter should be left for discussion and action at the next or some subsequent meeting. This should be done even if the request is made by a parent-teacher association, by teachers, or by pupils.

The board should be free to reject requests made by groups of the public if they seem unworthy of adoption. They may represent a minority of the people and in no sense the will of the community. If the board desires to learn the opinions held in the community, it can hold a public hearing or a referendum or call a mass meeting, but the board should act in accordance with the best judgment of a majority of its members after due consideration. Whatever action is taken, the secretary should acknowledge receipt of the petition if it is not formally presented by someone and should keep the petitioners informed as to action of the board on the request. If the petition is denied, the reasons for denial should be stated.

Hearings

Some board hearings are necessary because required by law; some are advisable as a source of information relative to community opinion; and some are improper and harmful to the management of a school system.

When a teacher on tenure is discharged for reasons such as incompetence, incapacity, or conduct unbecoming a teacher, the laws of most states require that the board shall grant him a hearing on request. The teacher often has the option of a public or private hearing and of being represented by counsel. The burden of proof is thrown on the board and its superintendent. Nevertheless, it is the board's duty to discharge such a teacher and to hear his testimony and bear the consequences.

In determining what is public opinion, a board can hear delegations to secure information, or persons can appear for the purpose of giving testimony, either as volunteers or on call by the board. The board should hear all sides of the question at issue. It should question witnesses but the members should not argue with them.

Sometimes a board hears groups or individuals on matters that can better be settled by administrative action. The right of appeal to the board should always be open, but the board should usually uphold the superintendent on such matters as the following: a request for or objection to the sending of pupils to schools in districts of the city other than those in which they reside; determining the residence or nonresidence of tuition pupils; constructing a new fence or sidewalk at a school; the nonpromotion of a pupil; or the use of school buildings by an athletic association. These and similar matters are proper for administrative action based on general policies of the board.

Adjournment

Like other deliberative bodies, most school boards have formal opening and closing procedures. Unlike most other motions, a motion to adjourn is always in order except that it may not interrupt a speaker nor be made when a vote is being taken. A motion to adjourn takes precedence over any motion or other business before the house and is not open to debate. However, it must be seconded before call for the vote on it. Many board members have developed the habit of leaving as soon as someone makes a motion to adjourn, before the motion has been seconded and without vote on it. Such procedure is not proper adjournment. It is true that if enough members leave so that a quorum does not remain, no business can be transacted, but, without a second or a vote, it should not be recorded in the minutes that the meeting was adjourned. It requires only a minute to call for a second and a vote; this should be done because a majority may desire to transact more business before adjournment and the motion might not pass. Actually, adjournment should not occur until after the vote, when the chairman should rap his gavel and announce that the meeting is adjourned.

CHAPTER 12

The Minutes of School Board Meetings

Legal Requirements for the Keeping of Minutes

The laws of some states specifically require the school board or its secretary to keep minutes of school board meetings. For example, it is provided by Chapter 71, Section 36 of the Massachusetts statutes that "The committee shall appoint a secretary who shall keep a permanent record in which all votes, orders, and proceedings shall be recorded." The laws of some other states make such requirements as that the board shall "record the proceedings of all meetings," "keep a correct and proper record of all the proceedings of the board," "keep a record of all the transactions of the board," "keep a record of its proceedings," "keep a permanent record of all proceedings of the board," or some other, similar provision. Whether or not specifically required by law, most boards provide for making and keeping some sort of records of their proceedings, though in some of the very small school districts this is not done and many boards keep only very brief and inadequate notations of school board actions.

Need for Keeping Minutes

The minutes of school board meetings are very important for several reasons. They furnish a history of the school district and of local school board policies and administration. There is often a need for records of meetings complete with: dates; names of members present and absent; names of members voting for and against particular motions; notations of approval of minutes by the board; and other notations which make the minutes complete.

The minutes are important because they are a record of all of the decisions and actions of the school board in the past. If properly prepared they will show all that has been done by the board in its meetings. They are almost the only source by which new members and a new superintendent can orient themselves by determining what problems have been met in the past, how they have been solved, and what constitutes the background of the policies of the board. The minutes are important because the rules and regulations of the board have grown out of the board's official actions over a period of years.

Complete records of the transactions of the school board are important because the minutes are a legal record of the activities of the school board as a public corporation having the specified legal purpose of maintaining public schools. They are important to the board and superintendent because the superintendent can act legally only as he has been delegated direct or indirect power to act by the board and the minutes will show what specific authority has been delegated to him. The minutes are the only record of board action that exists. The necessity for keeping minutes of school board proceedings was expressed by a Kentucky court as follows:

> The board of education can act only in its official capacity. It is made by the statute a body politic and corporate and all of its acts and doings should be made a matter of record. . . . We do not mean to hold that it is indispensable that these records should be kept with all the exactness of detail that is observed in the records of organized business institutions, but only that there should be some record kept showing that the board of education . . . acting in an official capacity, took action in respect to the matter under investigation.[1]

The minutes, if properly kept, approved, and signed as having been approved, are acceptable in courts of law as an original source of evidence in cases of litigation. The courts may use them both as sources of authoritative factual information and as

[1] Board of Trustees and Hartford Graded School v. Ohio County Board of Education. 174 Ky. 424.

evidence of whether or not the board acted legally and in good faith. In any case, it would require strong evidence to controvert evidence shown by complete and accurate minutes of a school board. Therefore, it is very important that the minutes be properly kept. For example, a court might question the evidence the minutes present if they do not show that a quorum of the members was present for a legal meeting, or do not show that a particular motion was carried, or that a particular meeting was legally held or legally adjourned by vote of the members.

Importance of Keeping Accurate Minutes

The minutes should be complete and accurate. They should be so prepared as to be models for minutes in the future and in such manner that the board members of the future will be proud of them when they refer to them or when they are submitted to a court as a source of evidence.

In a small city school district observed recently, the minutes were written in final form, in almost illegible handwriting, by a member of the board who had been elected by the board as its secretary. Only the briefest notes had been taken as the actions occurred and they had not been rewritten. The language used was bad grammatically and not clear as to meaning. Many faults could be cited with regard to the contents of the minutes, such as the frequent recording of motions without any statement of what action had been taken on them—whether they were put to a vote and, if so, whether they were passed or failed. So far as the minutes were concerned, no action had been taken on the recorded motions. Therefore the first of these must be before the board for its action to this day, and all subsequent actions taken by the board must have been out of order. Other motions that were not amendments or substitutions were recorded as having been made and passed when previously made motions were before the house for action. Sometimes the number of members present and whether or not there was a quorum were not recorded. An old school board minute book, dated 1846, was found in the archives of that city. It was in handwriting with many flourishes, but it was more legible than the current minute book. It was written in almost perfect language and furnished considerable detail of the transactions. It indicates that parliamentary practices had been better observed then than they were by the present board. This example of the inadequacy of board minutes is only one of many that could be given.

Another board decided that it kept its minutes too accurately. It had been sued on the awarding of a contract, and it lost on the basis of a true record of its action as shown by its minutes. After that, the board decided to keep only very brief records of its proceedings. Of course, it should have decided that in the future its acts would be legal. Many other boards have been upheld by courts on the basis of accurate minutes.

In one city, a board deliberately omitted from its minutes a motion to increase the salary of the superintendent—this in a state requiring the board to keep an accurate record of its proceedings. With one such omission from the minutes, whether made by action of the board or by adoption of the minutes without correction of an error, the proceedings of all meetings are suspect and may not be of great value in protecting the board in court. Most boards are very jealous of the accuracy of the minutes of their proceedings, but few have records that are fully adequate in serving the purposes for which they are designed.

Kind of Minute Book

The minute book should be a looseleaf book of convenient size with heavy, stiff covers. Books and paper fillers, such as $8\frac{1}{2}$ inches by 11 or 14 inches, are prepared by supply companies particularly for use by school boards. In some states, the state department of education furnishes a minute book and fillers to school districts, which is standard for the state. The paper should be such that typewriting will not show through the page and the record can be typed on each side. This makes the minutes compact and reduces the number of minute books to be preserved. Space is saved where minutes are printed. Four or five copies can then be preserved as official copies.

If the minute book has accumulated enough sheets to comprise a book and it is desired to begin a new one, and if all minutes have been properly approved and signed, they can be prepared for preservation by binding the pages into a book in chronological order. The looseleaf book covers can be continued in use for the minutes of the next period. Each bound volume should be given a consecutive number, and the years covered in any particular volume should be indicated on the back.

Form of Minutes

It is convenient to have pages printed or mimeographed as blank forms to be filled with regular and recurring preliminary data. Two hundred such pages would be enough for as many meetings and should serve for several years. One sheet would be used for each meeting and unprinted sheets of the same kind of paper should be used if additional sheets are needed. The form sheets might be printed at the top of the page as follows:

BOARD OF EDUCATION OF THE MIDDLETOWN SCHOOL DISTRICT

Middletown, N. K.

Minutes of the meeting of _____
Kind of meeting _____   Place of meeting _____
Time called to order _____   Time adjourned _____
Presiding officer _____

Members present:	Members tardy:	Time of arrival
_____	_____	____
_____	_____	____
_____	Members leaving before adjournment:	Time of leaving
_____	_____	____
_____	_____	____

Members absent:
_____
_____
_____

Others present:
_____
_____
_____

The minutes should record the manner of disposing of each motion before another motion is made and recorded. This does not apply to motions pertaining to the motion before the house, such as motions to amend, substitute, or lay on the table. Any unrelated motion is out of order when a motion is before the house. If the presiding officer does not remember that a motion is before the house, it is the duty of the secretary to inform him that such is the case.

The words "Passed" or "Carried," following the statement of a motion in the minutes, are not sufficient except for a motion to adjourn or motions considered to be of minor importance. On important business motions the notation should be "Carried unanimously," if such is the case, and, if the vote is divided and there is a poll of the members, the votes of the several members should be recorded.

Each separate action should be recorded in the minutes in one or more separate paragraphs.

All the board's resolutions, awards of contract, approvals of executive actions, and other actions should be numbered consecutively in chronological order of occurrence.

Marginal notations or brief subject titles should be used to indicate the location of the more important items. They will be useful in searching for specific actions. A relatively wide margin should be provided for that purpose and brief, well chosen, descriptive words or phrases should be used to locate the record of the different board actions. Center headings are sometimes used instead of marginal notations, but that requires the use of a heading for every item, or minor items will appear to belong to those having headings. For this reason, it is probably better to use marginal notations instead of headings.

For communications and other documents that are too long and bulky to be included in the minutes and still need to be preserved, it is suggested that references to the file and document numbers be made at the appropriate place in the minutes, so that the originals can be readily located. The documents should be filed, not left loose in the minute book or pasted in it.

The stenographic notes from which the minutes are prepared

should be preserved for a limited time. A year or two should be sufficient.

For more detailed discussion concerning the form and content of school board minutes, the reader is referred to *The Minutes of a Board of Education*, by G. W. Grill.

Contents and Preparation of the Minutes

There are wide variations among boards with regard to what is included in the minutes of school board meetings. In some cases, only the briefest possible records of actions are made. In others, the records are very complete, include a brief of the discussions, and contain copies of many documents and letters. Sometimes the originals are pasted into the minute books. These are the extremes. Most minutes are kept so that they include some details other than motions. These might include the following: briefs of hearings; copies of petitions and communications; a newly adopted salary schedule, or a record of the parts of a schedule that have been modified; lists of teachers newly employed, transferred, or placed on retirement; and other similar matters related to the business transacted by the board.

It is usually better to record fairly complete minutes, including not only motions and other actions, but also the main points emphasized in the discussion of important issues. Brief communications and documents that are important in nature may be included in the form of copies. Reference to the file and document number of larger communications and other documents may be made in the minutes.

The minutes should usually include the following:

1. Date.
2. Name of the board.
3. Statement that the meeting was called to order, by whom, the hour, and whether the meeting was a regular, organization, adjourned or reconvened, or special meeting, and, if a special meeting, its purpose.
4. Record of attendance and absence of members and a statement that a quorum was declared by the chairman.

5. Statement of action taken for approval of the minutes of the last regular and any special or other meetings that have been held since the last regular meeting.

6. Notation of the presentation and hearing of delegates or visitors who have oral communications or petitions to present and of any actions referring matters presented to special or regular committees or the superintendent for report, if such is done.

7. Statement of written communications and petitions read, such as those from churches, service clubs, parent-teacher associations, teacher organizations, pupil groups, or individuals, and a record of action on matters presented, when required.

8. Record of hearings and action on reports of special committees, any regular committees, and members of the board.

9. Record of hearings and actions on previously requested special reports from administrative officers such as the business manager, the architect, the athletic director, or the school nurse. If written, the reports may be numbered and filed as documents and reference made to them in the minutes by file and document number.

10. Record of the presentation of and action on reports of the superintendent concerning such matters as the following: change in the status of employees; nomination of candidates for employment; proposals of textbooks for adoption; proposals for changes in the curriculum; and proposals for buildings and grounds alterations, improvements or new construction, and building sites. These reports may also be numbered and filed as documents and reference made to them in the minutes by title and number.

11. Record of hearings and actions on resolutions introduced by various members of the board like those on the resignation or death of a board member or a principal, or a proposal to change the rules and regulations, board procedure, or some matter relating to the operation of the schools.

12. Record of motions and actions on unfinished business taken from the table by the board.

13. Record of motions and actions on matters of new business.

14. Record of the motion to adjourn.

This outline would not be complete for all meetings because some parts may not be represented in any particular one. It would not fit an organization meeting, for there would be no reports on hearings or unfinished business and the minutes of such a meeting must include a record of the taking of the oath, the names of new members, and the results of officer elections.

The names, addresses, and telephone numbers of all members should be included in the minutes of the organization meeting. It is a shocking experience to read the yearly minutes of school board meetings and discover that nowhere in them is there a list of members for that year—neither in the organization meeting minutes nor in the minutes of other meetings for which a notation has been made "All members present, except Mr. B." so that a member must be absent to have his name entered in the minutes.

Some meeting's minutes must include the budget for the year, either in summary form, in full, or by title as a numbered and filed document to which reference is made in the minutes.

Notes on meetings may be taken in shorthand by a capable stenographer, perhaps the secretary of the superintendent. The stenographic notes should be typed, and the minutes may be written or dictated for transcription soon after the meeting by the board's secretary, with the transcribed notes as a reminder. The minutes should be typed with duplicate copies, or otherwise duplicated, so that there will be copies for all board members. The typing of the sheets for the official minutes should be done after correction and approval of the minutes by the board, or the original and carbon copies will serve if there are no corrections.

Recording of Board Actions

Actions of the board should be recorded as motions, as action by consent of the board, by receipt and filing of communications, or by whatever method is used to determine board action. Many secretaries carelessly omit even important actions that are not determined by motions. Motions lost for want of a second need not be recorded.

It is sometimes a problem for a secretary to record in correct English motions made from the floor. The motions are often made incorrectly and the maker may not realize the errors in his statement. The secretary must make corrections without changing the meaning desired by the maker of the motion. Therefore, he should read the motion to the maker to determine whether or not his draft of the motion expresses the maker's intended meaning. Motions prepared by the superintendent will generally be prepared for the board in written form prior to the meeting and handed to the secretary.

The following is an example of a poorly made and recorded motion in the minutes of the board of a small city school system, given exactly as recorded. It is by no means an isolated example.

> It was moved and seconded that Miss K.... keep better discipline and that we inform her that such is the wish of the board. We believe that you should not let some pupils torment other pupils during school hours or steal his pencil and papers. We have tried to be patient with you and this is our last warning. We should send this notice to Miss K.... Motion carried.

Comment on the faults of either the motion or its recording would be superfluous.

Motions should be specific and exact. The motion "to fix the tax rate the same as last year" is not specific and definite. Persons referring to the minutes in the future would be unable to determine the tax rate from such a motion without searching through the minutes of the preceding year. The rate fixed should be shown, and, if the motion is made as indicated, the secretary should write in the rate and read the motion, as written, before the vote is taken.

Amendments are often made to motions and sometimes amendments are made to amendments. The latter sometimes cause the presiding officer to be confused. The secretary should record every amendment that is in order together with the vote and should reword the motion as the amendment directs. Disposition should be made of each amendment before a vote can be taken on any previous amendment or on the original motion. The disposition of all amendments should be shown in the minutes. The secretary should help to keep the chairman informed with regard to the order of amendments and the state of the original motion as amended.

Minutes of meetings should be recorded with the items in the chronological order of occurrence and should constitute running statements of all of the official actions of the board. They should be so accurate and complete that they will stand, if necessary, in a court of law as the complete record of the official acts of the board and can be ranked by the court above the memories of witnesses. They should be clear in statement but not excessively wordy. They should include all of the school board's actions because the board has no voice other than its minutes. However, an action omitted from the minutes, that complies with the law, is valid if fully substantiated as the legal action of the board. On the other hand, an action omitted from the minutes, requiring a roll call vote by law, may be declared null and void because the board's action is not recorded in the minutes.

The very poor practice followed by the secretary of one board may be briefly described. One notation, with only a change of the members' names, is as follows:

> Mr. Wolf requested that a correction be made in the following paragraph: "It was voted on motion of Mr. Lyon, seconded by Mr. Fox, to reappoint trade school personnel as listed." Mr. Wolf requested that the names of the trade school teachers as listed be made a part of the original motion. The names are as follows: J. M. Byrd, H. E. Pidgeon, M. A. Drake, ...

No correction was made in the original minutes as voted by the board. The incorrect motion remains in the minutes of the preceding meeting, though it has been recorded that the minutes of that meeting have been approved as corrected. To include the motion to make the correction in the minutes of the next regular meeting does not make the correction. It should have been made before the minutes were signed as approved.

On February 14 a motion was made and duly recorded to correct a minute of January 17, requiring a specific rather than a general statement of supply shortages. The secretary made a statement in explanation of the causes and kinds of shortages stated in the January 17 meeting. This was not acceptable to the board. At a special meeting on February 21, the statement included in the minutes of February 14 was ordered corrected by the board. No corrections were ever made in the minutes of the meetings of January 17 and February 14 as directed. The secretary wrongly held that the motion to make the correction constituted the actual correction.

After minutes have been approved, that fact should be attested by the signature of the chairman (or president) of the board under the word "Approved" at the end of each set of minutes. The date of approval should be shown. Unless all corrections voted have actually been made, it would be incorrect for the chairman to sign the minutes as having been approved.

Recording of the Discussion of Issues

A discussion of issues involved in an important proposal for a change of policy is vital because it stimulates thought on the part of the members of the school board and helps to prevent perfunctory action. The amount of discussion devoted to an issue will depend somewhat on the skill of the chairman's direction. Sometimes he can draw members into the discussion and secure the expression of opinions by direct questions or by asking them for their opinions on the matter. He should not permit some members to monopolize all the time, and he should not argue with members. As chairman he must preside impartially. If he desires to comment on the proposition, he can appoint a temporary chairman and ask for the floor, returning to his position as chairman when he is through.

Some boards provide for the taking of stenographic notes on

important issues. Parts that present factual data or reasons for stands taken on important issues are briefed and incorporated into the minutes. The preparation of such a brief or summary requires fine discrimination on the part of the secretary and the ability to grasp the essentials and separate them from the verbiage that usually accompanies such discussion. Some secretaries take *verbatim* reports of what has been said and use quotation marks. That practice results in needlessly long accounts with many repetitions of the reasons presented. A brief of the discussion, written in the third person and in correct English, is much to be preferred. Data on the discussions are useful as background for the interpretation of the policies after they have been adopted. Such data may also be useful in the future for showing the opinions and reasons expressed on an issue by each member.

The records of discussions do not necessarily need to be included in the minutes. Some boards keep these in bound, dated copies as documents to accompany the minutes. They are typed and preserved for reference use and are not official minutes. Their preservation would be a disadvantage if they should interfere in any way with free discussion by members who may not express themselves orally in the best "king's English." They may hesitate to express their opinions at all if they know that what they say will become a matter of record.

Correction and Approval of the Minutes

Complete and accurate minutes of school board meetings are important because they are the only records of actions taken by the board. They should be approved by the board to insure their correctness and to make them official. They can be approved only at regular meetings. It is not advisable to postpone approval of minutes because memories of what is correct as a record of transactions become dim with the passage of time.

The oral reading of the minutes of a previous meeting is a slow tedious process and a waste of the time that is available for board meetings. Instead of oral reading of the minutes of the preceding regular and any interim special meetings, the secretary of the board should mail a copy of the minutes as drafted to each member of the board soon after the meeting. Thus, the members will have an opportunity to read the draft carefully while the meeting is still fresh in their minds and to consider whether or not the minutes as drafted are complete and accurate.

If each member has a copy of the minutes as drafted, there will be no need for oral reading. A motion should be made to dispense with the reading of the minutes of the specified date and to approve them as submitted. A mere motion to dispense with the reading of the minutes will not be sufficient, for it does not approve them. After such a motion has been made and seconded, members may propose corrections or alterations that they deem to be necessary. If proposed corrections are sustained by the consent of the board, the chairman orders the corrections made and announces that the minutes of the specified date are approved as corrected, or as prepared if there are no corrections. It is important that the date of the minutes be included in the motion for correction or approval so that all members will be considering the same minutes. The secretary should be certain to include the date of the minutes approved in the record made of their approval.

The following are advantages of voting on prepared duplicated minutes instead of minutes read orally to the board: (1) the procedure will save the time of the board members; (2) most people receive more accurate visual than auditory impressions; (3) any errors in the draft will be more apparent when the copy can be reread than if heard only once; and (4) more time will be allowed members for giving consideration to the completeness and accuracy of the tentative draft.

If the board orders that a correction be made, it should actually be done in the typing of the minutes for the official copy or copies. Some secretaries make marginal notations, cross out parts that are wrong and write in the correct parts between the lines, or leave the minutes without correction, other than the record of a motion for correction made at a subsequent meeting.

None of these is satisfactory. There is no reason for retaining incorrect parts. Writing in corrections makes it appear that there has been tampering with the minutes, possibly after their approval. If the correction is not actually made, a person reading the incorrect action in the future will be misled because he will not know that consent or a motion for the correction was adopted at the next meeting. A motion to correct minutes is not a correction in itself, but an order that they be corrected. Incorrect parts are not true records and are in the minutes only because of the secretary's failure to understand the intent of the board or because of his omission of some part of the transactions. The page should be retyped as corrected. After approval, no change should be made in the minutes for any reason.

Publication and Distribution of the Minutes

The minutes should be drafted soon after the meeting and printed or otherwise duplicated. Copies of the draft of unapproved minutes should be furnished to the board members and the newspapers. The newspapers will want their copies before they have lost their news value. Hence, it is desirable that minutes be prepared the day after the meeting. Large school systems have a mailing list for the printed minutes which includes some members of the administrative staff, teachers' organizations, the public library, and other interested persons such as dealers who sell supplies to the school system.

The minutes, particularly those for meetings of the preceding year or two, should be open to inspection. Copies should be kept in the office of the secretary of the board and in the public library for use by the public.

Documents Relating to the Minutes

All originals or copies of documents relating to school board actions that are too bulky to warrant their being copied in the minutes should be carefully and systematically filed for preservation. It may be desirable to have a filing system separate from the administration files for documents relating strictly to school board business. This insures that the documents will not be destroyed in a year or two and makes possible the use of a separate and distinct numbering system for reference use in the minutes. Documents should be filed in numbered sequence to make their future use easy. They may be numbered and preserved in folders in steel files, in large envelopes, or in boxes. Whatever the method used, they should be kept in a vault for safety.

The documents are actually a part of the minutes and references should be made to them at appropriate places in the minutes. Some documents that are often too bulky to be copied in the minutes are the following: contracts and specifications; deeds; insurance policies; petitions; letters written to the board; lists of teachers; lists of high school graduates; reports of the superintendent or other officers of administration; and research studies on which actions are based.

Cumulative Index to the Minutes

Minutes may be indexed either on separate pages that can be bound with them or in a card file. In either case the items should be listed in alphabetical order. Use of the card index system has an advantage over the use of bound pages because a card for each new item can be inserted in its appropriate place without disturbing the alphabetical arrangement of the items. If the index is kept on pages of the minute book, the insertion of new items may require extensive alterations and the retyping of the page or of the whole index.

The index to the minutes should be cumulative and kept up to date by adding page numbers for the items as they appear in the minute book. This should be done as soon as minutes have been approved and the pages given numbers. Items should be indexed with cross references to other items selected for the index. For example, after the word, "counseling," the notation might be, "see guidance and counseling," with appropriate page references.

The cumulative index to the minutes will be useful for reference to official actions taken and policies established over a period of years, particularly where it is desired to have reference to all actions or items considered by the board. The index will be used by the secretary, the superintendent, or by board members (particularly new ones) who wish to know how issues have been met and resolved by the board in past years. They may desire a full and complete record of board decisions or policy with respect to such matters as the employment of married women teachers, teacher salary schedules, gifts from parent-teacher associations to the schools, and many more. It would be difficult and require much time to learn the complete history of a subject that may be a current issue without an index to the minutes. The cumulative, alphabetical index will also be useful for locating actions such as the bid quotations for supplies, for a repair job, or the form of contract previously used for a bus driver or for the painting of a building.

The index would be much like that of a book, with page number references, but, being cumulative, page numbers would be added to the index topics as required. Enough space should be allowed after and below each topic for the adding of page numbers as new actions are taken on the subjects. A section of such index might be organized as follows, each topic or subtopic being allowed a card.

Taxes:
  county
  district
Teachers:
  appointment of
  assignment of
  elementary
  examinations
  high school
  leaves of absence

married women
organizations
qualifications of
resignations
salaries
substitute
tenure of
unions (see teachers, organizations)
Technical high school
Telephones

Two index cards might appear as follows:

Teachers:
   appointment of, 12, 13, 50, 95, 186, 187, 189
Teachers examinations, 25, 171, 190

Custody of the Minutes

The board's official copy of the minutes, signed by the chairman as approved, should be kept by the secretary of the board in a fireproof vault adjoining the board room or the superintendent's office. Documents that belong to or with the minutes should be kept in the same vault. This also applies to old minutes as long as they may be needed for reference. Even after they are not needed for reference, they should be preserved through the years. They should be a systematic and authoritative record of all of the school board's official actions.

CHAPTER 13

The Employment of a School Executive

Importance of Employing a Capable Executive Officer

The laws of most states fail to require or even mention the employment of a superintendent of schools. Yet they make the school board responsible for the administration of the public schools. Obviously, a board that can act only when it is in session must depend on an executive officer—superintendent, principal, or head teacher—to act for it in performing the daily details of school administration. The board needs to employ a reliable superintendent to render it sound advice with respect to its legislative and ministerial duties and to administer the schools in accordance with its adopted policies.

Probably no function of a school board is more important than the appointment of an executive officer to administer the schools. Carelessness in this action may ruin a school system. It is too important to be decided by the toss of a coin or to permit the decision to be made on the basis of political or religious affiliation, or any other consideration than qualification for the work.

The author remembers a case in which the board failed to investigate, fully, the qualifications for the superintendency of an impressive appearing applicant. It was necessary to discharge the man six weeks after his assumption of the duties because he was mentally unbalanced. Disregard of the significance of an applicant's qualifications for the position is certain to result in a poor school system. The people of the school district will be right in holding the board responsible for such a situation.

All pressures for the employment of any specific person should be firmly resisted, whether from within or without the school district. In a certain city the board dismissed its superintendent. Since he was a loyal political party member, his friends appealed to the United States representative of the congressional district. This man interceded for the superintendent, telephoning the president of the board. The board members, all belonging to the same party, reinstated him at a special meeting held that evening. The board did not properly fulfill its duty to the school system by permitting itself to be intimidated and induced to place political party loyalty above the interests of the schools for which it was responsible.

Some Important Functions of the Superintendent of Schools

The work of the superintendent of schools is important to the board in securing an efficient, smoothly operating school system. Some of the superintendent's functions are so important that their effective performance determines the quality of the school system. As the board's executive officer, it is necessary that the superintendent be present at board meetings. It is the superintendent's duty to enforce the laws of the state within the school district, for and with the authority of the board. It is his duty to advise the board on the need for new policies or the modification of existing ones relating to the administration and operation of the schools. Whether or not the board sees fit to adopt his recommendations, it is the superintendent's duty to make effective such policies as have been adopted by the board to the best of his ability. Not only must the superintendent make the board's policies effective, but it is his duty, in matters not covered by stated policies, to administer the schools effectively in accordance with the dictates of his professional judgment.

In all school systems having a unified school administration, the superintendent is required to administer the system and be responsible to the board for the management of the entire enterprise in all of its phases—preparation of the budget for adoption by the board; accounting, purchasing, and other business activities; the operation and maintenance of school buildings; auxiliary agencies of the school district; and all phases of curriculum development and instruction. Some of these functions may not be under the direction of the superintendent in multiple headed school systems.

The superintendent should be responsible for the selection of teachers and other school personnel subject to approval of his nominees by the board. He should be held responsible for the effectiveness of the work performed by supervisors and other employees and for the organization of personnel for curriculum development duties.

The superintendent should perform the important function of providing leadership for the maintenance of public relations for the school system. He addresses service clubs and other organizations on matters relating to school accomplishments and needs; assists in the organization of parent-teacher associations; is active in movements for the improvement or welfare of the community; and informs the public of the work of the schools through annual reports and by press releases and public addresses.

Causes of Vacancies in the Position of Superintendent

The position of superintendent of schools is the most unstable and insecure of any of the professional education positions to be found in a school system. Although some instances can be cited of superintendents holding a single position for 30 or more years, that is rather the general rule for principals and teachers.

Though vacancies occur in the position of superintendent of schools due to death, disability, or retirement as in other school positions, the usual causes are the board's dissatisfaction with the superintendent, the offer of a better position in a larger school system, or his leaving the teaching profession. Although it is desirable for a school board to search for a superintendent who has been eminently successful as an administrator in a smaller school system, the practice of taking a superintendent away from another school district does create another vacancy that increases the total turnover in such positions. A vacancy may also occur when a superintendent is drawn into business. Indeed, cases have been reported of a member of the board taking him from the school district and placing him in his own business at a higher salary.

Sometimes a vacancy is caused by the discharge of the superintendent for what the board considers to be good reasons. Perhaps a majority of the board members are new, even having been elected as spokesmen for discontent in the community to oppose the superintendent and the policies of previous board members with whom the superintendent has co-operated and with whom the new members identify him. Therefore, it is difficult, or seemingly impossible, for the new members to accept him as the board's executive officer; sometimes it is difficult for the superintendent to co-operate with them. He may find it impossible to meet the desires of the new majority and at the same time maintain continuity and consistency with his administrative actions under the old one. The new members may view his actions and recommendations with suspicion.

Every effort should be made by both the superintendent and the board members to make such adjustments as are necessary to work together for the maintenance of a good and developing school system. However, if the board members find it impossible to have full confidence in the good intentions, good judgment, or capability of the superintendent, the proper course is to request or require his resignation as soon as legally possible, and to declare a vacancy in the position. There must be full and mutual confidence between the board and its executive officer, since he is charged with the function of executing the expressed will of the board. A change of superintendents is less detrimental to the schools than would be constant quarreling accompanied by acrimonious charges. However, unless a superintendent refuses to co-operate, is unable to convince openminded board members of the correctness of his contentions, or has in the past been a failure as an administrator and lost the confidence of the community or of the teachers, it is usually better not to make a change in superintendents. Rather, the board should strive to secure mutual co-operation in its relations with him.

The author has observed many changes in personnel of the position of superintendent of schools, made for various reasons. One superintendent died. Another retired from the position seven years after reaching the age of retirement. Another found himself in a nutcracker between the teachers and the board and decided to give his loyalty to the teachers and help them fight for higher salaries, but he was unable to help the board by recommending a satisfactory source of money for the higher salaries. After he had quarreled with the board and conducted a newspaper campaign for higher teachers' salaries, the board discharged him. Another superintendent resigned to establish a business with his son.

Several superintendents known to the author resigned to accept positions in larger cities at higher salaries. One left his position to accept a high ranking office in the army and the board decided not to re-employ him after his discharge because the assistant superintendent had become superintendent and the members preferred to retain him in the position. One superintendent had co-operated with a politically minded board that used the schools for making political appointments to janitorial and clerical positions, required clerical and other employees to act as ward workers in house to house canvasses for its political party, and made levies on employees for party contributions. That superintendent lost his position when the citizens caused the board members who supported him to resign and an opposition majority gained control of the board.

Several superintendents known to the author resigned to run for the position of state superintendent of public instruction or were appointed state commissioner of education. One superintendent was discharged when a change in the majority membership of the board altered the policy of the board with respect to constructing a central county high school building, which policy had been promoted by the superintendent. One superintendent resigned to become secretary of the state teachers' association and another to become state director of high school athletics.

One superintendent was discharged because he urged the teachers and voters to re-elect the present members of the board. In the course of two years, a majority of the members consisted of persons he had worked against. In two school districts, superintendents were discharged because they were clearly inefficient as leaders of their professional staffs and were also unable to maintain satisfactory public relations. Each refused to meet situations with positive action and permitted resentment to accumulate over a period of years. Another superintendent was displaced by a disloyal assistant superintendent who had undermined his standing with the board and insinuated himself into the good graces of the members.

The causes of discharge of superintendents are not always the large issues of policy and their execution, but are often the result of personal or professional maladjustments. Sometimes superintendents are even discharged for spite, possibly as a result of doing what is professionally right, such as supporting an efficient principal or teacher or the fixing of correct school attendance districts. As a rule, the salaries of superintendents are relatively very high compared with other positions in school systems or with other positions in local or even state government, but they may not be high enough to cover adequately the hazard of loss of position and the risk involved in purchasing a house in the district.

In spite of all that may be said for the retention of superintendents for long periods, the board is in duty bound not to retain an inefficient one. It is also bound to support an efficient superintendent and to stand by an inefficient superintendent until it has taken steps to discharge him. For the sake of the schools, any move to discharge a superintendent should be done quietly and with as little harmful publicity as possible. The inefficient superintendent should be given an opportunity to resign voluntarily. If necessary, he should be forced out as gently as possible.

Desirable Qualifications for the Position of Superintendent

A superintendent of schools should have broad interests in community, state, national, and world problems. He should be trained as a school administrator, preferably to the level of the doctor's degree and, as a minimum requirement, to one year of graduate study represented by a master's degree. Two years of graduate study of the work of a superintendent should be the minimum requirement for a superintendent of schools in a large school district where the problems are more complex. The mere level of training, *per se*, is not important; it is important that the training be preparation for the work of administering a school system. Specialization in a related field such as psychology, guidance, supervision, or athletics, is not adequate. A superintendent must be well-grounded in all of the important aspects of school administration so that he will be able to evaluate and approve the work of his staff and advise the board on the adoption of desirable policies and execute them.

The superintendent of schools must be generally prepared not only in the field of instruction and supervision, but also in personnel administration, business administration, physical plant administration, and public relations. He must be able to conduct practical research on the problems of administering the school system and in evaluating and drawing sound conclusions from organized data. He must be capable of presenting facts relating to the schools and plans for their improvement to public groups in a manner that will win such support if it is deserved.

The personal characteristics of a superintendent of schools are important if his administration is to be successful in maintaining an excellent school system. He should be intelligent, as indicated by relatively high grades received in his graduate study;

he should be capable of exercising good judgment with respect to the application of principles of administration to the practice of school administration; and he should be capable of planning courses of action and of taking the initiative in executing these plans.

The superintendent should be courageous in applying and executing adopted policies and impartial and unbiased in making administrative decisions. He should be tactful; conscientious and industrious; resourceful; energetic but not wasteful of energy; able to defend his position and to take, gracefully, criticism of his administrative actions; and willing to accept responsibility for the schools but also able to assign responsibility to members of his staff. The superintendent should have good health, self-confidence, good character and integrity, and a good reputation in the community and in educational circles. He should be frank in dealing with the public, co-operative, and able to dispel antagonisms. He should be loyal to the board, his staff, and the profession of education, subordinate only to loyalty to his country, his community, and his ethical standards.

As head of the school district's staff, the superintendent must have the following qualities of leadership: he must be able to inspire in others a feeling of loyalty to the schools and to develop good morale and attitudes of co-operative endeavor among the members of the school staff; he should be able to secure and to welcome participation of his staff in the determination of educational policies and plans for attaining the goals that have been co-operatively formulated and adopted; he should be able to view situations from the standpoint of others and help his staff to view matters from the standpoint of the board and the public; he should have the ability to select competent or potentially competent administrative assistants and develop leadership qualities in them; he should be able to inspire those working in the system to achieve great accomplishments in their several stations; he should be able to express himself clearly both orally and in writing; and he should be able to gain and retain the confidence of people in the community.

The successful superintendent of schools will consider his staff and himself as a team. True, he will be the captain, but a captain who consults the other members, heeds their advice, and acts on it when possible. He will recognize the accomplishments of the team as being more important than those of any member on it in maintaining an efficient school system. He should publicize the schools and the members of his staff but should avoid self publicity. Nothing could be more detrimental than a superintendent's seeking to improve his own position by taking credit for the work accomplished by his assistants and teachers. While giving credit to his assistants, he should be ready to take responsibility for the results. He should not be needlessly stubborn and should compromise when a vital principle of ethics or education is not at stake. When necessary, he should say, like the French revolutionist, "There goes the mob; I must find out where they are going for I am their leader." His leadership must be adroit. Unpopular actions should be popularized or, if necessary, avoided until the public, the board, or the teachers are ready to accept them.

Designation of Persons under Consideration for a Position as Superintendent

There seems to be no term that appropriately fits persons under consideration by a school board for the position of superintendent of schools. Some educators object to use of the term "applicant" because they think it has unfortunate connotations, suggesting selfish scrambling for a position. They hold that an "applicant" seeks the position and that the position should, rather, seek the man. It seems to them that it is unprofessional for a person to make known to a board that he is available for a better position. Nevertheless, some term is necessary to designate persons who are available for the position of superintendent, whether their availability is indicated actively or passively. It seems to be necessary to follow the common practice of using the term "applicant" to designate available persons for the position of superintendent, whether their availability has been discovered by the initiative of the person who is available or by the efforts of the board in discovering a qualified person who is available for, or can be induced to accept, the position. The term "candidate" will sometimes be used with the same meaning.

Policy with Respect to Promotion of a Local Candidate to the Superintendency

School boards often promote someone from within the school system to the position of superintendent of schools. Such a one might be an assistant superintendent, a principal, or an athletic coach. It is argued that employees are already known to the members of the board and the people of the school district, that they have been tried in the work they have been doing and found to be successful, and that promotion from within will create incentives in others to work for promotion. Also, local pressure is often brought to bear on the board to select a particular employee of the school system for the position.

On the other hand, it may be argued that appointment of a local candidate will not create incentive in others because few if any of them will ever have an opportunity to become superintendent of the local school system with the position filled. There is only one superintendent, and the board will not fill the position in anticipation of an early vacancy. The selection of a local candidate is more likely to create feelings of frustration and jealousy than incentive among the staff, particularly among the local candidates who were not selected. A superintendent selected from within the school system is likely to receive less loyal support from among his former associates than would someone from outside. Certainly, if the personnel are in a poor condition of morale and need leadership, it is likely that the leadership required can be better furnished by someone from outside the system.

Also, it is not certain that because a person was highly successful as an assistant superintendent, a principal, or a football coach he will be equally successful as a superintendent. The work is largely different and requires different capacities and training for its performance. Here, it is maintained that high qualifications for the position of superintendent are more important than previous employment in another position in the local school system, and that consideration should be given to qualified persons both within and without the school system.

Any lobbying by friends of any applicant should be resisted. The applications of local candidates should be considered along with those from outside the school district or state strictly on their merits. An assistant superintendent, principal, or supervisor who has prepared himself by training to become a superintendent should be given the same consideration as other applicants. He should not have preference because of his present employment in the school system. The sole objective of the board should be to select the candidate best able to serve the interests of the schools and community, whether or not he is a person already in the school system.

Practices of Selection to be Avoided

A board cannot use too much care in selecting the best qualified available person for the position of superintendent. The best qualified applicant is not necessarily the one who is most skillful in presenting his qualifications in the most favorable light. The latter ability is not related to the qualities required for administering a school system. The ability to promote himself, if continued after assumption of the responsibilities of the office, can easily lose to the superintendent the active support of his professional staff. The board must resist all pressures that are brought to bear in favor of a particular applicant. These are sometimes brought by the applicant or others for him, and they may be difficult to recognize. The selection should be made objectively on the basis of qualifications.

The school board must assume full responsibility for making

the selection of the superintendent. It should seek disinterested, professional advice, such as can sometimes be secured from officers of the state department of education or the outgoing superintendent if it has confidence in his judgment. However, only the board should finally determine who is selected.

The school board should be careful to avoid making its selection on the basis of irrelevant considerations or false inferences. A coach who can produce a winning football team will not necessarily be a winner as a superintendent. The coach may know football and not know public school administration. Some of the personal characteristics required for the two positions are the same, to be sure, but others are different. The same caution should be applied in considering the qualifications of a capable principal for the position of superintendent.

Though often considered as an indication of success, the length of service in a school system is an especially poor criterion for use as a basis for the selection of a superintendent. The selection of a person of many years service may place him in a position of great responsibility just at the beginning of his declining years. Instead of being the capstone of his career, it may end it in ignominy despite everybody's good intentions. The fact that a person has rendered many years of service to the school system does not necessarily mean that he has "stuck by" the school system; it may mean that he has been "stuck with" the school system and has had no opportunity to leave it. There is danger of making a mistake in discarding the application of a younger man in favor of that of an older one merely on the grounds of years of experience. Every criterion used for making the selection should be scrutinized for possible defects, and the selection should be made on the basis of all of the criteria for which valid data can be secured. After every caution has been exercised, there will still be a chance that the very best candidate has not been selected. The only certainty will be that the board has avoided selecting any of the poorer or more mediocre candidates.

Procedure in Selecting a Superintendent

The Machinery and Regulations for Procedure. A board should take its time in the process of selecting a superintendent. Unhurried action is the most likely to be right. Hasty action may result in a mistake that will be difficult and embarrassing to correct later. It may even be advisable to appoint someone to serve as acting superintendent for a few months, if that is necessary to avoid hurried action. The board should have sufficient time to search far and wide for suitable applicants and consider their qualifications impartially, on the basis of merit alone.

The board should proceed systematically and not become panic-stricken because the members feel the immediate need of someone in the position. It is better to proceed with care rather than to be sorry for the choice made. Unless the school board is very small, it will be advisable to appoint a small special committee on nominations to perform the details of the work for the board. Such a committee should make announcement of the vacancy, receive and acknowledge the receipt of applications and information data, give consideration to the merits of each application, and serve as a screening committee to select the applications of the better qualified candidates for consideration by the board.

It is also advisable for the school board to adopt regulations to guide the special committee on nominations in its work. Among matters that should be included in such regulations are the following:

1. A calendar of dates to be followed, including announcement of the vacancy, the cutting off of new applications, the completion of preliminary screening, the interviewing of candidates, and the like.

2. The setting of the time and place for special board meetings to be devoted to the work.

3. Establishment of plans and procedures for action.

4. Statement of qualifications the board desires to be met, if possible, by applicants for the position.

5. Assignment to the special committee on nominations of clerical service for writing letters, preparing minutes of the meetings of the special committee and the special meetings of the board, and keeping the special file of correspondence and applications.

6. Requirement that all correspondence and applications be kept in a separate file, inaccessible to all except the secretary assigned to the work.

7. Adoption of an information form to be filled by each applicant, and requirement that transcripts of graduate credits and photographs be submitted in addition.

8. Requirement that no personal applications be made to board members and that personal appearances of applicants be made only before the board or special committee at the times arranged with the applicants.

9. Provision for visitation, at the expense of the school district, by members of the special committee on nominations to the communities where promising applicants are employed, for the purpose of visiting them at their work or making such inquiries as are deemed necessary by the special committee on nominations.

10. Provision for the payment of expenses of the screened applicants to appear before the board at arranged times.

11. Requirement that all communications of applicants with the superintendent or members of the board be forwarded to the special committee on nominations for answer and be filed in the temporary file established for the papers of that committee.

12. Requirement that, after the selection has been made and the new superintendent contracted, all confidential papers and correspondence relating to applicants be returned to those persons concerned if return is desired, all other papers be destroyed, and the file completely emptied so that letters written about the new superintendent and other applicants will not be available

for him to read when he fulfills his duty of familiarizing himself with the filed materials of his office.

Announcement of the Vacancy and Sources of Applicants. Usually, when a position of superintendent of schools is vacant, it is desirable practice to announce the vacancy as a news item in state and national educational periodicals, where qualified persons are likely to notice it. Adequate time should be allowed for the receipt of applications. The announcement can also be made by letter to the state department of education and to the placement offices of the graduate schools of education in and out of the state, with a request for assistance in locating qualified candidates for the position. The placement offices may be requested to submit the credentials of three or four well qualified superintendents without informing the individuals that such is being done until the suitability of their qualifications has been determined. The special committee on nominations can select the better qualified persons from those submitted and request them to apply if they are interested. Superintendents in other school districts can be asked to suggest the names of well-qualified superintendents of their acquaintance, or they may themselves be considered for the position if they desire to make themselves available.

Qualified persons, invited by the board to submit their credentials for consideration for the position of superintendent, should be informed that others are also being requested to do likewise and that all candidates will be given careful consideration by the board. Properly filling the position of superintendent of schools is important enough to warrant the board taking the initiative in securing available candidates. The board will not be able to fill the position properly by merely waiting for applicants and making its selection from them. The board should search for exceptionally well-qualified and successful superintendents of smaller school districts and assistant superintendents, supervisors, and principals in larger school districts who have qualified themselves by training and have proved themselves to be leaders in the communities in which they work.

Preparation of Specifications for the Position. The board should prepare and adopt specifications for the position of superintendent of schools in accordance with the qualifications it considers to be its requirements. It should specify: the level and kind of graduate education required for the work of administering its school system; the amount and kind of experience required; age limits; character traits; and many more. It may even be deemed desirable to specify certain subjects the candidate shall have studied in preparation for the work. These might include supervision of instruction, curriculum development, achievement testing, public school administration, school building plans and specifications, school finance, and the like. The board may require a minimum number of years of experience as an administrator. If the state issues certificates to superintendents of schools, the board should require that the applicant hold, or be fully qualified to obtain, a state certificate as superintendent of schools.

The specifications should be adopted as the standards the board desires to be met and intends to use in making its selection. However, it should be made clear that the candidate most nearly meeting the board's specifications, in the judgment of the members, will be the one selected. If this is not done, the high standards set may be a block to securing some good applications because of the self elimination of some who fall short of one or more of the standards. Prospective applicants should be made to understand that their applications are desired even though some of their qualifications fall short of the specifications in minor respects. The board should state the salary to be paid in the specifications. Many qualified persons would not care to apply for a position if that factor is left indefinite.

Sample Specifications for the Position of Superintendent of Schools. There are many ways in which specifications for the position of superintendent of schools may be prepared. The following is an example of specifications that might be prepared for a city or county school district of perhaps 20,000 pupils.

The board of education of Aurora, N. K. anounces that applications will be received for the position of superintendent of schools of the Aurora public school district between the dates of March 15 and May 15, inclusive, on a three-year contract, beginning July 1, 1954. Salary $13,000 per year.

The applicant who, in the opinion of the board of education, most nearly meets or exceeds the following qualifications will be offered the contract. Applicants not meeting some one or more of the specifications may qualify by exceeding the minimum of other specifications.

Age: Between 35 and 44 years, inclusive, preferred.

Education and Training: A master's degree or better, granted on the basis of specialization in public school administration, with preference given, other qualifications being equal, to such training at the level of two or three years of graduate study. The university granting the degree must give training in school administration, equivalent, in the opinion of the board, to that given by the University of N. K.

Experience: The position requires five or more years of experience as a superintendent of schools, an assistant superintendent, a supervisor of instruction, a principal of a public school of 35 or more teachers, a school business manager, or some combination of such positions. The experience must have been highly successful and the applicant must have maintained co-operative relations with his immediate superior, namely the board of education or the superintendent or assistant superintendent of schools.

Character and Personal Qualities: The applicant must have both good character and good reputation. He must be reliable, honest, sincere, tactful, energetic, and judicious. He must have qualities of initiative, perseverance, patience, and professional leadership.

Investigation of Qualifications of Candidates. Through its special committee on nominations, the school board should spare no time and effort in its investigation of the qualifications of candidates for the position of superintendent of schools. There need be no investigation of applicants whose data show clearly that they are unqualified for the position, but those who appear to be well-qualified, as indicated by their credentials, should be fully investigated. Letters of inquiry should be sent to members of school boards under whom the applicants have served. Information that has been omitted from the application form or is not clear or complete can be requested from the applicant.

Better than a letter to board members of other cities is a trip by a member of the special committee on nominations to interview members of boards who are familiar with the work of applicants under consideration. Whether the information is secured by letter or interview, answers should be secured to definite, appropriate questions, prepared in advance. The questions should concern the ability, success, and personal characteristics of each person whose credentials indicate that his qualifications merit further investigation. Each applicant's strengths and weaknesses should be learned and made a matter of record. All data secured by letter or interview should be kept confidential by the members of the school board so that those who furnished the information will not be embarrassed.

If some of the candidates have studied recently at a university, it is likely that the placement bureau of that institution will have collected letters and other data and assembled them for use by school boards. If such credentials do not include an applicant's transcript of credit, such a transcript, showing the subjects studied and the grades received in each subject, can be requested from the university registrar's office. The titles of the subjects studied and the grades received are valuable supplementary information concerning the training of applicants.

Screening for the Best Qualified Applicants. After reading data on their application forms, and the other credentials that have been submitted by the placement office, the special committee on nominations should eliminate some of the applicants from further consideration without additional investigation. The ones to be thus eliminated will be those wholly unqualified for the position.

The special committee on nominations should sift the applications of those investigated to determine which are the five or six better qualified applicants. These should be invited to come to the school district, at its expense, to inspect the school system and to confer with the school board. It will probably be better to conduct the interviews in two or three sessions, so that the board members will not be hurried and sufficient time can be devoted to each applicant to enable the members to estimate his capabilities.

The applicants should be conducted about the school district, through some of the school buildings, and given such information as will be of interest to them. The retiring superintendent or some other administrative officer who is not himself under consideration for the position can best conduct applicants about the school district. Previously, each of the screened applicants should have been sent a copy of the latest school report and the rules and regulations of the board. After the applicants have rested from the tour, they should meet individually with the school board.

A list of practical school administration problems may well have been sent to each applicant about a week before the date set for the meeting, with a request that he select one of the problems for a quarter hour's report at his conference with the board. Such problems as the following will serve the purpose: the steps to be followed in constructing a high school building; steps in making a school budget; steps in making a salary schedule; the objectives of the elementary school; or a method of controlling athletics. The applicant's discussion should be followed by questions from members either relating to the problem under discussion or to other problems bearing on the educational philosophy and experiences of the applicant. These may be spontaneous or previously prepared (as the individual board member prefers), but each member should make it a point to participate with one or more questions. The applicant should be given an opportunity to ask questions of the board members concerning the school system and its policies for guiding the superintendent in the administration of the schools. He may want to know such things as the tax rate and valuation of property in the school district, the number of pupils by grades, plans for school building construction, or what the members of the board conceive to be the board's functions and the superintendent's duties.

The whole procedure of interviewing candidates should progress with as little publicity in the community as possible. All interviews, whether there be five, ten, or any number, should be held in the course of a single week or even in two or three days. The interviews should be held in accordance with an adopted schedule, one applicant at a time. The board members will want to make mental note of such matters as each applicant's apparent knowledge of the principles of administration, his educational philosophy, his ability as a speaker, the apparent strength and congeniality of his personality, and his poise.

Election of a Superintendent. Within a week after all interviews have been concluded and while they are still fresh in the minds of the members, the board should meet in formal session to select one candidate to serve as the board's executive officer and superintendent of schools. The members will have their estimates of the results of the interviews as a guide in making a choice. They will have the report of the special committee on nominations and perhaps a rating of the candidates by that committee derived from the collected credentials and information relating to their professional qualifications. The board members may desire to read the compiled information and evaluation of each candidate remaining after the sifting process has been completed. They may want to discuss the relative merits of the several candidates and to question the members of the special committee on nominations. The members should be careful not to give too much weight to the results of the interview; it is the only part in which those not on the special committee have participated. The quality and extent of special training in school administration, the kind and quality of experience, and an evaluation of the character traits of the selected candidates may be far more important than what was learned about the candidates from the interview.

After careful consideration of the relative abilities of the selected candidates, the board will be ready for the vote. Voting probably should be done by ballot. A process of elimination of the candidates receiving fewest votes on each ballot should be used until only two are left. A motion should be made to select the candidate receiving a majority of the votes unanimously.

Instead of a board committee on nominations, sometimes an outside committee of educators from colleges and universities or of principals or others from the local school staff is appointed to accept applications and screen applicants, selecting the best qualified five or six for consideration and action by the board.

Terms of Contract with the Superintendent

The school board would be placing the welfare of the schools in jeopardy if it employed a superintendent on a long term contract at the start. The first employment of a superintendent should usually be for a period of three years. If he is successful to a degree that meets the expectations of the school board, he may then be given a longer term contract, perhaps five years. It would be better to offer him the long term contract before his probationary contract expires, but the board should not offer him such a contract unless and until it is fully satisfied that it desires to retain him in the position. After a trial period of three years, it may be deemed better to employ the superintendent on indefinite tenure or a continuing contract instead of a long term one. Such a contract would be subject to termination on six months' notice by either the board or the superintendent, but continued until after notice of termination is given.

Permanent Tenure for Superintendents

A few states include superintendents in their permanent tenure laws for teachers. Others make it optional with the board whether or not superintendents shall be granted permanent tenure. However, most states do not provide by law for the permanent tenure of superintendents of schools. Although insecurity is as bad for superintendents as it is for teachers, and worry as to the continuance of his employment may prevent a superintendent from performing his functions effectively and making long range plans for the schools, yet it is impracticable to grant permanence of tenure to a superintendent. In fact, insecurity of position is one of the explanations for the relatively high salaries of superintendents compared with personnel whose employment status is permanent.

As the board's executive officer, it is necessary that the superintendent co-operate very closely with the board. The membership of a board frequently changes, and a superintendent who is able to work co-operatively with the board at the time he is selected may not be able to work well with it at a later date, after most of its members may have been changed. Such co-operation is necessary even if it should require a change of superintendents. If the state, by law, or the board, by resolution, places the superintendent of schools on permanent tenure, the board will be able to dismiss the superintendent only by bringing charges against him for some definable cause, and it will be unable to place full responsibility on him for executing the policies of the board. In a democracy, the board's executive officer should always make effective the will of the board, for the board represents the people. If he fails to do so, he must be subject to dismissal by the board or the people's desires may not prevail. For these reasons the members of the board at any one time should not be empowered to place a superintendent on permanent tenure. Such an action might handicap the board some time in the future.

CHAPTER 14

Relations of the Board to the Superintendent and Other School Personnel

Interrelationships of the Board and School Employees

The contacts between the school board and its employees are made largely through the superintendent of schools. He is and should be the chief employee because he is the board's executive officer as well as the spokesman for the staff that serves under his direction so far as the school operations are concerned. He holds the key position between the board and the school employees. Articles and chapters in books on school administration have been published which consist largely of diatribes against board "interference" with the exercise of administrative authority by the superintendent, principals, and other staff employees. Noninterference is important, but the board is the legally responsible body; the superintendent and his staff are employed to execute the will of the board, under the law, in the administration and operation of the schools. It is not the function of the superintendent as spokesman for the staff either to browbeat the board into submission to the staff's will or to kowtow to the members to gain favorable action for the schools or the employees.

Sometimes the board may find it necessary to set financial limits at which the superintendent and his staff must stop or proceed more slowly in improving the schools or the status of the employees. It is not undemocratic, as sometimes charged, for a school board to modify educational policy if it conflicts with community desires. The board represents the majority of the school district democracy. It is answerable to the whole community, not to the employed staff. It is the staff that must conform to community desires. The mere fact that funds available for expenditure may be limited will limit what can be done for the improvement of the schools and the welfare of the employed staff. But the board should be guided in professional matters and within reasonable possibilities by the superintendent and, through him, its other employees in so far as the board members are convinced that such advice is in the interests of the schools and the school district community.

A few writers on school administration maintain that it is the professional duty of the school staff to work for the election of "desirable" school board members. Most authorities on school administration hold that the school staff should be neutral except for exercising the right to cast their individual ballots. It would seem that the latter view is the sounder, both on grounds of ethics and professional education policy. The organized support of a candidate for board membership by employees of the board is ethically wrong because the interests of the staff are given precedence over the welfare of the community to the extent that their interests conflict. It is poor policy from the standpoint of the school staff because it will be generally recognized that the staff may be self-interested in the election of certain board members. For that reason, organized support by the staff may arouse community opposition and serve to cause their candidate's defeat. If a really "undesirable" candidate is likely to be elected because several "desirable" candidates may split the opposition vote, some civic group may be able to induce some of the candidates to withdraw.

Fortunately, campaigns for membership on a school board need not be very costly as a rule. Expenses for posters, public halls, radio or television programs, automobile service for taking voters to the polls, and other expenses may cost a few thousand dollars in a large city if there should be a bitter contest for membership. Under no circumstances should school employees be organized to support or be solicited for contributions to the expenses of a candidate for re-election or a candidate to replace an existing member. Civic organizations and persons who do not have and cannot be charged with having a personal interest in the outcome of the school board election may properly contribute to the election of their favorite candidates as a civic duty.

Personal Relations between Board Members and School Employees

The personal relations between school board members and school employees, particularly the superintendent and other administrative officers, should be cordial and friendly but not so intimate as to make other board or staff members jealous. Intimate relationships might result in charges of favoritism or undue influence one way or the other. A superintendent should not consult one board member to the exclusion of others or take certain members into his confidence outside of board meetings. He may give information concerning the schools to individual board members outside of board meetings, as he would to other persons of the school district, but to discuss controversial matters or special problems of the board with some members and not with others is likely to be construed by the neglected members as "undercover" activities and to cause the superintendent to lose their good will. It is not advantageous for a superintendent or other school employee to appear to have special friends or confidants among the board members. A superintendent may request advice on matters on which he already has authority for discretionary action, but if he does seek such advice he ought to consult all board members or perhaps consult other members on other matters of equal importance.

No school employee can be expected to act on the authority of one board member, for added to the inability of one member to speak for the board would be the unprofessional act of by-passing the superintendent. It sometimes happens that a new member of the board, elected to perform a mission and before he has found his proper place as merely one member on the board, will issue directions to the superintendent, principals, or teachers. He has no more legal or ethical right to issue such directions than has any other resident of the school district. In fact, any individual member is nothing more than a resident of the school district. In such case, it is the duty of someone on the board, preferably the president, to inform him kindly but firmly of his place as a member of the board.

Sometimes a board member of long standing has assumed a place of authority on the board for his own personal gratification. It is not advisable for a superintendent to recognize such assumption of power to the exclusion of the other members. Such an action places the school system in the unfortunate position of having, in effect, a lay superintendent above the professional and regular appointed one. Also, new members may displace old ones at any election and may challenge the patriarch's authority, as they have a right to do. Under such conditions the superintendent may find it impossible to extricate himself from his record of compliance and will find himself out along with his mentor and sponsor.

School board members should not make special efforts to do business with school employees. Banker members should not solicit their accounts; insurance members should not canvass them to sell them life insurance; automobile dealer members should not try to sell them automobiles. Board members should not take unfair advantage either of the school employees or of their own business competitors to secure the patronage of school employees. If businessmen find it desirable to promote their business with school personnel, they should not make themselves available for membership on the school board.

School board members should not expect or even tolerate any special privileges for their children. A person whose philosophy of life will permit the acceptance of special favors because of his position as a member of the school board is not worthy of being a school board member. One might say that such a person is not fit to live in a democracy. He is out of harmony with social ethics in America and is unfair to the school employees, the school children who are not so favored, and actually, most of all, to his own children, for whom he demands or permits the favors.

Relations among School Board Members

There is great satisfaction in being a member of a school board when the members work together harmoniously. Harmony does not imply that the board is dominated by one member or the superintendent, and it does not mean that all members think and act alike. It means that the members recognize the authority of the board as a body and their own lack of authority as individuals except as the laws or regulations require specific formal duties of the board's officers or as the board assigns specific duties to certain members. It means that the members have a common desire to place the interests of the community and its developing children ahead of any other interests, and that they respect the opinions of one another and willingly support the actions of the majority. It means that in case of differences of opinion and even of dispute, members will be tactful, respectful, and argue in a dignified manner for the policies and actions they deem best, will avoid discourtesy and bluster as a substitute for reason, and will not attempt to bulldoze other members.

Membership on a school board is not pleasant when factions develop and prevent co-operative efforts for the advancement of education in the school district. Such factions sometimes develop from business, political, social, and even religious rivalries and personal contests for power. In such cases, the majority usually supports and the minority opposes the superintendent (both sides with little reason for their stand), but, when there are such divisions, woe to the superintendent who has been partial if an election of new members causes the former minority to become the majority.

Factions are particularly harmful because the real views of individual members are subordinated to the leader of the faction. As long as members use their own judgments in deciding questions at issue, it is probable that each will vote with various different members on the different questions and factionalism will not develop.

Factionalism is often encouraged by press reports of divisions among members in board meetings or by the gossip of members or others about such disagreements. When factionalism enters, honesty, courtesy, and good sportsmanship tend to disappear, and the interests of the small group take precedence over the interests of the larger whole community group.

Relations of the Board to the Superintendent of Schools

Practice of Employing a Superintendent. In some states having many small school districts, most boards do not employ a superintendent. All school districts employ superintendents in other states. In Virginia, the superintendent is a constitutional officer, and in a few states the statutes provide for the office and make him the board's executive officer. Usually, there is no requirement that a superintendent be employed, but it is within the board's discretionary power, and the need for a superintendent is generally recognized. In one state having both county and independent school districts, the county superintendent is elected by popular vote but is made responsible to the county school board by law—a most unsatisfactory relationship. A superintendent elected by popular vote usually considers himself responsible directly to the people, as indeed he is, regardless of the provision of the law. Instead, the school board should appoint its executive and administrative officer in order to secure his full responsibility to the policy-making body.

Board Appraisal of the Superintendent. A school board is

responsible for evaluating the work of its superintendent and for judging the results of his and his staff's administration. The board should perform this function carefully and fairly and avoid prejudice and the making of arbitrary judgments. It should tolerate occasional mistakes (which are bound to occur), but the board and superintendent should make each mistake a lesson in bringing the control and administration of the school system nearer to perfection. If it is evident that the superintendent is not functioning effectively and probably will not learn to do so, he should of course be replaced. The turnover of superintendents is a disruptive factor for school systems, and the board should give its superintendent ample opportunity to prove his worth as an administrator before discharging him.

Division of Functions. The division of functions between the board and superintendent is not only customary in the control and management of school systems but is in harmony with sound principles of control and management for industrial and for other public enterprises. A board of directors of a business corporation does not perform the administrative details of the enterprise and a board of a hospital does not attempt to perform operations, determine diets, or manage the laundry. Boards of various public and private enterprises employ a president or a superintendent as their executive officer, give him considerable freedom to manage the enterprise subject to the restrictions of their adopted policies, and hold him responsible for results. A school board, consisting of laymen in education, should do likewise.

This is all very clear in theory, but the line between policy making and approval functions on the one hand, and executive and administrative functions on the other, is difficult to determine. The board's rules and regulations and other adopted policies can help to make the distinction clear. Executive and administrative functions can begin only where legislative functions end. Generally, it may be said that legislation should deal with principles; requirements should be general rather than specific; and methods of effectuating the required results should be left to administration. On the other hand, administration should be concerned with executing the laws and the board's regulations and orders in the most effective manner possible.

The board and its members are obligated to refrain from interfering with the execution of its policies to an extent that will make it impossible to hold the superintendent responsible for results. It has the further obligations to support the superintendent in the execution of its policies, to study his reports and recommendations, and to refuse to act on complaints from other employees or the public until the superintendent has made a report to the board on the matters at issue. School boards should and often do aim to divide the functions in this manner. A regulation of the Portland, Oregon, board reads:

> It is the aim of the board of directors to leave in the hands of the superintendent of schools all matters of decision and administration which come within his province as an executive or as a professional educator. It reserves to itself the ultimate decision in all matters concerning general policy or the expenditure of funds; but even in these fields it will proceed only after receiving reports or recommendations from the various departments affected. It is the duty of the superintendent towards the board to keep it steadily informed concerning the welfare and progress of the schools; to submit promptly and frankly all school reports asked for by the board; and to carry out the decisions of the board in all faithfulness to the public and its children.

Board Performance of Administrative Duties. The school board should be very circumspect about performing administrative duties or designating anyone other than the superintendent of schools to do so. The superintendent cannot be held responsible for actions performed by committees of the board or by the president acting as the board's agent. To the extent that the board relieves the superintendent of authority in administration, it also relieves him of responsibility. The main reason for employing a superintendent is because a board is in no position to perform direct administrative duties. However, it is a rare board that confines its activities to its peculiar functions. Even if the board has adopted regulations, it may spend a part of its time in considering cases for exceptions and in dealing with situations that should be administered under the general regulations or left to the judgment of the superintendent if none apply. Examples are: the board's selection of employees in some school systems; its dealing with matters of conduct of teachers or pupils in particular situations instead of in general; its passing on the grade placement of a pupil referred to it by a parent; its acceptance of a student teacher for practice work with a particular teacher; and its renting of a gymnasium to a businessmen's club. Other examples are furnished by Olsen, as follows:

> The board that passes on each separate expenditure for books, that considers each individual tuition case, that weighs the desirability of each separate request for the installation of a telephone, that debates the desirability of each purchase of coal, that discusses how the soil of each school garden should be prepared for seeding, that authorizes each purchase of postage stamps, that evaluates each proposed purchase of kindergarten supplies, that decides the merits of each request for leave of absence, that determines whether or not a given school piano shall be tuned, that passes on each and every request for the use of school buildings by non-school groups, that considers the installation of glass in each of the doors or broken windows, etc., of necessity sees only a mass of details.[1]

Such matters as these should be delegated to the superintendent and through him to his staff. With such matters to decide in monthly or semimonthly meetings, the board would not be able to see the forest for the trees; the school system as a whole for its small parts.

The misconception of the function of a school board was expressed in the Boston school survey report as follows:

> This division of responsibility between the School Committee and the professional staff employed to administer the schools is not always recognized by the School Committee. It would seem that the members have the mistaken notion that it is their duty to assume directly the actual administration of the schools. The Committee spends time in dealing with administrative details which pertain to its executives while at the same time it

[1] Olsen, Hans C. *The Work of Boards of Education and How It Should Be Done.* New York; Bureau of Publications, Teachers College, Columbia University, 1926.

fails to give necessary time and deliberation to major plans, policies, and issues which are its major responsibility. It does not seem to have definite policies. Each problem as presented is considered in the light of the immediate emergency without recognition of the effects of the decisions reached on future policy. . . .

. . . .

There are times when the Committee seems to consider itself a board of executives and the professional staff of superintendents its servants who, leaving all initiative to the Committee, are to operate in accord with its whims and desires. This is poor administration and results in lack of that co-operation which is essential in the conduct of the school system. Efficient operation of the schools calls for the closest and most co-operative consideration of problems by the School Committee with its executives. Each has important contributions to make in arriving at sound decisions.[2]

Superintendent's Authority for School Administration. In most states, the superintendent's authority is derived wholly by delegation of authority lodged in the school board by law. By sufferance of the board, the superintendent assumes functions for which the laws make the board responsible. All this is sound in principle, for the executive authority should be subordinate to the legislative body.[3]

The relationship places on the board the responsibility for defining the functions of the superintendent in general terms. It is not necessary that the board define his duties in great detail or that it formally approve all of his actions. Of course the board's authorizations should be stated clearly and should place full responsibility upon the superintendent for administration of the schools, but such responsibility will be directly to the board.

[2] Finance Commission of the City of Boston. Strayer, George D., Director of Survey. *Report on a Survey of the Public Schools of Boston, Massachusetts.* Ch. I, 1944.

[3] This relationship generally holds in large measure in industrial organizations and for the Government of Great Britain and its commonwealths. In the Federal Government of the United States and the several states, the executive authority is elected by the people and is largely independent of the legislative authority. Many political scientists believe responsibility of the executive authority to the legislative body to be, universally, the sounder system.

There is some danger that a board will permit a very successful superintendent who has served for a great many years to assume too many responsibilities, so that the school system will be operated without board control. This is a real danger, for the very smoothness of the operation may be an indication that the schools are drifting and may be falling behind the educational procession. Such a school system may need a more active superintendent. In any case, the board should not relinquish its functions as the policy making body.

Advisory Functions of the Superintendent. As the trained expert in school administration, the superintendent should fulfill the important functions of rendering his informed opinion and furnishing professional advice to the board on matters of policy that he believes need to be considered by it for adoption, modification, or repeal. His advice should grow out of his recognition of the needs of the school system, based on sound principles developed from his professional training and his professional experience. Of course, the board should be convinced of the soundness of any recommendations it adopts, and the superintendent should be required to present reasons for his recommendations, backed by reports giving full data relative to each. The board has no obligation to adopt all recommendations made, though it should give considerable weight, other things being equal, to the superintendent's professional judgment and should look to him for educational leadership.

On his part, the wise superintendent will carry his board—all members of it—along with him as far as possible in his consideration of important problems and will not be impatient at possible slowness in their perception of the needs as he sees them. He will encourage discussion by the members. Such ideas as the following may require time and patience because they are changes in the traditional plan of the school system: the establishment of kindergartens, a vocational school, or special classes for defective children; the construction of a new school building; or the establishment of the 6–3–3 plan of school organization. Some may cost additional money, others may save money, but the financial as well as the educational effect should be carefully considered.

The superintendent should be very careful to present only those recommendations which he has considered thoroughly from all angles and is convinced are sound. He should be frank and honest in presenting to the board both the favorable and unfavorable aspects of his recommendations, and not leave the unfavorable ones for the board to discover after they have been adopted. He must be sure of his ground before making a recommendation for action. The board's confidence in the soundness of the professional advice of its superintendent depends largely on his past performance and his ability to present the merits of his recommendations clearly. The board should not act on important proposals without a convincing defense of each, accompanied by full data relating to the matter at issue.

The complaints by some superintendents that boards will not accept their advice arises from the lack of confidence in the soundness of the superintendent's judgments and a suspicion that his proposals may have been made on impulse or without full consideration of all facts or results. The board members should have confidence in the soundness of the superintendent's professional and practical judgment and should rely considerably upon his advice to guide their deliberations and decisions.

Duties and Responsibilities of the Superintendent. The duties and responsibilities of the superintendent of schools are much the same in all states, but they vary somewhat depending on state laws concerning the functions of the local school system, the size of the school systems, and the form of organization. As the chief administrative officer, the superintendent should be responsible for the performance of all activities of the school system not handled by the board. This presupposes an ideal form of organization and excepts possible duties of the board officers. A complete list of the activities and responsibilities he assumes for the board would be very long. A few of the more usual ones, some of which are subject to specific approval by the board, are to:

Serve as executive and chief administrative officer of the school board in the conduct of the schools and of their auxiliary activities.

Enforce the state laws in the school system and the rules and regulations of the state board of education and the school district board of education.

Attend school board meetings and, in some districts, serve as secretary of the board.

Prepare rules and regulations for consideration for adoption by the board.

Furnish the board with information relating to the schools, advise the board on professional and business matters, and recommend changes in, additions to, and deletions from, policies.

Initiate or pass along from his assistants, educational, financial, physical plant, and other policies for board consideration and action.

Make special reports to, and surveys for, the board.

Keep the board informed on the execution of adopted policies.

Accept requests and complaints, submitted by patrons and the staff, for official presentation to the board.

Prepare agenda for board meetings.

Make and send to board members copies of minutes of meetings prior to their approval.

Provide employees with copies of board rules and regulations.

Keep official files and have custody of official documents.

Prepare the annual report of the board to the public.

Direct the school's public relations program.

Address community organizations.

Co-operate with parent-teacher and other organizations interested in the public schools.

Provide for administering the use of school facilities by outside agencies, in accordance with the provisions of school board regulations.

Organize the personnel of the school system with clear lines of authority and responsibility, subject to approval by the board.

Issue administrative directives in supplementation and amplification of the board's rules and regulations.

Plan and conduct educational research.

Assume responsibility for the development of the schools in accordance with sound principles of organization, administration, supervision, instruction, plant management, and business administration.

Supervise and direct the supervision of employees in all schools and at other posts.

Determine qualifications necessary for each class of position.

Accept all applications for employment that are worthy of consideration.

Establish machinery for determining the relative merits of candidates for school positions.

Select teachers and other employees and recommend candidates for employment.

Make duty assignments and transfer teachers and other employees.

Determine the relative efficiency of employees and establish machinery for ratings.

Recommend promotions and demotions to the board for action.

Recommend the continuance of employment, or the discharge, of probationary employees.

Accept resignations and applications for the retirement of employees for board action.

Provide means for the inservice training of teachers and other employees.

Provide for the holding of professional meetings of groups of employees.

Administer sick leave regulations.

Grant leaves of absence, subject to regulations of, and approval by, the board.

Determine the school calendar, length of sessions, and teaching periods, subject to board approval.

Determine school admission requirements, subject to board approval.

Determine school attendance district boundaries, subject to board approval.

Keep the education program up to date in subject matter and instruction technique.

Determine the philosophy of the school system, subject to board approval.

Recommend textbooks for adoption and specify kinds of equipment and supplies needed for instruction.

Recommend subjects and courses of instruction to the board.

Organize the professional staff for developing curricula, teaching guides, courses of study, and other materials for use in teaching.

Recommend worthy courses of study for adoption by the board.

Prescribe and direct programs for testing and examining pupils.

Supervise the enforcement of the compulsory school attendance laws and the issuance of work permits.

Direct the administration of a guidance and counseling program.

Direct the school health program.

Direct the pupil transportation program.

Direct the athletics program and the programs of other extra-curricular activities.

Direct the operation of special schools and special classes for atypical children.

Plan the physical plant construction program.

Recommend sites and kinds of school buildings required after school building studies and on the advice of the school staff.

Report to the board the condition of school property and recommend plans for new buildings and alterations.

Provide for the supervision of plant operation and maintenance.

Direct the business affairs of the school district.

Prepare, with the help of assistants, the annual school budget for consideration, possible modification, and adoption by the board.

Administer and direct the administration of the adopted school budget in accordance with the provisions of law and the regulations of the board.

Direct the purchase of equipment and supplies.

Direct financial and pupil accounting.

After reading this list, which is far from complete, the reader will say, "The superintendent certainly must be a versatile individual." That is true, but, except in very small school systems, he will have assistants to perform many of the functions. The assistants will be expert in their particular fields of school administration, and the superintendent will depend largely on their opinions and advice in directing the performance of special functions.

Preparation of School District Reports. The board should depend on its executive officer, the superintendent of schools, for its information about the schools. To furnish such information, the superintendent or his staff must make surveys and studies and present the results to the board in the form of written and oral reports. Reports can be made on subjects requested by the board, or the superintendent can make them on his own initiative to accompany and support recommendations he makes for board action. Some can be made merely to furnish the board information relative to the schools and their activities.

Reports should consist of factual material or of opinions and reasons, as necessary. The factual material may include tables, charts, and pictures. The reports should present the results of the superintendent's and his staff's research briefly. They should deal with various problems facing the board and with the progress and conditions in the schools. They may include information on such subjects as: school attendance; enrollment trends; curriculum changes; teaching technique changes; the supply of materials of instruction; pupil failures and retardation; provisions made for individual differences in the interests and needs of pupils; plans for education week; experiments being conducted in the school system; per pupil costs; or pupil transportation regulations and costs. However, the superintendent should make certain he does not monopolize the time of board meetings and should present much of his report material in duplicated form for reading.

The superintendent should bear in mind the fact that his reports are made to laymen in education. He should not be discouraged if the board members show lack of interest or do not understand the full significance of parts of them. In such cases he should strive, in the future, to make his reports interesting and concrete for comprehension by board members who have their own business interests and can give but a part of their time to their duties as board members. He should not be too modest to explain elementary principles of school administration and instruction to members of the board, although recognizing the fact that at least some of the members will know the principles of general administration as well or better than he knows them.

The superintendent should have a stream of carefully prepared facts flowing to the board. These should be presented clearly and concisely to save the time of members in digesting them. Such material as: maps of the school district which show the locations of schools and school attendance district boundaries; school population spot maps; summary of the budget; graphs and charts showing the purposes of expenditures; pupil enrollment trends; pupil cost trends; schedules; curriculum subjects; bond payments schedule; insurance coverage on plant; and many other basic data can be kept in a looseleaf manual supplied to each member of the board.

The superintendent and his staff should prepare an annual report on the schools. This may take the form of a report from him to the board, from which he can produce a report by the board to the public. It may be a report of the board to the public, of the superintendent to the public, or of both the superintendent and the board to the public. Since the board is the legal authoritative body representing the public, the annual report should be addressed to the public and presented as the board's report. The report should be attractively prepared and published in printed or otherwise duplicated form for distribution to interested persons.

Board Support of the Superintendent. The school board should support its superintendent's actions as long as he holds the position, but it should insist that his actions be in conformity with the adopted policies of the board. Board members should refrain from criticizing the superintendent to the school staff or the public. Criticism of the superintendent reflects on the board since it is responsible to the public for his actions. The board members should hear the superintendent's views on matters concerning which there is criticism by patrons, teachers, or others in the community. However, it should sever his employment if he is consistently wrong on important matters.

Special Relations of the Board to a New Superintendent

The school board should furnish a new superintendent with a statement of both of their functions, duties, powers, and responsibilities. Such a statement will provide immediate working relationships to give him the confidence needed to begin his work. The statement should make clear to him that the board considers itself to be the policy making body and will adopt or modify its policies in order that the schools will better provide for the needs of the community. The board should make it clear that the superintendent is to render professional guidance as occasion requires, but that it will hold itself free to accept or reject his suggestions.

The statement should make it clear that the superintendent is the board's executive officer and that it delegates to him, and through him to the administrative and supervisory staff, the authority and responsibility for administering the schools. It should place on the superintendent the responsibility for operating the schools within the requirements made by the state and the board of the school district.

The following is a statement made, June 29, 1942, by the Glen Ridge, New Jersey, Board of Education:

> In its desire to be a constructive influence in the community, to make the greatest possible use of the time and effort of its members, and to start the new superintendent of schools in an administrative situation that is clean cut and sound, the Glen Ridge board of education presents the following statement which relates to the division of basic responsibility. . . .
>
> I. *Policy Formation and Control*
> The board of education has the major responsibility of forming and/or changing policies to meet satisfactorily the needs of the community in relation to a public school system. Such policies must likewise be progressive and practical. Beyond the formation of policies it is the function of the board to con-

trol their operation through a system of inspection and report.

The superintendent of schools is expected to guide the board in policy matters and to represent accurately the attitudes and contributions of the staff, the students, and the community.

Policy is defined as a basic plan of action which establishes objectives to be attained and limits within which freedom of judgment can be exercised.

II. *Action Required by Law*

The board of education will take such specific actions as are required of it by law.

The superintendent of schools is expected to present such actions to the board in proper form and to insure the legality and adequacy of board action on such matters.

It is the desire of the board that all board action required by law be studied carefully as to the possibility of delegating certain powers to fully qualified individuals within the school system.

III. *Administration of Operating Functions*

Once the board of education has established an adequate policy, it delegates to the superintendent of schools the responsibility for operating the school system within the limits of such policy. This should keep from the board much operating detail and many routine decisions which otherwise would consume its time.

The superintendent of schools has the privilege of asking guidance from the board on operating matters whenever he so desires, but that is not a requirement. When faced with the necessity of making exceptions to an established policy, he is, of course, expected to submit such matters to the board of education.

IV. *Reports*

It is the responsibility of the board of education to set up such reports as are needed by that board to perform properly its policy making and legal functions. The board will likewise indicate the form and content of such reports.

It is the responsibility of the superintendent to see that such reports are made out properly and rendered to the board on schedule.

V. *Immediate Course of Action*

Therefore, it would appear that the first objective of this board would be the formation and adoption of a revised set of rules and regulations.

Although the board adopts its rules and regulations, it probably should not formulate many of them. Rules affecting the staff and pupils should grow out of the experience of the persons affected, subject to the approval of the board.

We shall look to the counsel and guidance of our new superintendent in this task and shall expect him in turn to seek the
advice of all staff members in matters of policy. Each one should
be made to feel that any suggestion he makes is worthy of
consideration.

The above statement illustrates a step a board should take
in inducting a superintendent into a position as head of the
district's school system.

Relations of the Board to Administrative and Supervisory Assistants

In some school systems, parents, principals, teachers, and
others bring to individual board members questions or complaints concerning such things as school administration, personnel relations, or building management. Board members
sometimes call administrative officers or teachers in for conference concerning these matters. This is wrong. Grievances
should be presented to the superintendent or the assistant in
charge of the matter in question. Board members should refer
complainants to the superintendent who should deal with the
complaint or refer it to his assistant best qualified to deal with
the matter. In case a change of policy is needed for its settlement, the superintendent must refer it to the board for action.

The board and its members should not usually bypass the
superintendent by dealing directly with his assistants. However,
the board may be informed of the work of the schools by these
assistants and others such as the head nurse and the directors of
physical education, music, art, or guidance, but directions to
them should follow the line of authority.

Relations of the Board to Teachers and Other School Employees

The adopted policies of the board largely determine the conditions of employment of teachers and other employees—their

work loads, depending on the number of persons employed, the salary schedule, provisions for sick leave, the furnishing of a duplicating machine in each school, and others. In its policies, sometimes not formally adopted, the board determines who is eligible for employment with regard to such things as residence, marital status, and church or political affiliation. Many such requirements have little concern for the education of children and should be given no consideration. It is usually a safe rule for a conscientious board member to base his judgment of a question at issue on what he believes will be best for the education of the children.

As a rule, teachers, principals, and other employees should bring matters to the attention of the board only by way of the superintendent. The line of responsibility from teacher or custodian to principal, to superintendent, to school board, and the reverse for the line of authority, should usually be observed for official matters. It is only by maintaining the lines of authority and responsibility that the superintendent can be held responsible by the board for the administration of the school system and he, in turn, can hold his assistants responsible for the administration of the parts assigned to each of them. The board should refuse to deal directly with teachers and other employees except in cases of formal appeal to the board over the superintendent's decision. The possibility of appeal to the board over the decision of the superintendent should be kept open, but appeals on trivial matters should be discouraged, and the board should be certain the superintendent is in the wrong before reversing his decision.

Boards are restricted by the laws of most states from arbitrarily discharging teachers. A typical law provides that the board may discharge teachers and other professional employees "upon sufficient proof of improper conduct, inefficient service, or neglect of duty; provided that no one shall be dismissed without first having been given in writing due notice of the charge or charges and an opportunity for defense." It is important that good teachers feel secure in their positions and that the board develop respect for the teaching profession in the community.

Only by such means can the best quality of young people be drawn into the teaching profession. However, a board should not hesitate to discharge a teacher if it is convinced, everything taken into account, that such a course will be in the interests of education in the school district. The same holds for employees other than teachers, but they usually do not have tenure except when they are employed in the classified or "civil" service.

CHAPTER 15

Public Relations and the School Board

Public's Need for Information on Its Schools

The people in nearly all communities are interested in their schools as an extension of their homes, existing to furnish a special form of aid in the development of their children. The instinctive desires to love and protect their children, and to feel pride in their achievements, constitute the basis for an emo ional attitude on the part of parents that is not evidenced in like degree toward the fire department, the public works department, or any other agency of government. In a measure this special interest persists after children have been graduated by the schools and left the home. The schools touch the lives of all persons in the community very closely. With such a setting, the maintenance of good public relations becomes a fine art, too often neglected though it is.

Public opinion is replete with incorrect or partially incorrect ideas concerning the schools. Most adults have attended public schools and their concepts are largely those of the schools of 20 to 50 years ago. Most schools are far superior to those of the past in many respects—teachers are usually college graduates now, instead of only eighth grade or normal school graduates; textbooks have been greatly improved concerning the selection and organization of subject matter, illustration, and clarity of expression; the curriculum consists of more useful and more interesting pupil experiences; school buildings are generally better in most school districts; instruction equipment has been and is being improved; the psychology of learning is better understood and is being used by teachers more effectively than formerly; and the philosophy of education is more soundly based than in the past. Few adults fully appreciate these changes and most of them conceive of the schools as still being such as they, themselves, attended.

On the other hand, the teachers of today are no more devoted to their work than were those of the past when strikes by teachers had never occurred. Then, there was no radio or television to compete for the time and attention of children, divert their attention from their studies, and sometimes present to their developing minds false and misleading impressions. The public and often even teachers need to appreciate more fully the changes in education, both good and bad, that have occurred in and out of school and are still occurring.

Distinctions should be made among the activities pertaining to public relations, publicity, and propaganda. The maintenance of good public relations is necessary to the survival of the schools. The public is entitled to information about the schools, and this must be obtained through modes of publicity. Good public relations conditions are not secured by propaganda or by "selling" the schools to the public but rather by working with the public on the problems of maintaining good schools. It should not be forgotten that the schools are the public's—not the board's and not the teachers'.

The maintenance of good schools requires publicity. The people must be led to understand not only the successes of the schools but also the difficulties that stand in the way of their improvement. This can be accomplished by means of frankness and completeness in the presentation of facts concerning the schools. There are good public relations when the people in genral have a sympathetic, co-operative, and helpful attitude toward the schools, and when they understand the objectives of the schools and help to promote their attainment. Publicity is necessary to the maintenance of good public relations; the people have a right to access to information concerning their schools. Propaganda has come to mean the presenting of favorable and the withholding of unfavorable information in an attempt to prejudice public opinion. Public relations units have done this in some school districts. It has resulted in a loss of public confidence in the correctness of the information furnished. Good public relations is built on understanding—by the public of the schools and by the schools of the attitudes of the public toward the schools and of the need of the public for what the schools provide.

Public Bias in School Attitudes

The opinions held by the people of a community are not always balanced and sound and sometimes vary among persons. Some parents want painless education for their children; others want discipline. Often they do not have a clear perspective of the schools as they relate to all children. They may see their one child, the one classroom where he attends school, the one teacher, and the one school building, and they may draw their conclusions concerning the whole school system from this limited knowledge.

Small problems which affect the children and are large in their estimation may become large to the parents vicariously. If a parent has only a partial view of the schools, the emotional element of a single situation may be the basis of an attitude that will be applied widely to the schools in general. It is necessary to the maintenance of balanced attitudes that the people of a community have many experiences with the schools and that they be furnished information about them from many sources. As the chosen representatives of the people of the school district, it is the responsibility of the board to see that information is furnished the people to whom the schools belong and that the causes of antagonistic attitudes, where such exist, be eliminated and co-operative attitudes toward the joint enterprise be developed.

Special groups sometimes look upon the schools with a bias based on their own limited objectives, and they sometimes try to control the schools for purposes extraneous to those for which the schools exist. These are sometimes worthy, but they are not school purposes and usually distort the work of the schools. Patriotic groups wish to have their particular brand of patriotism inculcated, and social groups want to have the kinds of social movements in which they are interested disseminated. Sometimes public utilities or other industries desire to form certain public opinions by furnishing material for instruction in high schools. Business enterprises sometimes wish to use the schools for advertising chewing gum, soft drinks, or other products. Even agencies of the Federal Government have sometimes used the schools for propaganda purposes to promote the work of their special agencies. Many private and government agencies furnish excellent free curriculum material to the schools in the form of films, film strips, pamphlets, and the like.

The problem confronting school authorities is where to draw the line in the use of free advertising or propaganda materials. Should an insurance company's useful health material be used? If so, should other material having more obvious advertising or propaganda purposes be used? Should material advertising soft drinks, cigarettes, or intoxicating liquors be used? Should collections of children's pennies be made to memoralize a war hero? A board must base its policy on such considerations as the following: (1) Where is it practicable to draw the line? (2) Will use of the material be fair to the competitors of an industry or the opponents of the theory advocated? (3) Will use of the material or the activity be harmful to children? (4) Will use of the material or activity give undue weight to matters of relatively minor importance? (5) Will what is desired interfere with the regular instruction for which the schools exist?

Although some boards may be too strict in excluding matter extraneous to achieving the objectives of the schools, it appears that boards in general have probably been too lenient in permitting outside agencies to use the schools for propaganda and advertising purposes. The professional staff has also been too ready to accept materials from agencies having special purposes, good though many of the purposes may be.

Public Control of School Boards

The public exercises control over the board, whose members it elects (or who are appointed by officers it elects), in several ways:

If the public approves of a board's actions it re-elects the members; if it disapproves, it replaces them at the expiration of their terms.

Instructions on certain matters are sometimes given the board by the people in town meetings or by ballot.

The force of public opinion serves to control the actions of school boards if they neglect or refuse to make effective the will of the people as formulated by the press, by parent-teacher associations, by community advisory councils, by taxpayers' associations, and others.

Traditional practices have been developed by various agencies in the community which influence or restrict the actions of the school board.

The public exercises an influence on board actions by submission of petitions to it. A petition may induce a board to bring a matter to a vote which otherwise might not be considered or might be permanently laid on the table.

Public hearings, when held on the budget, change of district boundary lines, location of a school building, and other matters, give persons in the community an opportunity to influence board actions by the expression of their opinions.

Requirements that board meetings be open to the public may serve as a means of control by preventing secret or unpublicized actions by the board.

The right of the public to inspect certain records that are not confidential by nature may serve as a means of public control over board action.

Public control over school board actions is secured by the legal requirements for posted or advertised notices of meetings, elections, opening of bids on materials or services for purchase by the board, or publication of the school budget or receipts and expenditures.

Function of Maintaining Good Public Relations

One of the most important functions of a school board is that of maintaining or providing for the maintenance of good public relations for the school system. Of course, it is necessary that the board and school personnel strive to make the schools deserving of good will. Good public relations cannot last for long if developed by propaganda for an unworthy school system. It is necessary that deserved public confidence be the result of wise policies, progressive administration, and a devoted staff.

Confidence is developed in a board that presents a united front. Such a board is more likely to be able to resist pressures when necessary and is better able to judge whether or not any specific action will be in the interest of the whole community to which the board members owe their allegiance. A united board is not necessarily one that always passes or rejects motions by unanimous vote but rather is one of which all members, even those on the losing side of an issue, defer to the action of the majority and earnestly strive to make the board's action effective. If some members actively oppose an action after the board has made its decision, the board is disunited and will soon develop public doubts concerning the wisdom of its decisions. This attitude by the public will make the board's task of acting for the people more difficult. It is well to discourage divisions and to try to secure co-operative efforts for better schools. A superintendent is usually unwise to insist that a board come to a decision when the vote is likely to be nearly evenly divided. The minority may be guided by a considerable segment of the public, and the vote may divide the community on the issue.

The members of the board cannot provide all of the information concerning school policies, administration, and operation required by the public. The superintendent and the staff working under his direction should serve as the main source. The function of supplying information to the public is one for board members, administrators, teachers, and other employees. The function of providing leadership in public relations rests largely on the shoulders of the superintendent even·though he may have a director of public relations to perform the details of the work.

The board represents the people in acting in the interests of the development of their children. The members are a part of the community and can properly determine school policies only if they are informed concerning both the work of the schools and the opinions and desires of the public. Being the natural link between the people of the community and the professional staff, and being laymen of the community and employers of the staff, an important function of the members of the board is to "run interference" while the staff "carries the ball" for public relations. Also, the superintendent will need to take an active part in community activities, make numerous addresses to community groups, and organize his staff to render similar services because he and his staff have more accurate and detailed first-hand information concerning the schools than has any board member.

The public schools belong to the people who support them and their only purpose is to help in the development of the children of the community. The people have a right to be informed concerning the policies, administration, operation, objectives, and successes and failures of the schools. It is the function of the school board to provide the means for furnishing full and accurate information, favorable and unfavorable, together with interpretation and explanation, in terms the lay public can comprehend. Failure to furnish such information, either by design or neglect, leads to possible misinformation and a questioning of the motives of the board or staff.

Relations of Board Members with Community Groups and Individuals

Parents and others sometimes bring complaints to individual board members instead of to the superintendent, the principal, or other administrative officials. For example, Jones, a friend of board member Brown, complains to Brown that his Mary was not passed from the fourth grade to the fifth. He maintains that Mary is a bright girl and that the teacher is prejudiced against her. The teacher told him that Mary didn't work well enough, but Mary has attended school regularly and Sally Smith was out of school a month and she was passed. He reminds Brown that he helped elect him to the board.

Brown requests the teacher to come to his office for a conference. Awed by the intercession of a member of the board and knowing that Mary's grades were near the passing line, the teacher agrees to pass Mary. The principal learns of the matter and calls it to the attention of the superintendent because a school board member has interceded. The superintendent and principal consult the teacher, the school psychologist, the school nurse, and the pupil's scholastic, health, psychological, and other records. It is shown that Mary is somewhat mentally immature and physically malnourished. She has not performed well in the fourth grade class and is a half year younger chronologically than the average fourth grade pupil. When these facts are made known to Jones, and it is explained that Mary would be happier and better able to develop her personality if transferred from the class of older children to the younger group, he readily agrees that Mary should spend another year in the fourth grade. Suggestions are made for co-operation by the home in Mary's development.

The fault of procedure was that the board member should not have attempted to settle the matter. He wanted to be helpful and felt an obligation to his friend, Jones, but he was not professionally trained to settle the matter, and he did not have time to study the records, even if he had had access to them. He did not have such access because pupil records are confidential. Besides, as an individual board member he is only a citizen and had no authority to act for the board or the superintendent. He should have referred the matter to the superintendent as an administrative problem. If it had been a policy matter, he should have referred the matter to the board through its secretary. The secretary might well be the superintendent.

If a board member is elected on a platform pledging school reforms, he may find himself alone. His mistake is that of making a pledge. After he has access to more complete information, he may find that his pledged "reforms" were educationally unsound and that what looked from the outside like a need for change proved to be a vital part of the educational services when viewed from the inside. The new member may have pledged himself to eliminate the fads and frills from the schools, but now he can find none—at least none that all of his supporters will agree are fads and frills. Not all will agree that art, music, physical education, or athletics are fads and frills.

Suppose a board member stated that he would eliminate socialism from the schools after his election. The public seemed to agree that this was a worthy aim. However, when he attempted to eliminate school lunches, health service, physical education, and playgrounds as being socialistic when assumed by the schools rather than the homes, a demand for the member's resignation as being unfitted for school board membership arose in the press and in mass meetings of indignant parents. Segments of the public considered the member's opinions to be indicative of opposition to the schools more than opposition to socialism. He might have concluded that he was wrong in classifying these activities as socialism; he could have decided that the public wanted that much socialism and dropped the matter; he might have resigned as demanded; or he might have continued as an obstructionist member of the school board.

Board members should not pledge action before they have full information. Caution is the part of wisdom in making changes in the schools. Members should maintain an open-minded attitude and refrain from basing their actions on prejudices and fallacious reasoning in order to avoid wrecking a part of the school system. An open-minded attitude produces a smoothly running system.

As a representative of the public, a school board member

should be sensitive to the kind of schools the people want and can afford to maintain. He should protect the schools against what he considers to be unjust attacks. If he considers attacks are justified, it is his duty to try to influence the other board members to act with him in having faults corrected or, if the school district cannot afford the necessary expense, to let people know why the board cannot perform its functions more satisfactorily. In determining the validity of criticisms, the board member should try to separate the "wheat from the chaff" and be able to distinguish those that are valid from those that are merely irresponsible gossip. Such gossip may be motivated by political demagoguery, by grudges held against someone, such as a teacher, the superintendent, or a board member, by selfish interests, or by some other extraneous motive. The reason for the criticism may determine how the criticism can best be met.

It is well to require a critic-petitioner of the public schools to present his specific charges and desires in writing. This will enable the board to pass his document on to the superintendent and thence to members of the superintendent's staff for facts to report to the board. It will enable the board to evaluate it and to determine whether or not it has been motivated by indefinite opinions and general ill will. If the charge appears to have validity, the board can direct the superintendent to have the matter investigated by the proper school authorities for report and possible publication of results.

The board, itself, should hear representatives of community groups with courtesy and should act on their petitions, but it is not proper for such representatives to present their petitions to individual board members or to attempt to secure pledges of action in advance of its presentation to the board. It is a member's duty to refrain from committing himself and to refer petitioners to the superintendent. In such reference, it is not necessary to give them the brush-off rudely. The reason should be stated to them.

Board members have many opportunities to help maintain good public relations by making addresses before community groups and in private conversations. The public has many reasons to have confidence in board members' individual opinions since they render service to the community without pay, are laymen with knowledge of the public schools, and are interested in the development of the community and its children. Members can create goodwill for the schools if they find time to attend some of the many school events such as the principal athletic contests, music programs, school exhibits, dramatic productions, and commemorative programs. Also, in his club, church, and business activities, the board member can often discuss school needs and obtain the opinions of others on the general effectiveness of the schools. However, the member will have no right to speak for the board, except as authorized, nor to predict its actions in such contacts. It is unwise for a member even to commit himself to his action, for that will make it difficult for him to change his mind if he needs to when full information has been furnished the board as the basis for determining its action.

School Board Interpretations of Public Opinion

It is difficult for the members of a school board to interpret public opinion correctly concerning school issues. Usually many people lack basic information necessary for the forming of sound opinions. The board is often confronted by groups desiring to: use the schools for raising funds to build a memorial; promote some cause by holding essay or oratorical contests; request that the law be better enforced providing for the teaching of the evil effects of alcohol and narcotics on the human system; present a plan for organizing the whole faculty for the promotion of art, music, or health education; request the sponsorship of spelling contests; or request the teaching of thrift in 30 minutes of school time a week and the collection of children's savings for deposit in the banks. Many organizations and individuals desire that the schools adopt such special objectives.

Most or all of the proposals may be worthwhile, but their promotion as special objectives unbalances and distorts the curriculum. Each is a pull in one direction at the expense of other elements of children's curriculum experiences. All provide that the details of the work be performed by classroom teachers in addition to their regular instruction duties. It would be intolerable to permit anyone else to perform them on school time. It is a mistake for a board to consider such plans as representative of public opinion. Each is representative of only a small segment of public opinion. Most lay citizens don't sense the curriculum distortions and the problems concerning the time allowances for other pupil experiences that result from the schools' trying to meet the desires of community groups.

It is easy for school board members to be confused in determining what the public desires. Petitions may or may not be representative of public opinion. Many pressure groups may be unorganized, such as those to promote school athletics, to increase enrollment in vocational or commercial courses, or for the establishment of nursery schools. Some pressure groups may be led by cranks, bigots, or egotists, playing for personal publicity and power. The schools belong to all of the people, not to certain groups. The board is the agent of all, not merely those in a member's political party, church, parent-teacher association, or taxpayers' association. In case of divided opinion, it is difficult for a member to determine which view best represents majority public opinion. A board should guard against being misled by the noise of a small minority of persons who may consider themselves to be the public.

School Board Guidance of Public Opinion

Public opinion on school issues is difficult to interpret because it is often not definitely formed and it changes from time to time as different issues are forced to the attention of the public and as different persons assert their interest in the problems of maintaining the schools. The board members, being of the community and serving without compensation, often are and should be a stabilizing influence in the forming of public opinion. The people naturally look to their chosen representatives for information, guidance, and leadership on school matters. A reciprocal relationship is proper. The board should accept guidance from the community and make its will effective in so far as it can determine the real desires of the people. If the relationships are good, the community will have confidence in the judgment and good intentions of the board, and community opinion will lean toward acceptance of the board's actions.

Through the superintendent and his staff, the school board must furnish the public with information and with the correct interpretation of its meaning. Of course, it should not especially select the information that is favorable to the board and the schools or color the facts to favor actions the board has taken or the desires of teachers and other employees. The presentation of facts and their interpretation should be honest or the public will soon come to look on what is furnished with suspicion, as propaganda. Honesty in dealing with the public will help the public to form sound opinions.

The public may sometimes express a desire for something other than that which the board members think is best. It is fickle and its expressed opinions are changeable and often inconsistent as different people become spokesmen for it. It seldom accepts responsibility for what it has demanded after the board has acted on its demands. If the public demands what is not in its best interest, it is the responsibility of the board to stimulate and direct public opinion through discussion, explanation, and publicity of the truth. Of course, the board will have to accept responsibility for its actions, whether or not they are those dictated by the more vocal part of the community. Public apathy is probably the greater danger to the schools. Apathy will permit the schools to drift along without adequate moral and financial support, resulting in unenthusiastic time-serving by many members of the staff and also in a low level of efficiency.

School board members are representatives of the people. They serve without personal gain as a service to the community. As such representatives they are in a position to exercise leadership in promoting the interest of public education. The people and state legislative bodies will rely on the opinions of school board members if they have sufficiently informed themselves concerning the needs of the schools so that they can speak authoritatively. The people generally realize that the members have no narrow, selfish interests to serve. When teachers or school administrators speak for the schools they are too often suspected of having selfish motivations. If the public schools are to maintain their position of importance, it will be necessary for school board members to accept leadership in maintaining the financial and moral support of public education.

Means of Maintaining Good Public Relations

Some of the means of maintaining, or making possible the maintenance of, good public relations in a school district may be listed as follows:

The board can invite the public to contribute suggestions for the improvement of the schools as a means of determining what the people think about the schools and their needs.

The board can encourage the organization of parent-teacher associations, which will serve as a source of information concerning a part of the public's attitudes toward the schools.

The board can organize school advisory councils of representatives of community organizations to furnish information concerning public opinion.

News releases may be prepared for the press and radio. Motion picture films may be made of school activities for showing at such meetings as those of parent-teacher associations, women's clubs, and businessmen's clubs, or for showing on television.

Good public relations can better be maintained by means of a continuing program of furnishing information to the public than by spurts of high pressure publicity after long periods of quiescence.

The board can sponsor a news sheet for parents and lend encouragement to high school publications.

The annual report of the school board to the public should furnish much information concerning the schools that will be the basis for good public relations.

The board's publications of various kinds can be produced in color, harmony of design, and in good literary style, so far as financial limitations permit, as a means of encouraging people to read them.

School programs can be broadcast over the radio.

Musical and dramatic programs, art exhibits, athletic contests, and other activities produced for public entertainment can be encouraged by the board and attended by its members.

Products of school learning activities can be placed on display.

The schools can hold open house for the public during education week or, better, visitations can be encouraged throughout the school year.

School board meetings can be open to the public from the call to order to adjournment except when the board deems it necessary or advisable to recess for an executive session or to hold a meeting of the committee of the whole.

Announcement of board meetings can be furnished to the press.

The school board can encourage reporters to attend its meetings and co-operate with them in preparing news of the board's and schools' activities.

Every action of the board and superintendent has public relations significance. For example, care used in the selection and approval of teachers for employment is important because attitudes of many people toward the schools are formed by their experience with classroom teachers.

The board and superintendent should not ignore matters, sometimes seemingly trivial, that cause ill will. They should seek to make corrections or should show why corrections should not be made.

Members of the board and the superintendent, as well as principals, supervisors, and others in the school system, can address community groups on the accomplishments and needs of the schools.

Participation of teachers and principals in community activities is valuable for maintaining public relations.

Contacts with the homes by classroom teachers, principals, visiting teachers, and school nurses are important in the maintenance of good public relations.

An adult education program of subjects desired by adults will help to maintain good public relations with those in classes, such as mothers, business women, bankers, engineers, various groups of skilled workers, and persons interested in hobbies.

A policy can be adopted of encouraging community use of school buildings with reimbursement by the users for extra expense for heat, light, custodial service, and supervisory service that must be furnished by the school district, and adequate supervision can be supplied so as to avoid an undue amount of deterioration of the buildings, equipment, and grounds due to community use.

These are not all of the means available for maintaining good public relations by the board and members of the school staff. Others could be listed, such as the placement of high school pupils and graduates in part time and full time positions in the community, services rendered to parents of preschool children in preparing their children for admission, guidance of parents in co-operating with the schools in developing children, testing of commercial products for local businessmen in the school laboratories, and many other contacts with the public. All of these things are important, as all experienced school board members and superintendents must agree.

School Reports as an Aid in Maintaining Public Relations

In some parts of the nation annual school reports are made to the public by all school districts or other units of school organization. In other parts they are made only by the larger school districts or not at all. Good reports are a valuable aid in furnishing information concerning its schools to the public. They often contain not only discursive matter but also tables, graphs, and photographs. Some school districts have the board's reports printed in the high school print shop, if there is one, or by commercial printers. Some have their reports duplicated by other means. However this is done, the annual school reports should be widely circulated in the district.

In addition to annual reports, some boards have prepared for public circulation regular news bulletins or occasional brochures presenting the results of studies made of some parts of the school system by administrative or supervisory officers of the staff or committees of teachers. In some states boards are required to publish a report of the receipts and expenditures of the school district for the year in a local newspaper. Whatever means of reporting is used, the board has the obligation of keeping the public informed of the accomplishments and needs of the schools.

School Board Relations with the Press

The local press usually has considerable influence in determining the attitudes of the public toward the schools. Representatives of the press should be urged to attend all open meetings of the board. Sometimes the relationships between the board and the press are sufficiently good to make it possible for the board to permit reporters to attend executive sessions with the understanding that certain parts of what transpires will be considered entirely "off the record." This was the practice in a certain West Coast city, but a similar invitation extended to reporters in an East Coast city was refused on the grounds that reporters must keep themselves free to publish whatever they learn. Such a confidential relationship is sometimes difficult to maintain, but a relationship of mutual trust should be maintained if possible.

Usually the press is friendly toward the schools, but it has a function to perform for the public, that of furnishing it with true and newsworthy information. The board and superintendent should be courteous and co-operate with representatives of the press in obtaining the news relating to the schools. Any tendency of the school authorities to withhold news, or to distort or color it, will cause a suspicious and possibly a hostile press.

A newspaper will go after the news and get it from whatever source is available. It is necessary that the board, the superintendent, and others having charge of public relations be frank and honest in dealing with the press and banish any notion that they can control the newspapers or withhold news from them. The press will not tolerate school authority censorship of school news. The public relations functions of school authorities are to help the press to ascertain the truth and to advise as to what true news, if published, may injure some innocent person or the schools. They should not try to determine what shall be published themselves. The decision to publish or ignore news must rest with the editor. Antagonism between the schools and the press, each a great public agency, will result in a losing battle for both.

The school authorities should consider the relationships from the standpoint of the newspapers as well as of the schools. A community consists of persons having many interests. The reporter and editor represent the public for the collection and sifting of news for truth and newsworthiness and for determining whether or not its publication would be good public policy. In editorials, the editor is no more bound to take one side than another. An editorial opposing an increase in salaries of teachers and policemen in one city caused much consternation among the teachers. They forgot that a newspaper may be quite as much interested in lower taxes as in higher salaries.

Some news stories will probably be uncomplimentary to the board or the schools. The board and school personnel should not be oversensitive to unfavorable news or even editorials. They should not be considered as an indication of hostility of the press toward the schools. The press has an obligation to the public and no condition of personal friendship for members of the board or of regard for the schools is likely to prevent the discharge of its functions except in exceptional circumstances. Only unreliability, worthlessness as news, or lack of fitness for publication is likely to prevent the press from publishing the news.

The press will have to judge what to print in each case. It

may be expected to refrain from jumping at conclusions not warranted by the facts and to defer publication pending investigation in case an innocent person or a child may be injured by premature publication of a story. But the press cannot be expected to protect the board or any member of it or members of the staff against criticism, nor can it be expected to serve as a tool to promote any cause of the board, the superintendent, or the staff. However, the press has a right to promote any cause it deems to be desirable. Criticism of individuals by the press should not be construed as criticism of the schools. To avoid errors of fact or conclusion, the public spirited press will freely consult the appropriate school authorities concerning any newsworthy event.

Usually, announcements and such local news items as teacher assignments, lists of graduates, honor rolls, and athletic schedules are prepared and released to the press by school principals, supervisors, or others in charge of the activities or situations in the schools. Matters dealing with policies of the board, feature articles on some school activity or accomplishment, or a story on some unusual school event are prepared by the director of public relations or by some one appointed by the superintendent. The press usually prefers to write its own news stories but sometimes will accept a feature article.

School Board Relations with Parent-Teacher Associations

Any agency that helps to make contacts between the school and the home has at least one feature worthy of encouragement. In most school districts large enough to employ a superintendent of schools, parent-teacher associations are in operation at some or all of the schools. One difficulty is that many parents do not join the association. Often, some of the parents lack interest or feel a lack of ability to participate in the activities of the association. Also, most parents belonging to the association are usually mothers. If fathers belong, many do not attend meetings, though there are some associations that have good attendance by fathers.

Some school authorities do not encourage the organization of parent-teacher associations because they fear the criticism such organizations sometimes engender. This policy is unworthy of a superintendent or principal. Good public relations are developed by meeting criticism in the open and not by hiding one's head in the sand to make believe that no criticism exists. While parent-teacher association meetings often present a forum for criticizing the objectives or work of the schools, the associations are also usually quick to defend the schools against unwarranted attacks leveled at them by other community groups or individuals.

Some parent-teacher associations experience difficulty in finding a part to play in the support and operation of the schools. Besides attending programs staged by pupils, hearing talks by school officials on the work of the schools, visiting classrooms, appointing home room mothers, conducting round table forums on school problems, providing entertainment for pupils on Halloween, providing a Thanksgiving dinner or helping with the Christmas program, and the like, many associations feel an urge to devise plans for raising money to purchase such equipment for the schools as a motion picture machine, pictures for the classroom walls, flags, band uniforms, pianos, or playground apparatus, and other similar items. The practice sometimes leads to difficulties because the association's committee may purchase materials not standardized by the school purchasing division and the school system's films and phonograph records, for example, may not fit the machines purchased, or the equipment may be a hazard to children. A few school boards have adopted a policy of accepting only such gifts as have been purchased from standard lists made for the local school system.

School Relations with City Officials

In most school districts, school boards have no special relations with city officials other than the co-operative relationships that should be maintained with officers of the fire department, the police department, the recreation department, the public works department, the public library department, and other departments discussed in Chapter 3 of this volume. However, a few school districts, usually having boundaries coterminous with city boundaries, are not financially independent of the city governments, and the boards in such districts usually have a lively time sidestepping responsibility for matters on which the mayor or the city council exercises authority. These relationships were discussed in Chapter 3 also.

In the case of fiscal dependency on a city authority, the school board must sell the school program to persons who have the power to reduce the budget proposed by the school board. Antagonisms between the school board and the mayor or city council in such cases are often at white heat. Such a condition is not good for the schools. Friction should be reduced to a minimum.

School Board Hearings

In some states, hearings are required on the discharge of certain employees or on budget proposals. There is no reason that a board should limit the use of hearings to matters stipulated by law as a protection against board action. The board can use hearings to gather information or opinions on important issues for its own purposes in considering or acting on specific issues concerning policies affecting the schools.

Legislative bodies such as the Federal Congress, state legislatures, and city councils often hold hearings. Some school boards use hearings also, but many do not. Hearings are held: (1) to obtain information pertinent to a problem faced by the board; (2) to discover opinions of the public on school issues; (3) to gain the good will of citizens by furnishing them opportunity to express their opinions and the reasons for them; or (4) to develop interest in the schools and their problems.

Hearings may be used as a democratic method of determining

whether or not a large part of the public desires or does not desire that the board take some particular important action. The achievement of this purpose is limited since not all persons can be heard. Such proposals as the establishment of a junior high school, the establishment of kindergartens, an increase in the tax rate for the purpose of raising the salaries of teachers, or the transfer of school nursing service from the city health department to the school board, or vice versa may be important enough to warrant the board's holding hearings on the issues. The issues must be important enough to warrant the expenditure of the time devoted to the hearings.

Hearings furnish the people with a channel for participation in helping the board to make its decisions on controversial matters. Of course, the board itself must make the decisions after the hearings, taking account of the validity and weight of the facts presented and arguments advanced. Hearings do not in any way reduce the responsibility of the board for making its decisions. The board should be guided by what it learns from witnesses but should guard against making its decisions merely to satisfy a minority group whose interests are not in harmony with the interests of the general public.

A disadvantage in the practice of holding hearings lies in the opinion that may be developed in the minds of those supporting or opposing a position that the board has been convinced by their arguments and will act accordingly. Of course, the board cannot act both pro and con even if it should desire to please all of those who testify. Another disadvantage is that hearings may lay the board open to acrimonious abuse from cranks, bulldozers, propagandists, and lobbyists. However, such persons can be restricted, in the hearings at least, to presenting opinions and reasons relating to the matter at issue. A value of hearings lies in the fact that they afford an opportunity to persons to express indignation if they have pent-up emotions. The expression of their feelings calms them and may forestall a later explosion under less favorable circumstances for the board and the schools.

Hearings may originate with the board that desires information or to hear expressions of public opinion or they may grow out of petitions presented by community groups such as parent-teacher associations, taxpayers' organizations, the churches, teachers, alumni of the schools, or pupils.

The board must decide whether or not the subject and purpose are worthy of a hearing and who shall be called to testify. A school board member should preside at the hearing and the board should be in charge. Board members may merely listen to what is presented or may direct questions to the witnesses. Above all, the board members should be receptive to the facts and opinions expressed and should avoid being drawn into any arguments with witnesses, regardless of how much some of them may disagree with their opinions. Board members should not be expected to listen to long and irrelevant discussions or to a propaganda barrage.

School Advisory Councils

School advisory councils or other organizations of citizens date to the First World War. Some were formed for promoting defense training in the Second World War. Others were required as a condition of qualification for Federal aid for certain kinds of vocational education. Since the Second World War, there has been a trend toward the organization of school advisory councils, advisory committees on education, or community organizations under other names whose purpose is the rendering of advisory service to school boards. Stimulation for the organization of what is termed "citizens committees" has come in recent years from an organization called the National Citizens Commission for the Public Schools.

The objectives of school advisory councils are not as yet well defined. There is no common pattern for membership, and the methods of forming such bodies vary widely among communities having them. Some councils have many members and others have only a few. In a study by Hull,[1] it was found that the num-

---

[1] Hull, J. H., *Lay Advisory Committees to Boards of Education in the United States.* Los Angeles: University of Southern California, 1949.

ber of members ranged from 5 to 1,210 and the usual number was from 20 to 30. From 80 to 90 per cent of the members were laymen. The rest were educators but these did not usually play a prominent part in the activities of the councils. Some school boards have many advisory committees dealing with specific matters (up to 30 or more), but the general practice is to have just one council to render advice on all school problems.

In some school districts advisory councils have been organized by outsiders as opposition groups to interfere with the work of the board or to attempt to force the board to adopt such policies as they desire. Sometimes advisory councils are organized by the board. Their members usually represent organized groups such as service clubs, parent-teacher associations, veterans' organizations, taxpayers' associations, the chamber of commerce, women's clubs, labor organizations, religious organizations, and other groups that are interested in the schools.

School advisory councils should be formed by the board rather than by outside groups that oppose the board. It is assumed that such a council will represent a large segment of public opinion in the school district, but it cannot be permitted to dictate the actions of the board, which is the responsible body by law. Such councils should be composed of persons from the principal organizations or occupational groups of the community as determined by the school board, but the number of members should lie between 20 and 30 in order that the group will be large enough to be representative of the community, yet small enough to be effective in action. If the representation of all important organizations will require too many members, some can be selected to represent combinations of groups, such as one to represent all service clubs, all labor organizations, or all professional organizations. Preferably, all members of the council should be laymen. If representatives of teachers or other school organizations are on the council, they may be suspected of exerting undue influence.

The council should not reduce the responsibility of the board for policies adopted, the administration of the schools by the superintendent and his staff, or the operation of the schools by the principals and their assistants. The board should keep itself free to accept or reject advice as the members see fit. The proper place of the advisory council should be made clear by the board from the beginning. Although the members of the advisory council should be selected by the various community organizations as their representatives, they should understand that the advisory council is an agency existing to serve the board and that it can be disbanded by the board if it does not serve its purpose, for its existence is extralegal. Of course, the council cannot make decisions for the board since it does not assume responsibility. Obstructionist members cannot be tolerated. The board must not relinquish any authority, and there is no legal way it can escape full responsibility for the schools.

It must be recognized that citizens' committees have been organized in some cities to aid those cities in ridding themselves of inefficient or corrupt boards of education or to secure changes in school laws. These have their proper place, where needed, but they are not the kind of committees needed to furnish the board with the information it needs for co-operative public relations. The work of the board with an advisory committee is a two-way process. The advisory committee helps the board to secure information about community desires and it helps the people to understand the conditions and potentialities of the schools.

The organization of an advisory council is not the easiest way of providing for educational planning or acceptance of the plans by the community, but it is often the surest way. The actions of an advisory council may be unpredictable and its advice may be feared by the members of the school board, the superintendent, and the employees, but it will bring issues into the open, and there can be little doubt of the acceptance of a board's actions by the community if it has an advisory council's full support.

The purpose of an advisory council should be to interpret community desires for the information of the school board and to co-ordinate and define community opinion so that the board can act on the advice if it deems it to be desirable. Although an advisory council has no legal status, it may have great influence in promoting what is generally desired by the representatives, such as promotion of visual education, vocational and social guidance, recreational facilities, school libraries, vocational placement services, and financial support. It can help to make the schools the center of community interest and action, and it can serve to prevent the making of expenditures for the schools beyond the financial means of the district.

The president of a board may be directed by formal action of the board to organize an advisory council. He may send invitations to the organizations selected by the board for each of them to send a representative to a meeting called by the board to discuss the possible desirability of forming a school advisory council. The organizations should be selected to represent as many different community groups as possible. The reasons for the organization of such a council should be explained to the representatives and also by the press to the public. If the representatives at the organization meeting decide to form such an organization, they will report the fact to their respective organizations. If these organizations desire to be represented, they can select official representatives to the council. The council can meet regularly three or four times a year to discuss the needs of the schools and take action on recommendations to be made to the board, and they can meet jointly with the board to render advice or consider problems on call of the board.

The school advisory council should avoid falling under the domination of one or more strong leaders. Each representative of a community group should be equally a leader with the other representatives to best represent the community. Representatives should be selected annually and sometimes changed by the organizations they are selected to represent.

CHAPTER 16

The Development of School Board Efficiency

Some Possible Causes of School Board Inefficiency

School boards are either more or less efficient and can seldom be separated into dichotomous classes of efficient and inefficient. Where it seems to predominate, school board inefficiency often arises from a combination of causes, but usually one or two factors stand out as being more causative of the inefficiency than others. Some of the causes of inefficiency or of conditions leading to such a state may be stated as follows:

Selection of an incompetent superintendent of schools—one who: (1) has had inadequate training in and has not otherwise learned sound principles of school administration; (2) cannot analyze educational situations so as to distinguish the elements that constitute problems; (3) is temperamentally unfitted to deal with teachers and other personnel so as to secure teamwork; or (4) is mainly interested in only one part of school work to the neglect of other parts, such as a superintendent's special interest in athletics, carried forward from a former position held as athletic coach.

The board members do not trust the superintendent to perform such administrative acts as preparing the budget, purchasing supplies, or selecting the teachers, but try to perform such acts themselves.

One or more of the members of the board tries to administer the schools personally or to direct the superintendent in his administration of them.

The board does not permit the superintendent to attend its meetings and does not request his advice on matters requiring action.

The board and superintendent are incompetent in financial administration or the school district is financially poor and the public's demands are not in line with the financial ability of the board to meet them.

Board committees determine policies in various fields and the board merely approves their recommendations, inconsistent though some of them are with the recommendations of other board committees.

There is frequent change of board membership due to election for short terms, failure to re-elect members, resignations or refusals to run for re-election, or other causes, so that there are but few experienced members on the board.

The board devotes insufficient time to deliberation on school problems and acts hastily, usually due to waste of the time allowed for board meetings.

The board is divided into two factions, the members of each faction having personal animosities toward the members of the other faction. The factions do not co-operate in the interests of securing an efficient school system.

The board members are divided by partisan politics, by different religions, or in some other way, and tend to vote on nearly all issues in the interests of their blocs.

Board members are selected by geographical divisions, and there is rivalry between the different sections of the school district.

The board is under the domination of an outside agency or a very powerful local politician and, on demand of such a dictator, rescinds its decisions even after they have been made and publicized.

Custodial and stenographic positions, and in some cases teaching positions, are used for purposes of political patronage.

The board members use the schools for private gain.

The board members have been selected by a small minority of the electorate at a separate time from the general election, and the members have the same lack of interest as was shown by the voters.

Some of the board members have unsuitable personal characteristics, such as a desire to dominate the board or a quick temper that discourages co-operative effort by the members.

Inservice Improvement of School Board Members

Need for Furnishing Information to Members. Some of the literature on school control and school administration points to a need for "educating" school board members. "Education" is not the proper term; the members are educated men and women. What is meant is that they need to be informed about the principles and techniques of the work of school boards and to be brought to appreciate the fundamental place of the school board in the control, administration, and operation of the public schools. They need to know what constitutes the acceptable practices by which school boards conduct their business.

Board members are representatives of the people and their thoughts about education before assuming office have been like those of the usual citizen, limited largely to matters arising from the contacts they have had with some particular school their children attend, to the taxes they pay to support schools, and perhaps to what they have learned from the few school administrators and teachers they know. Most of them know little of the business practices of the school system before taking office. They know little of the means used for financing the schools. They know only in a vague way the possibilities in such a thing as audiovisual education and what, if anything, the school system is doing to make use of it. They are only vaguely aware of the future requirements for school buildings. They think of the curriculum as the kinds of experiences provided by the schools for learning 30 or 40 years ago.

School boards and their associations recognize the need for sources from which members can secure valid information about public education in general and their own school districts in particular. Members should be aware of the possibilities for improving education in the future. A resolution on "Information for School Board Members" was adopted some years ago by the Illinois Association of School Boards, as follows:

Whereas the American school board is charged with the government of the public schools of this country, with the laying of taxes to support these schools, with the responsibility of approving courses of study and of employing faculty ·and nonteaching staffs and is directly accountable to the citizens for the conduct of the schools; and

Whereas rapid changes in social life are pressing upon the public schools for appropriate changes in educational policies and responsibilities, thus requiring careful evaluation of the work of the schools by the school board in order to bring educational policies and procedures into harmony with our social needs;

Therefore Be It Resolved that the Illinois Association of School Boards advocates that every possible effort be expended to develop among all school board members in the state a lively understanding of their serious responsibilities; that every agency of education consciously undertake the inservice training of new school board members to the details of their duties, and more particularly that the following steps be recommended:

1. All professional administrative officers of the public schools should consciously assist school board members to obtain information adequate to their responsibilities;

2. All educational associations—local, regional, statewide, national—should adopt definite policies to further the work of democratic self government of the public schools by advocating that the school board members be adequately informed in educational affairs;

3. All editors of educational magazines should be requested to adopt an editorial policy encouraging the inservice training of the school board members under the leadership of the local professional administrative officers and the state and county or regional school board associations (with such assistance as can be obtained);

4. All teacher training institutions should advocate with all candidates for teaching or administrative employment this same professional aid to the school board; in addition, governing authorities of such institutions should seriously consider making compulsory for all candidates for administrative positions a reasonable knowledge of school board government before recommending them for such positions and for candidates for teaching positions at least some knowledge of school board government before recommending them for teaching positions.

Orientation of New Board Members. New school board members are usually inducted into the board at the organization meeting in which they take the oath of office. There should be more than the administration of the oath of office for the preparation of a board member to participate fully in the work of the board. Upon the election of a new board member, the following steps might well be taken to orient him:

The president of the school board and the superintendent of schools (who might well be secretary of the board also) can write the newly elected member letters of welcome.

In his welcoming letter, the president of the board can invite the newly elected member to attend board meetings as a visitor until the time of organization.

The president of the school board should outline for the newly elected member the problems and methods of the school board prior to his taking the oath of office and before pronouncing him a member of the board.

The superintendent can take the new member to visit the schools and explain to him their peculiar features, purposes, and problems.

The new member can meet in individual conferences with the superintendent, assistant superintendents, supervisors, school physician or head nurse, school attendance director, principals, and others of the administrative staff to learn about their work and the objectives and purposes of the schools.

The superintendent can furnish the new member with a folder containing a copy of the state school laws, a copy of such rules and regulations as the state board of education has made available, a copy of the local school board's rules and regulations, the latest local school report, copies of the minutes of school board meetings for the latest year, the administrative code for the schools if there is one, a map of the school district showing the locations of schools and the school district boundaries, maps showing densities of school and preschool populations, tables showing tax rates for recent years, bonded indebtedness and retirement dates for bonds, budgets, tables of per pupil costs, teacher qualifications, school building ages and efficiency scores, and statements on the philosophy of the school system, the curriculum, and extracurricular activities.

The process of instruction of new members of the school board is needed even more if the new members have been elected in a contest with present members. Of course, it should not be expected that the new members will be indoctrinated into the opinions held by the retiring members; that would not be desirable. They have their own contributions to make in representing the public that selected them. Their orientation should be the attaining of knowledge of the conditions and problems facing the schools and the available resources of the schools for meeting them. They should learn of the means the board has used in performing its functions, whether good or bad.

It is assumed that new members come to the board as amateurs in the principles of school control and administration, though some of them may be expert in the control and administration of other enterprises. It is assumed that new members can apply such principles of control and administration as they know, but not always wisely unless they have a background of facts relating to the school system, the laws and rules by which it operates, and ability to evaluate the soundness of the recommendations of the superintendent. The purpose of the orientation is to give to the new member information basic to the rapid learning of the duties and responsibilities of the school board, so that he will have some basis for making judgments in the formation of his opinions.

Board Room Bookshelf. All members of school boards will need to read to gain information on the principles and practices of school control, school administration, and the more general principles of teaching and learning. To make it convenient for them to secure reading material, the secretary of the board should make available late periodicals and books dealing with education on a table or shelf in the board room. They can be charged out to members either at meetings or during the month. The secretary should call the attention of the members to new materials available to them.

The following matter can be placed on the shelf: current copies of three or four periodicals published for school board members and superintendents; the state teachers association journal; copies of the state school laws and other publications of the state department of education; surveys and special studies of other school systems; handbooks and other publications of the national and various state school boards associations; school reports of other school systems; some such books as are listed in the bibliography of this book; and such other material as may be instructive to the members of the school board. Some boards consider such reading important enough to warrant the board's subscribing to at least one magazine and the purchase of one or two books a year for each member. The cost need not usually exceed $50 to $75 a year, and the books will be of great aid to members in performing their functions. Copies for individual use, however, would not eliminate the need for the bookshelf for other materials they may desire to read.

Conferences and School Visitation. The school board's functions are not limited to monthly meetings, the approval of properly audited bills for the purchase of goods, and the rubber stamping of the recommendations made by the superintendent. The board should act intelligently as a legislative and approval body, reject recommendations it considers unsound or impracticable, initiate desirable measures, and accept responsibility for the administrative actions of its executive officer and his assistants.

Just as the state and Federal legislative bodies have machinery for investigating the needs for legislation by maintaining research staffs, holding committee hearings, and traveling to secure firsthand information, so should school board members secure information to aid them in acting intelligently. They should hold conferences with the administrative and supervisory officers and should visit schools to consult with principals, to inspect school buildings, and to observe classes and pupil activity groups in operation. They should visit the schools to learn about the schools, not to supervise them. In some cases it may be advisable to visit the schools accompanied by their respective principals so as to cause less disturbance.

Attendance at School Board Association Meetings. School board members ought to avail themselves of the opportunities to attend meetings of their associations—regional, state, and national. Such attendance will give them perspective if they will study the problems and apply the solutions of others to those faced by the boards of which they are members. It will give them the educational views of other laymen members of school boards, and it will help them to appreciate the fact that their board is not working alone but is a part of a very large enterprise. Attending members will profit most if they participate in the discussions. Boards sometimes send only one representative to such meetings because they desire to be economical in the use of the school district's funds. In such cases the representative should learn all he can about the work and responsibilities and the particular problems currently facing the boards of the region, state, or nation, and report to the other members whatever he has learned that will be useful to them.

Educational Consultation Service

In order for a school board to improve its efficiency, it must first learn what is wrong and what are the possible steps to be taken to secure improvement. One of the best ways of doing this is to employ a competent educational consultant to make a thorough study of the school system. Not only should he and his staff be competent, but they must have the time available to spend in residence in the school district. A "survey" of the surface problems that can be discovered by a few brief visits to the school system with a report written away from the system will have but little value. Such a "survey" is so general in character that it could apply to almost any school district merely by changing the name.

A consultant must have a thorough understanding of the backgrounds of problems if he is to find sound solutions. Such a consultant should not have unproved theories in some limited area of education which he wishes to propagate. He should discover what lies at the root of each problem and take a balanced view of the whole school situation. Such a detailed evaluation of a school system might well be made at intervals of 10 or 12 years. The findings and recommendations can be vital to the development of school board efficiency.

Sometimes much can be accomplished by organizing committees of school personnel and residents of the community to analyze the problems, with the consultant employed to help the committees plan the work and examine the results critically. Such a study will be meaningful to the people who prepare it, so that a high percentage of the recommendations are likely to be made effective. On the other hand, a thorough study and report on a school system made by an experienced consultant will have the advantage of giving the board and school staff outside viewpoints, will draw upon knowledge of successful practices in other school systems, will furnish frank and independent opinions that cannot often be secured in self surveys, and will be based on records, such as those of pupils and teachers, that can be made available to outside consultants but cannot be made available to committees of teachers and parents. The outside study and report is certain to be more impersonal and objective than the self survey because outside consultants have no personal interest in the personalities of the school system. The board should plan its program of improvement of the school system on the basis of the study and report, however made.

School Board Associations

Development of School Board Organizations. School board associations have been organized at various levels. In a few states having small school districts, the boards are organized into county or regional associations. At this time, there are state associations in 44 of the states, some of which also have county or regional associations. One state has regional associations only, and these are making an effort to secure legislative authorization for the organization of a state association.

School board organization seems to have been started in Pennsylvania in 1896. In some states, school board associations which were formed later were discontinued and have lately been re-established. There have been changes in the names of associations through the years, but the principal functions have not been greatly modified. The following table shows the dates of organization and the names of present state associations, as indicated in literature of the National School Boards Association:[1]

State	Year	Name
Pennsylvania	1896	Pennsylvania State School Directors Association
Illinois	1913	Illinois Association of School Boards
New Jersey	1913	State Federation of District Boards of Education in New Jersey
Kansas	1918	Kansas Association of School Boards
New York	1919	New York State Association of School Boards
Nebraska	1919	Nebraska State School Boards Association
Wisconsin	1920	Wisconsin Association of School Boards
Minnesota	1921	Minnesota School Board Association
Washington	1921	Washington State School Directors Association
Utah	1923	Utah State School Boards Association
Montana	1926	Montana School Boards Association
North Dakota	Before 1927	North Dakota School Officers Association
Iowa	1928	Iowa Association of School Boards
Florida	1930	Florida School Boards Association

[1] The titles of state associations and year of organization of some of them is given in brief items in the *American School Board Journal* as follows:

Tuttle, Edward M., "A Roll Call of Progress Among School Board Associations," July 1952; "Continuing the Roll Call of State School Boards Associations," August 1952.

State	Year	Name
Rhode Island	1930	Rhode Island Public School Officials Association
Vermont	1930	Vermont State School Directors Association
California	1931	California School Trustees Association
Virginia	1934	School Trustees Association of Virginia
Wyoming	1934	Wyoming School Trustees Association
Kentucky	1936	Kentucky School Boards Association
North Carolina	1937	North Carolina School Boards Association
Connecticut	1938	Connecticut Association of Boards of Education
Louisiana	1938	Louisiana School Boards Association
South Dakota	1938	Associated School Boards of South Dakota
Tennessee	1939	Tennessee School Boards Association
Colorado	1940	Colorado Association of School Boards
Texas	1941	Texas Association of School Boards
Idaho	1942	Idaho School Trustees Association
Missouri	1942	Missouri Association of School Boards
New Hampshire	1944	New Hampshire School Boards Association
Delaware (Reactivated)	1944	Delaware Association of School Boards
Oklahoma	1946	Oklahoma State School Boards Association
Massachusetts	1946	Massachusetts Association of School Committees
Oregon	1948	Oregon School Boards Association
Arizona	1948	Arizona School Board Association
Alabama	1949	Alabama Association of School Board Members
Indiana	1949	Indiana School Boards Association
Michigan	1949	Michigan Association of School Boards
New Mexico	1949	New Mexico School Boards Association
South Carolina	1950	South Carolina Association of School Boards

State	Year	Name
Ohio	1950	Regional associations, only, at this time
Georgia	1951	Georgia School Boards Association
Mississippi	1951	Mississippi School Boards Association
Arkansas	1951	Arkansas Association of School Boards
West Virginia	1952	West Virginia School Board Association
Nevada	In process of organization	
Maine	None	
Maryland	None	

Many of the state associations have now been incorporated by the respective state legislatures, but many of the earlier associations were merely loose organizations that met for mutual benefit without legal authorization. Some met with district superintendents of schools associations. Some meetings were called by the chief state school official. Most of the larger states now employ full time executive secretaries. Most of the other states employ part time executive secretaries or have the free services of secretaries elected to the office by the members.

A proposal to form a national organization as a federation of state school boards associations was made at a meeting of a National Council of School Board Associations, in 1938, in Chicago. The proposal was discussed further at a meeting the next year in Knoxville. The organization was accomplished in 1940 and conferences of the new organization were held in 1941 and again in 1942. The meetings were then discontinued due to difficulties of travel during the war years. The prewar organization was revived in 1945 and a meeting was held in Springfield, Illinois, attended by representatives of 21 of the then existing state associations. In 1948, the name of the national organization was changed to National School Boards Association. The association was incorporated in 1949 by the legislature of Illinois, and headquarters were established at 450 East Ohio Street, Chicago, which is still the headquarters address of the national association.

Functions and Objectives of School Boards Associations. Some of the early school boards associations were affiliated with the professional education associations of superintendents or teachers. Most, if not all, school boards associations are now independent of associations of professional employees. They should not be so affiliated because school board members are laymen and have a different relationship to the public than have employed personnel. Although many of the problems met by school boards and superintendents or teachers are the same or similar, others are different. In some cases the interests of the two groups are in opposition. If the school boards associations were to affiliate with organizations of school administrators or teachers, it might cause the public to lose a measure of confidence in the intentions of members to serve the interests of the public. However, there should be close relationships between an association of professional education employees and the lay school board organization, and each should help the other. School boards associations sometimes hold their conferences at the time and place where school administrators or teachers meet, to the advantage of both in arranging programs and attending meetings.

The functions and objectives of state school boards associations may be stated briefly as follows:

To devise means for securing public support of the schools and for maintaining good public relations on both local and statewide bases.

To stimulate capable people to accept school board membership and the public properly to appreciate the services rendered to their communities by school board members.

To make school board members more keenly aware of their duties and responsibilities.

To develop interest in, enthusiasm for, and secure co-operation in statewide plans for effecting improvements in the schools.

To provide for the discussion of plans for effectuating economies in co-operative purchasing, building insurance, building maintenance, and the like.

To furnish information on current legal, financial, and educational matters for the mutual benefit of the members.

To secure co-operative efforts by boards in solving problems of school control.

To hold conventions and conferences for the mutual exchange of ideas and experiences among school board members.

To prepare and distribute to members of school boards, bulletins and other published material containing information concerning the schools such as salary schedules, employee relationships, financing of school buildings, apportionment of school funds, and sources of revenues.

To gather and circulate information on school activities and needs.

To disseminate the results of research to member boards and individuals and indicate how they can be used.

To support research activities on important matters related to school control and administration for the benefit of the boards.

To make studies of current problems facing school boards and their possible solutions.

To promote needed legislation and prepare bills for legislative consideration or enactment if necessary.

To decide what legislation is needed and to support or reject educational bills proposed.

To discuss methods of enforcing and taking advantage of the provisions of state school laws and to discuss their effects upon the schools and the communities.

To analyze the meaning and importance of school laws.

To provide a headquarters office and, as a rule, a secretary, full time or part time, to effectuate the wishes of the members of the organization.

Functions and Objectives of the National Organization. The preamble to the Constitution of the National School Boards Association sets forth the purpose of that association as follows:

> Recognizing that the nation's future is dependent on the complete education of its youth, that in unity there is strength, and that exchange of ideas is important at all times; that co-ordination of effort on the part of all educational forces interested in the betterment of education is necessary; and also recognizing that school boards are in a strategic position to bring about needed improvement of public education, we be-

lieve a National School Boards Association will aid in accomplishing these ends.

The purposes of the national association are specifically stated in its constitution as follows:

1. To work for the general advancement of education for the youth of the United States and its possessions.
2. To study the educational programs of the different states and disseminate this information.
3. To work for the most efficient and effective organization of the public schools.
4. To work for the adequate financial support of the public schools.
5. To study educational legislation proposed in Congress to the end that the various state school board associations may be informed of such legislation.
6. To accomplish such other purposes as may be approved by the membership of this organization acting in annual or called meeting, or by the Executive Committee.

The functions and objectives of the national association have been stated to be:

1. To aid state school board associations to improve and strengthen their state organizations in effective service to local school boards.
2. To maintain channels for exchange of ideas and to prepare and distribute to state associations and, through them, to local school boards, educational information and literature, as well as to encourage workshops and study groups where school board members may prepare and qualify for more effective service to the public schools.
3. To inform state school boards associations and, through them, local school boards, on successful techniques of school board operation, school administration, educational trends, and solutions to current school district problems arrived at in the various states.
4. To give the school boards of America, through their state and national associations, a voice in educational policy making at all levels.
5. To foster such objectives and policies of education as will preserve our American concept of democracy and develop each individual child for successful living and good citizenship.
6. To improve the quality of school programs toward the highest types of education offered in the various states, seeking a balance in curriculum content and instructional methods which

will utilize the best ideas of modern education while retaining established and proven techniques.

7. To encourage the most desirable and efficient working relationships on the local level between boards of education, school administrators, the school staff, and the public.

8. To provide a constructive program of information and good public relations on national, state, and local levels in order to inform parents, communities, states, and Congress in Washington of the aims, potentialities, and needs of our public schools.

9. To work in cooperation with every national agency, educational and lay, which is sincerely desirous of advancing universal public education to higher levels of effective service to the children, youth, and adults of America.

Provisions for Membership in Associations. The trend is toward membership in state associations by boards, but in a few states membership is still open to individual members of boards. Fees are generally charged for membership of school boards and are paid from school district funds. In some states, courts have decided that dues to the state associations are legal expenditures of school districts.

Provisions for the payment of dues vary greatly in details among the state associations, but dues are generally charged according to the size of districts as indicated by the average daily attendance of pupils, the number of teachers employed, or the assessed valuation of the school district. The number of size groups ranges from 3 to 14. The amounts are as low as $1 for each board of any size to from $15 to $250 or more, according to size.

States having large school districts and few boards as well as some having small school districts have 100 per cent membership. Some states having many school districts have only a relatively small proportion of the school boards in their associations, but usually most of those are boards of the larger school districts.

Work of the Associations. Much of the work of school board associations is indicated in the preceding statements of their functions and objectives. Their purposes are often stated in the laws incorporating them. They adopt constitutions and bylaws stating the nature of their work. Some of them maintain a headquarters office with a full time secretary in charge.

They study the effects of school laws and initiate desirable school legislation. Their voice is one the legislators will heed since they are laymen who have no selfish personal interest to serve in their proposals.

The state associations make and submit annual financial reports to member boards. They conduct some research of a practical type and make it available to their member boards. They arrange for meetings of school boards and study and discuss current problems and hold conferences in which they compare their experiences. The members discuss such problems as the following: financing of school building construction; equitable distribution of state school funds; testing and purchasing of equipment and supplies; securing teachers in times of shortages; teacher salary trends; teacher tenure laws; relation of the board to the superintendent; school board procedures; maintenance of good public relations; school district consolidation; pupil transportation; school district organization; and school board rules and regulations. They serve as sources of information for member boards. Some of the state associations employ a full time secretary to co-ordinate the efforts of member boards, and the National School Boards Association employs a full time secretary and co-ordinates the efforts of state associations.

Publications of the Associations. State school boards associations vary greatly in the number of member boards and in the activities conducted. This is to be expected in states that vary from fewer than 20 school boards (Delaware) to several thousand school boards (Missouri, Illinois, Minnesota, and several other states). Most of the state associations publish materials either in printed or otherwise duplicated form, such as regular monthly, bimonthly, quarterly, or irregular bulletins, journals, newsletters, and announcements. These are designed especially for the members of the particular state association that produces them. Some of these have been published by state associations, as in New York, for 30 or more years. Publications are more likely to be produced by those states employing full time secretaries. Others produce occasional brochures, such as reference material for boards or reports on the activities of the association. They usually publish reports of their conventions.

Handbooks or manuals for school boards are produced in many of the states having associations. Some of these are now old and are being revised. They have usually been published by state departments of education or state universities. These generally present some of the school laws and their significance, board organization plans, board functions and duties, and other information needed by board members.

The national association publishes a directory of the state associations; proceedings of conferences and conventions; a semimonthly release on state and national association activities; releases for publication in educational periodicals; and, jointly with other organizations such as the American Association of School Administrators, booklets on subjects of concern to school board members.

School Board Members' Creed

As a guide to school board members in improving the work of boards, a school board members' creed was compiled from the written contributions of superintendents of schools and members of school boards, by the Epsilon Field Chapter of Phi Delta Kappa educational fraternity, of Los Angeles, California. The creed is as follows:

As a member of the school board:
I will listen.
I will recognize the integrity of my predecessors and associates and the merit of their work.
I will be motivated only by a desire to serve the children of my community.
I will recognize that it is my responsibility together with that of my fellow board members to see that the schools are properly run—not to run them myself.
I will work through the administrative employees of the board—not over or around them.
I will recognize that school business may be legally transacted only in open meeting legally called.
I will not "play politics."

I will attempt to inform myself on the proper duties and functions of a school board member.

In performing the proper functions of a school board member:
I will deal in terms of general educational policies.
I will function, in meeting the legal responsibility that is mine, as a part of a legislative, policy-forming body—not as an administrative officer.
I will consider myself a trustee of public education and will attempt to protect and preserve it.

In maintaining desirable relations with other members of the board:
I will respect the opinions of others.
I will recognize that authority rests with the board in legal session—not in individual members of the board.
I will make no disparaging remarks in or out of meeting about other members of the board or their opinions.
I will recognize that to promise in advance of a meeting how I will vote on any proposition which is to be considered is to close my mind and agree not to think through other facts and points of view which may be presented in the meeting.
I will make decisions in board meeting only after all sides of the question have been presented.
I will discourage the use of standing committees and insist that all members of the board participate fully in board action—delegating detail matters to administrative employees.
I will insist that special committees be appointed to serve only in an investigating and advisory capacity.
I will consider unethical and will thus avoid "star chamber" or "secret" sessions of board members held without presence of the school administration.

In meeting my responsibilities to my community:
I will attempt to appraise fairly both the present and the future educational needs of the community.
I will attempt to procure adequate financial support for the schools.
I will interpret to the schools as best I can the needs and attitudes of the community.
I will consider it an important responsibility of the board to interpret the aims and methods of the schools and the materials used in them to the community.
I will insist that business transactions of the school district be on an ethical, open, and above-board basis.
I will not buy for personal use at "school" prices.
I will not consider a position on the school board as a "stepping stone" to political power.

In working with the superintendent of schools and his staff:

I will hold the superintendent of schools responsible for the administration of the schools.

I will give the superintendent of schools authority commensurate with his responsibility.

I will expect the schools to be administered by the best-trained technical and professional people it is possible to procure.

I will elect employees only on the recommendation of the superintendent.

I will participate in board legislation only after considering the recommendations of the superintendent and only after he has furnished complete information supporting his recommendation.

I will expect the superintendent of schools to keep the board of education adequately informed at all times through both oral and written reports.

I will expect to spend more time in board meetings on educational programs and procedures than on business detail.

I will give the superintendent of schools friendly counsel and advice.

I will refer all complaints to the proper administrative officer or insist that they be presented in writing to the board as a whole.

I will present any personal criticisms of employees to the superintendent.

I will provide adequate safeguards around the superintendent and other personnel so they may perform the proper functions of education on a professional basis.

APPENDIX A

A Summary of the Ethical Principles
for School Board Control

Purpose of Codes of Ethics for School Boards

Some school boards and state school boards associations have adopted codes of ethics for the guidance of the boards and their members in the performance of their official functions. A code of ethics for a school board is a prepared statement of principles of what is considered by the board to be desirable conduct for the guidance of the board and its members, formulated into a system of provisions, and formally adopted by the board as its code of ethics. The statement of definite principles of conduct and their formal adoption, publication, and dissemination among the members of the board makes easier the application of the principles to the situations met by the board and its members.

The general knowledge that a board is being guided by a code of ethics of its own or has adopted its state association's code will inspire public confidence in the board's integrity and improve public relations. To be able to point to a specific principle, such as No. 5 or No. 38, as a guide to an action, contemplated or taken, will explain the action and reduce undesirable pressures brought by persons or groups desiring that the board grant special advantages or favors to themselves or their schools —pressures that sometimes are difficult to resist—and will make the board more confident in its actions.

It should be generally assumed that the members of school

boards will exhibit ethical conduct as citizens, though this may not always be the case. However, the board is the composite of the individual members associated for action in formal meetings. What is accepted as a right action for an individual may not always seem to hold for a board, particularly when the welfare of the public schools is concerned. Guiding principles need to be formulated. Each member should have knowledge of the ethical principles that have been approved by the corporate body, the board.

This appendix is indicated as a summary of ethical principles because the actions of school boards and their members and the ethical implications of their actions have been discussed in the various chapters of this book. The following list of principles of ethical conduct may be useful to school boards for suggestions in the formulation of their own codes of ethics or in checking already adopted codes for possible omissions. It is not maintained that this list or any list that could be devised could be complete for all possible actions and relationships. The list of reformulated principles, roughly classified, follows:

School Board Relationships:

With the State. The school board will:

Provide for the observance and enforcement of the state school laws and the laws affecting schools from the health, criminal, public buildings, and other codes.

Observe state regulations made under the laws, such as those applying to qualifying for state funds, raising local tax moneys, expenditure of funds, audit of school accounts, issuance of bonds, transportation of pupils, school attendance, state school reports, certification of teachers, and the curriculum.

Take steps to have corrected any existing state laws or regulations that need repeal or amendment and to have needed new laws enacted.

Toward Other School Boards. The school board will:

Not employ a teacher or other person who is under contract with another school board without first securing release of the employee from the contracting board.

Not enter into competitive bidding with another school board for the services of teachers or others for employment, but will determine salaries by the application of adopted and published salary schedules for the different classes of positions.

Avoid turning over confidential letters and personal evaluation sheets to persons considered for employment, and make certain that confidential materials are returned to their sources immediately upon filling a position.

With the Community. The school board will:

Transact school board business only in regular or legally called meetings and not in rump sessions called without proper notification to all members.

Open all meetings of the board to the public except when it is necessary or advisable that the board adjourn to executive session or meeting of the committee of the whole.

Strive to maintain schools as good in quality and as economically as possible.

Study educational movements and standards on a statewide and national basis and apply them to the local school system to determine its excellencies and deficiencies.

Provide the means for keeping the public informed about the conditions and work of the schools and keep informed concerning the community's attitudes toward and desires for the schools.

Not permit, in the maintenance of public relations, any misrepresentation of the objectives, accomplishments, problems, or needs of the schools.

Represent the people of the community and, so far as possible, make all decisions on the basis of what will result in the most good to all the people rather than to any particular group, such as political party, race, religion, occupation, or geographical section of the school district.

Place the educational development of the children above the desires of any adult group as a criterion for determining action, so far as it is possible and practicable to do so.

Avoid favoritism in performing its duties and refuse to adopt policies that will discriminate against certain persons considering only the operation of good schools.

Not ignore, but rather deal wisely with persons registering complaints against the schools or employees, either orally or by written petition.[1]

Call for opinions of the community, by ballot or public hearings, on controversial school issues on which there appear to be a considerable division of public opinion.[2]

With the Board's Executive Officer. The school board will:

Select the best qualified superintendent of schools available for the salary the school district can afford to pay.

Encourage its members to maintain frank, open, and friendly relations with the superintendent.

Recognize the division of functions between the legislative, which require approval by the board, and executive, which require administration by the superintendent.

Expect the superintendent to attend all school board meetings except those in which the board acts on matters concerning the salary, tenure, or conduct of the superintendent.

Not perform administrative actions itself, nor delegate their performance to members or committees of the board.

Give consideration to recommendations made by the superintendent and his reasons for making them in its determination of policies.

[1] The injury to a school system when complaints multiply due to lack of attention by the board was stated in a report of a committee of educators, appointed by the mayor of Chicago, prior to the reorganization of the school system in 1947, as follows:

"The Chicago schools have for many years been a subject of controversy. This does not create a healthful atmosphere for education. Continual criticism of the schools is a serious handicap to the future of the city and destroys the confidence of the citizens. It is a serious injustice to the students in the schools and to thousands of competent teachers who are doing first class work."

[2] Controversial school questions that might need to be referred under certain conditions and in some localities are those such as: Shall schools be dismissed for two hours a week to enable pupils to meet at their respective churches for religious instruction? Shall sex education be taught and, if so, in what grades and in what school subjects? Shall facts about the United Nations be taught? Shall facts on communism be taught? What shall be taught concerning labor unions and management? What shall be the site of the new high school?

Give the superintendent sufficient authority to match the responsibility placed on him.

Hold the superintendent responsible for results but allow him to exercise considerable freedom in directing staff actions.

Encourage the superintendent to present to the board, for its information, administrative problems he meets that are not fully covered by the policies of the board.

Support the superintendent of schools in the administration of the schools, whether in executing the adopted policies of the board or exercising the initiative allowed him in managing the schools.

Depend on the superintendent and his properly authorized assistants to select for nomination for employment the persons who in their opinion are best qualified for the particular vacant positions.

Refer to the superintendent any applications for positions received directly by board members.

Refer complaints concerning the schools or their personnel to the superintendent for investigation and report and act on his recommendations concerning such complaints.

With the Teachers and Other Employees. The school board will:

Refuse to employ personnel on grounds of political, religious, fraternal, or other extraneous considerations, but employ each person on the basis of his particular qualifications for the vacant position.

Not employ teachers without adequate information concerning their qualifications and abilities.

Avoid susceptibility to personal influence in approving the superintendent's nominations, assignments to duty, recommendations for promotions and dismissals, and other actions or recommendations relating to personnel.

Notify nontenure teachers and other employees of the continuance or severance of their employment thirty or more days before the expiration of their contracts.

Refuse to dismiss any employee to make a vacancy to which a friend of some board member can be appointed nor for any reason other than one that is ethically acceptable and notify the person dismissed of the real cause of dismissal.

Not employ any relative of a board member.

Take legal steps to retire or discharge teachers who are unfitted physically, mentally, or morally to perform their duties satisfactorily.

Refrain from placing on teachers or other employees humiliating or unreasonable restrictions.

Encourage teachers to belong to and participate in community activities but expect them to use discretion in their choice of activities and not to injure the schools nor handicap their own work thereby.

Not require teachers to participate in good community activities but view with favor their voluntary participation.

Recognize that the conduct of teachers is usually a matter for guidance by principals and supervisors and seldom for disciplinary action by the board, unless and until referred to the board through administrative channels.

Recognize the existence of teachers', custodians', and other employees' unions but discourage strikes against the schools; allow no advantage to, and impose no penalties against, union members.

Try to maintain friendly relations with employees and to avoid a management-labor attitude by either board members or employees.

Protect teachers of science, social studies, and other subjects, who teach controversial issues fairly and without bias, from persons in the community having strong emotional leanings toward particular sides of controversial issues that need to be taught objectively.

Support teachers accused by parents or others of inefficiency or misconduct pending investigation by the superintendent of the facts and their significance to the schools.

Concerning School Business Transactions. The school board will:

Expend school moneys in the most economical manner possible, considering price and quality of goods and services purchased.

Not, as a rule, delegate to individual board members the authority to make purchases but, rather, delegate this function to the superintendent for action by himself or an assistant charged with the function of purchasing, the actions being subject to board approval.

Pay no commission nor grant any other reward to any board member or employee for services rendered in making purchases for the school district.

Make no purchases of supplies or equipment from board members.[3]

Not enter into contract with a member of the school board or a member's firm for making school building repairs or altering or constructing school buildings.[4]

Purchase a tract of land from a board member only if necessary and then only at a price determined by outside and disinterested appraisers.

Not serve for pay as the school physician, school dentist, board's attorney, or in any other capacity.[5]

Not permit board members or school employees to order goods such as fuel, food supplies, and Christmas candies for private use at reduced prices as a part of an order for the schools; nor to take advantage of special prices or discounts offered to schools on goods or services billed to schools; nor to receive any other pecu-

---

[3] The author has noted a case in which a school board member organized a "supply company" under a firm name but without capital and located in his home. The school board was his only customer. He ordered paper and other supplies for the schools by telephone from a wholesale supply company in an adjoining city. The supply company delivered the goods to the schools and billed him in the name of his company. He paid the wholesale price and in turn billed the school board for the cost to his company, plus 10 per cent profit. Another case is known of a school board member in a large city school district who became very wealthy, over a period of years, in part by securing the contracts to supply many schools with fuel.

[4] An Arkansas court held that

". . . a director is disabled from making a binding contract with a school district, not because the thing contracted for is itself illegal or tainted with moral turpitude, but his personal relations to the district as its agent requires he should have no self-interest antagonistic to that of the district in making a contract for it. The contract, however, in such case is not absolutely void, but is simply not a binding agreement and may be avoided by the district. . . ." (Smith v. Dandridge, 98 Ark. 38.)

[5] The author has known of several instances in which a school board member served under the board of which he was a member as teacher, custodian, school physician, or school dentist.

niary benefit, direct or indirect, that is not open to all persons of the community.[6]

Look with disfavor on the practice of agents of commercial concerns seeking to sell textbooks or supplies to the schools through the intercession of school board members.

Not permit its members or employees to accept compensation or valuable gifts from salesmen or firms benefiting from school business.

Not withhold information concerning specifications and time for receiving bids from certain responsible vendors while furnishing it to others.

Not give preference to local suppliers of goods or services over outside suppliers unless their bids are better.[7]

Refuse to split purchase orders at prices fixed by bidders in collusion, but place the orders with one firm only, to the extent that it is able to fill the orders, providing consideration is given to (1) the quality of the goods or services offered, (2) the prices bid, and (3) the bidders' records of responsibility in fulfilling the terms of their contracts.

School Board Members' Attitudes and Conduct:

Toward the Board. The school board member will:

Not seek nor accept his office for the purpose of selfish aggrandizement or personal gain.

[6] The author knows of a superintendent and business manager who purchased their staple groceries as a part of cafeteria orders and reimbursed the cafeteria fund for the wholesale cost plus a share of delivery charges. They were stopped by the school board after a report had been circulated in the community that they were stealing cafeteria supplies.

[7] Merchants and contractors often hold that they should be given preference in the letting of school contracts because they are local taxpayers. This opinion is not based on sound reasoning. Other persons who have nothing to sell the schools are also taxpayers. The board has no ethical right to use the money collected from all taxpayers to pay higher prices to a local firm than would be required by a firm from elsewhere and thus waste the funds to which all have contributed in taxes. If one taxpayer is entitled to a subsidy then all are, and a part of the tax money collected was not needed and should have been left in the taxpayers' pockets. Fairness requires that the best possible use be made of the money collected from all of the taxpayers. The board's obligation is to all of the taxpayers for the most economical expenditure possible of their money, not to one or a few taxpayers at the expense of the others. A local bidder has no ethical claim beyond equal treatment with all other bidders.

Not hold another public office in a local government of which the school district is a geographical part.[8]

Not represent or identify his membership with any organization or faction in the community and not accept dictation from any group.

Inform himself as to the responsibilities and functions of board members and strive to meet them to the best of his ability.

Try to prevent a division of the board into factions which may prevent members from voting on issues before the board in accordance with their convictions.

Not enter into collusion with other members to promote certain features of the public schools at the expense of other equally worthy features.

Refrain from announcing the probable action of the school board on an issue before the board has taken action.

Not pledge his action in advance nor place himself in a position such that it will be difficult for him to modify his stand on an issue during the period of board deliberation.

Not assume the authority of the board, nor individually perform administrative functions, nor personally assume any directive authority over school personnel.

Not act as an individual in settling complaints registered with him, but refer the complainants to the superintendent for investigation of and administrative action on their complaints or to pass on to the board with recommendations for policy legislation.

Be courteous to other board members and respect them for the expression of their honest opinions even though they may differ from his own.

Recognize the integrity of his colleagues and predecessors on the board and refrain from impugning their motives.

---

[8] In some states, it is illegal for a school board member to hold either a state or Federal office, but the necessity for such a rigid restriction is doubtful. In some states, state and Federal officers such as postmasters are sometimes elected to school board membership. In some school districts, mayors or city council members are designated as *ex officio* chairmen or regular members of school boards, often with disastrous results due to their lack of time, competing interests, and sometimes domination of the boards.

Present views and arguments to the members of the board without bitterness or antagonism.

Attend school board meetings regularly and punctually.

Not bring up matters for action at board meetings without warning the other members but rather have the matters included in the agenda for meetings.

Observe correct parliamentary usage in participating in board meetings and co-operate with other board members in securing decorum and orderly procedure.

Refrain from using the time of board meetings for the discussion of matters unrelated to the problem at issue and irrelevant to the solution of the problem.

Not influence the action of any other board member by a promise of a return of favors or by threats nor convince him that an action is in the interests of the schools or the people of the community in any other way than by force of argument.

Not have pet schemes for promotion to the exclusion of other more urgent or more important matters, but have well rounded interests in the schools; avoid developing interests in certain school subjects or special hobbies to the exclusion of other issues of equal or greater importance and maintain balanced interests and outlooks.

Accept the board's decisions and disregard whatever of a personal nature was said against the member or his opinions.

Maintain an attitude of loyalty to the board and its decisions.

Not disclose information the board desires to hold confidential pending negotiation or investigation, such as its desire to purchase a particular school building site or determination of whether or not a teacher's employment should be continued.

Exercise discretion about participating in gossip concerning the school board and its actions and not be a source of information on matters that may be embarrassing to the board or harmful to the schools.

Toward the Schools. The school board member will:

Accept membership on the school board with the purpose of rendering unselfish service to the community and its schools and not as a step on the political ladder nor as an aid to him in his business or profession.

Try to appraise the requirements of and for education in the school district fairly.

Not intervene in the administration and conduct of the schools on his own initiative but seek board action for the correction of conditions where there is need for such.

Not permit personal interests to take precedence over the welfare of the schools in deciding matters of policy.

Not accept a reward or gift from any salesman or from an applicant for a position.

Not accept any favors or special privileges from the schools for himself or his children, such as permission for his children to attend school A when he resides in school X subdistrict unless similar permission for transfer is allowed to other children.

Uphold the schools before the public or strive to make them good enough to be worthy of such support.

Guard against the board's exploitation of the schools or the pupils in them.

Accept, as the guiding principle for policy formation, the fact that the sole reason for maintaining public schools and all of their activities is the education of children.

Toward Employed Personnel. The school board member will:

Not urge the superintendent of schools to nominate to the board a particular candidate for a position in preference to other candidates.

Not accept "kickbacks" for securing placement of persons in school positions.

Not urge appointment of a person to a school position who is a close relative or personal friend of the member. Whether or not a person should accept school board membership if he already has a close relative employed by the board is open to question, and is a problem for the board to decide.

Not seek the business of teachers or other employees.

Not assume a dictatorial attitude toward the principal, teachers, or other employees of any school or the central administration offices.

Toward Other Boards. The school board member will:

Not write open recommendations of teachers or other employees addressed "To whom it may concern," but will write directly to those making inquiry.

Refuse to recommend a teacher or other person for employment by another board if he has been discharged for inefficiency, misconduct, insubordination, or other cause, except after full explanation of the circumstances and after being satisfied the discharged employee will not repeat the offense or inefficiency if employed elsewhere.

Remember the golden rule of school board relationships, which is that the education of the children in the school district of another board is as important to that board as the education of the children in his district is important to the board of which he is a member, and give to an inquiring board the kind of appraisal of a teacher or other person seeking a position that he would expect to receive from that board if he were making the inquiry.

APPENDIX B

Check Lists for School Boards and School Board Members

Two check lists or rating scales are presented here in the form of questions. The answers are to be evaluated and scored numerically. The first list is for the evaluation of the school board's efficiency (including school district organization), and the second is for the evaluation of the potential and actual contributions of a school board member to the board's activities.

No standards for answers to the questions are presented, for it is considered that the text of this book contains very comprehensive standards for the conditions and practices that should obtain. After reading the chapters, one will have fairly definite standards in mind. Questions of minor importance have been omitted or consolidated into more comprehensive questions.

The lists can be used to best advantage as self-rating scales because some of the items can be scored properly only by a person intimately familiar with the board at work and with the personal attributes, reactions, and contributions of its members. Other than the school board members, the superintendent or the secretary of the board should be sufficiently familiar with the board's work and its members to assign proper scores to the items.

The scores will be useful to board members as a basis for improving the work of the board and each member's participation in its activities. The check lists are analytical and will point to specific strengths and weaknesses. The results would be useful to voters in selecting board members, but a board cannot be evaluated until it is organized and in operation, and the services of members can only be evaluated after they have been elected (or appointed) and have served.

CHECK LIST FOR SCHOOL BOARDS

	None or Poorly Developed	Average or Partly Developed	Excellent or Highly Developed
	Score 0–2	Score 3–5	Score 6–8

Characteristic:

I. *School District Organization and School Board Authority*

1. Does the school district constitute a unit sufficiently large for effective and economical administration?

2. Does the board have under its control both public elementary and secondary schools and, if there are any, also kindergartens and junior colleges?

3. Are the school board and school district corporation considered to be a unit of government distinct from the departments of city or county government? Does the board operate independently of the mayor and city council or of the county board of commissioners or supervisors?

4. Does the board exercise full control over school property and school business affairs?

5. Does the board exercise full authority over the public schools and accept full responsibility to the public for their efficient and economical operation?

6. Does the board enforce or secure the enforcement of school laws that require action by school authorities and take advantage of permissive laws when to do so would be to the advantage of the schools or taxpayers?

CHECK LIST FOR SCHOOL BOARDS (*Continued*)

	None or Poorly Developed	Average or Partly Developed	Excellent or Highly Developed
	Score 0–2	Score 3–5	Score 6–8

II. *Circumstances of School Board Membership*

7. Are members elected or appointed at large instead of from, and to represent, the separate precincts or wards of the city or divisions of the county? Is the membership free of *ex officio* members?

8 A⁻e there 5, 7, or 9 members on the board? Are fewer than one-half of the normal board vacancies filled in any one year?

9. Is the term of office four or more years? Are the terms of members overlapping?

10. Are the members of the board taxpayers for the support of the public schools? Do they have children or grandchildren in the schools?

11. Is the average length of service of past board members (total years served by all members, divided by the number of members) reasonably long, such as 6 or 7 years for members whose service has been completed, or is there frequent change in membership?

12. Do the members work together and co-operatively for the schools' and people's benefit, and without division into rival factions along political, religious, national origin, or occupational lines?

CHECK LIST FOR SCHOOL BOARDS (*Continued*)

	None or Poorly Developed	Average or Partly Developed	Excellent or Highly Developed
	Score 0–2	Score 3–5	Score 6–8

III. *Organization of the School Board*

13. Are from 10 to 18 regular board meetings held each year with adjourned and special meetings held as required?

14. Is the board's business conducted without the use of standing committees other than the committee of the whole?

15. Who is secretary of the board? (1) A full time secretary or the superintendent? (2) Some other employee such as the business manager or a part time secretary? (3) A board member?

16. Are the duties of the chairman (or president) and other officers of the board properly performed?

17. Does the board recognize the superintendent of schools as its chief executive officer, although retaining to itself the function of determining board policies? Does the board grant to the superintendent sufficient authority to match the responsibility placed on him so that the board can hold him fully responsible for securing results?

18. Is the superintendent made responsible, under the board's general direction, for all administrative functions, including those relating to instruction, pupil services, school buildings, school business affairs, school research, and public relations of the schools?

CHECK LIST FOR SCHOOL BOARDS (*Continued*)

	None or Poorly Developed	Average or Partly Developed	Excellent or Highly Developed
	Score 0–2	Score 3–5	Score 6–8
19. Are the administrative functions logically and functionally divided among the administrative and supervisory personnel under the direction of the superintendent?	———	———	———
IV. *Relations with the Superintendent*			
20. Does the board use great care in selecting for employment the best qualified and most capable superintendent available to it?	———	———	———
21. Do the superintendent and his administrative staff make the executive decisions in conformity with legal requirements and adopted policies of the board?	———	———	———
22. Does the board require, permit, or prohibit the superintendent's presence at board meetings except when his own status, tenure, or salary are under consideration?	———	———	———
23. Does the board refer matters at issue to the superintendent for investigation, report, and recommendation as to action?	———	———	———
24. Does the superintendent definitely and soundly advise the board, and is the board's action taken in consideration of his professional advice? Does he confer with and seek the advice of the board in executing its adopted policies?	———	———	———
25. Does the board act, in filling all vacancies in positions, only with reference to the superintendent's and his assistants' investigations, selections, and nominations of persons for employment?	———	———	———

CHECK LIST FOR SCHOOL BOARDS (*Continued*)

	None or Poorly Developed	Average or Partly Developed	Excellent or Highly Developed
	Score 0–2	Score 3–5	Score 6–8
26. Does the board fully support the superintendent in the performance of the duties it has delegated to him?	————	————	————
V. *Relations with Individual Board Members*			
27. Do the members of the board sincerely work for the best interests of the schools, as they view them, within the practicable limits of the school district's financial ability to support its schools?	————	————	————
28. Does the board prohibit the purchase of goods or services from any of its members? Does it prohibit members or employees from ordering goods as a part of school orders at reduced prices for purchase in quantity lots?	————	————	————
29. Does the board refuse to employ board members or their close relatives except such relatives as were on tenure prior to the time the membership began?	————	————	————
VI. *Policy Making Functions*			
30. Has the board adopted rules and regulations (1) for its own procedure, (2) which define the organization of the staff, and (3) which define the general duties and responsibilities of employees?	————	————	————

CHECK LIST FOR SCHOOL BOARDS (*Continued*)

	None or Poorly Developed	Average or Partly Developed	Excellent or Highly Developed
	Score 0–2	Score 3–5	Score 6–8
31. Do the board's rules and regulations deal with general policies, leaving detailed instructions on administrative matters for administrative directives? Are they based on sound principles of organization and procedure?	——	——	——
32. Has the board adopted a code of ethics as a guide for itself and its members?	——	——	——
33. Does the board adopt general policies to be applied by the administrative staff to specific cases, refusing, itself, to deal with the specific cases as they arise from time to time?	——	——	——
34. Does the board consider only the qualifications of applicants for performing the duties involved in the positions, refusing to give consideration to matters not concerned with efficient performance of the duties involved?	——	——	——
35. Does the board insist that sound business practices be used by its business staff?	——	——	——
36. Does the board authorize only such purchases as will be to the best advantage of the school district and show no favoritism in placing orders and awarding contracts?	——	——	——
VII. *Board Meetings and Records*			
37. Does the board have a properly equipped board room for its meetings?	——	——	——

CHECK LIST FOR SCHOOL BOARDS (*Continued*)

	None or Poorly Developed	Average or Partly Developed	Excellent or Highly Developed
	Score 0–2	Score 3–5	Score 6–8
38. Is adequate preparation made for board meetings? Are members sent copies of the agenda and unapproved minutes of the previous meeting prior to the time of the meeting?	——	——	——
39. Is board business transacted in accordance with accepted principles of parliamentary procedure?	——	——	——
40. Has the board adopted a satisfactory official order of business? Are board meetings conducted with dispatch and in accordance with a satisfactory form of procedure?	——	——	——
41. Are the minutes of board meetings kept in satisfactory form and comprehensiveness? Are they indexed?	——	——	——

VIII. *Public Relations*

42. Does the board maintain freedom from the undesirable influences of pressure groups?	——	——	——
43. Are meetings of the board open to the public except when occasional executive sessions are deemed to be necessary?	——	——	——
44. Are sufficient means provided by the board for securing expressions of public opinion on school issues of major importance? Does the board act on petitions and hold public hearings?	——	——	——

CHECK LIST FOR SCHOOL BOARDS (*Continued*)

	None or Poorly Developed	Average or Partly Developed	Excellent or Highly Developed
	Score 0–2	Score 3–5	Score 6–8
45. Does the board have an effective plan in force for maintaining good public relations? Are the board's relations with the public satisfactory?	———	———	———
Score (each column)			
Total score (all columns) _____			

The range of possible total scores is from 0 to 360 points. Of course, no board would have a total score of 0 and it is unlikely that any board would score as high as 360 points. The scores of the boards of 12 representative school districts, as scored by the author, are as follows:

Population of School Districts	I	II	III	IV	V	VI	VII	VIII	Total
Possible score	48	48	56	56	24	56	40	32	360
City, 400,000	46	33	32	44	18	32	25	17	247
City, 330,000	48	38	48	48	19	45	29	25	300
City, 250,000	40	24	49	46	12	31	21	7	230
City, 120,000	30	25	35	37	13	26	27	15	208
County, 50,000	40	12	44	43	14	9	11	2	175
City, 30,000	33	22	37	32	13	27	28	15	207
Town, 22,000	30	24	40	20	8	6	14	3	145
City, 20,000	25	19	20	6	0	2	12	2	86
Town, 10,000	21	21	26	10	7	8	2	4	99
City, 6,000	37	30	38	39	12	6	4	7	173
Town, 4,000	32	22	31	43	10	10	10	12	170
Township, 1,000	36	25	19	4	2	4	2	8	100

The above scores are for school boards in 8 different and widely scattered states. Only group scores are given. They indicate on which points the board is strong, weak, or average and point to the characteristics in which improvement is possible.

CHECK LIST FOR SCHOOL BOARD MEMBERS

	None or Poorly Developed	Average or Partly Developed	Excellent or Highly Developed
	Score 0–2	Score 3–5	Score 6–8

Characteristic:

I. *Relation to the Community*

   1. Was the member of the school board selected by and to represent the school district at large?

   2. Did he secure his office for the purpose of working in the interests of the community and its schools so that he owes no prior allegiance to any other community group? Does he hold office in some other government agency such as the city?

   3. In seeking or accepting the office was he primarily interested in benefiting the community and its schools rather than in promoting his own interests?

   4. Are his opinions highly regarded by the people of the school district? Is he a community leader?

   5. Does he resist the pressures of political, religious, fraternal, and other groups when their demands would be detrimental to the interests of the community and its schools?

II. *Attitude toward Education and the Schools*

   6. Do the school board member's actions show that he comprehends the importance of education in conserving the social inheritance and in providing for the future progress of society? Does he have a layman's conception of what is included in a modern school curriculum and what are effective techniques of teaching?

CHECK LIST FOR SCHOOL BOARD MEMBERS (*Continued*)

	None or Poorly Developed	Average or Partly Developed	Excellent or Highly Developed
	Score 0–2	Score 3–5	Score 6–8
7. Does he take a well balanced view of all phases of the school system, with broad interests in the schools, without special hobbies?	——	——	——
8. Are his official actions sincere, free from prejudice, and performed in the interest of the people of the school district and for the development and welfare of their children? Is he interested in the progress of every child in the school district regardless of his creed, race, national origin, or mental ability?	——	——	——
9. Does he concern himself about appointment of only the best qualified candidates for teaching positions as determined by the superintendent without preference for teachers with influence?	——	——	——
III. *Attitude toward Board Members and Staff*			
10. Does the school board member maintain satisfactory relations with other members of the board?	——	——	——
11. Does he recognize the superintendent as the chief executive officer of the board and not try, himself, to direct the superintendent or assume some of his functions? Does he refer complaints to the superintendent?	——	——	——
12. Are his relations with administrative officers, teachers, and other personnel under the direction of the superintendent satisfactory?	——	——	——

CHECK LIST FOR SCHOOL BOARD MEMBERS (*Continued*)

	None or Poorly Developed	Average or Partly Developed	Excellent or Highly Developed
	Score 0–2	Score 3–5	Score 6–8
13. Is his attitude directed toward holding employees responsible for securing educational results of a high quality and against laziness and inefficiency? Does he have a high regard for teaching as a profession and act to help rid the schools of teachers designated by the superintendent as inefficient?	———	———	———
IV. *Possession of Desirable Character Traits*			
14. Is he intelligent, honest and sincere, willing to assume responsibility for board actions, and able to take criticism of both the board and himself?	———	———	———
15. Is he agreeable, good natured, courteous, tactful, frank, patient, and co-operative in working with other board members and not egotistical, domineering, or quick tempered?	———	———	———
16. Is he interested in the improvement of the schools? Does he judiciously reach independent decisions?	———	———	———
17. Is he able to form opinions and at the same time retain an open mind subject to change of opinion when convinced his opinion is wrong?	———	———	———
V. *Refusal to Exploit the Schools*			
18. Does the board member avoid the use of the position for political control?	———	———	———
19. Does he object to the appointment of close relatives of himself or other board members to positions in the schools?	———	———	———

CHECK LIST FOR SCHOOL BOARD MEMBERS (*Continued*)

	None or Poorly Developed	Average or Partly Developed	Excellent or Highly Developed
	Score 0–2	Score 3–5	Score 6–8
20. Does he keep his office as a board member separate from his private business or profession and not solicit business or patronage, directly or indirectly, from teachers or other employees?	———	———	———
21. Does he refuse to conduct business with the school board for profit or to work as an employee of the board for compensation?	———	———	———
22. Does he refuse to accept special favors from the schools for himself and prohibit special considerations and privileges being granted his children?	———	———	———
VI. *Contributions to the Work of the Board*			
23. Is the board member well informed on the laws concerning the functions, powers, duties, and responsibilities of the school board?	———	———	———
24. Is he active in improving himself for the more effective discharge of the duties of his office as a board member?	———	———	———
25. Does he attend board meetings regularly and punctually and generally participate in school board deliberations? Does he contribute to the planning of future school improvements?	———	———	———
26. Does his participation in the work of the board follow the rules of parliamentary procedure, and does he conserve the time devoted to board meetings by observing prescribed routines and making his contributions with dispatch?	———	———	———

CHECK LIST FOR SCHOOL BOARD MEMBERS (*Continued*)

	None or Poorly Developed	Average or Partly Developed	Excellent or Highly Developed
	Score 0–2	Score 3–5	Score 6–8
27. Does he insist on having facts as a basis for forming his opinions on important issues and avoid making snap judgments in contributing to the board's decisions?	———	———	———
VIII. *Loyalty to the Board and the Public Schools*			
28. Does the board member conduct himself in a dignified manner and avoid association with persons of questionable character?	———	———	———
29. Does he refrain from gossip about the board, board members, and the schools and from making public any confidential information he may have relating to employees or pupils that should be held confidential pending board action?	———		———
30. Does he refuse to predict board action in advance or to pledge his own vote on issues before the board meets for action?	———	———	———
31. Does he support all policies adopted by the board unless they are unethical regardless of whether or not he favored or opposed them when they were before the board for consideration?	———	———	———
Score (each column)			
Total score (all columns) ———			

The highest possible score would be 248. It is unlikely that any board member would be scored as low as 0 or as high as 248, if the conditions and member's actions on the board are known and competent judgments are used in awarding the scores. The efficiency of board members ranges from very low to very high. It will surprise some to find that this is the case even among the members of their own boards.

Selected Bibliography

American Association of School Administrators, National Education Association. *School Boards in Action.* Twenty-fourth Yearbook. Washington: National Education Association, 1946. 413 p.

Campbell, Roald F. *Handbook for Utah School Board Members.* Salt Lake City: Utah School Board Association, Capitol Building, 1946. 75 p.

Carpenter, W. W., A. G. Capps, and L. G. Townsend, *Suggestions for Procedure for Missouri Boards of Education.* (Revised) Bulletin, Education Series. Vol. 51, No. 44. Columbia, Mo.: University of Missouri, 1950. 88 p.

Chesney, L. W., *School Board Handbook,* Publication No. 147–52. League of Kansas Municipalities. 1951. 141 p.

Cubberley, E. P., *Public School Administration.* (Revised) Chapters XI–XIII. Boston: Houghton Mifflin Co., 1929.

Davies, David R., and Fred W. Hosler, *The Challenge of School Board Membership.* New York: Chartwell House, Inc., 1949. 153 p.

Davies, Daniel R., and Elwood L. Prestwood, *Practical School Board Procedures.* New York: Chartwell House, Inc., 1915. 195 p.

Edwards, Newton, *The Courts and the Public Schools—The Legal Basis of School Organization and Administration.* Chicago: The University of Chicago Press, 1933. 591 p.

Gilland, Thomas McDowell, *The Origin and Development of the Power and Duties of the City School Superintendent.* Ch. VI. Chicago: University of Chicago Press, 1936.

Grill, George W., *The Minutes of a Board of Education: A Handbook for Public School Executives.* Milwaukee: The Bruce Publishing Co., 1932. 215 p.

Hull, J. H., *Lay Advisory Committees to Boards of Education in the United States.* Los Angeles: University of Southern California, 1949.

Hunkins, Ralph V., *Superintendent and School Board, A Manual of Operative School Administration*. Lincoln: University of Nebraska Press, 1949. 132 p.

Lamers, William N., "Are You a Superior School Board Member?" In *The American School Board Journal*. May 1952.

McLaughlin, F. C. "Local Government and School Control." In *School and Society*. April 5, 1952.

Messick, John D., *The Discretionary Powers of School Boards*. Durham, N. C.: Duke University Press, 1949. 147 p.

National Education Association, Research Division. "Fiscal Authority of City School Boards." *Research Bulletin*. Vol. XXVIII. No. 2. Washington: The Association: Apr. 1950. 78 p.

National Education Association, Research Division. "Status and Practices of Boards of Education." *Research Bulletin*, Vol. XXIV, No. 2. Washington: The Association, Apr. 1946. 53 p.

Olsen, Hans C., *The Work of Boards of Education and How It Should Be Done*. Contributions to Education, No. 213. New York: Bureau of Publications, Teachers College, Columbia University, 1926. 170 p.

Sears, Jesse B., *City School Administrative Controls: An Analysis of the Nature, Placement, and Flow of Authority and Responsibility in the Management of a City School System*. New York: McGraw-Hill Book Co., Inc., 1938. 281 p.

Sears, Jesse B., "School Board Procedures, With Special Reference to the Use of Hearings." In *The American School Board Journal*. Vol. 107–108. Nov. and Dec. 1943; Feb., Apr., and June 1944.

Shannon, J. R., "What 1,000 Terre Haute Citizens Look for in Voting for School Board Members." In *The American School Board Journal*. Feb. 1947.

Stapley, Maurice E., *Attitudes and Opinions of School Board Members in Indiana Cities and Towns*. Bulletin of the School of Education, Indiana University. Vol. XXVII, No. 2. Bloomington, Ind.: Published by the Division of Research and Field Studies, Indiana University, 1951. 42 p.

Stapley, Maurice E., *Story of a Workshop*. Bulletin of the School of Education, Indiana University. Vol. XXVIII, No. 1. Bloomington, Ind.: Published by the Division of Research and Field Studies, Indiana University, 1952. 47 p.

Thomas, M. J., and Others, *The School Board and Public Education*. Pittsburgh: University of Pittsburgh Press, 1951. 155 p.

Tuttle, Edward M., "Progress Among School Board Associations." In *The American School Board Journal*. July 1952.

Virginia Association of School Trustees, *The Virginia School Boards: A Manual for the Guidance and Help of Members*. Richmond, Va.: The Association, 1948. 82 p.

Index

Evolution of school districts, 21–22
Executive:
appointment of, 234–235
authority of school boards, 23–24
directives, 41
employment, 234–255
functions, 234
importance of capability, 234–235
meetings of board, 126, 197–199
officer of school board, 23–24, 41–43, 129–130, 261 (see Superintendent of schools)
responsibilities of board, 152–153
Ex officio:
chairman of board, 112
designation of members, 86
Exploitation of schools by board members, 347–348
Extravagances caused by dependency, 54

F

Factionalism, effect on board actions, 261, 305
Federal authority over education, 10, 19–20, 38, 40
Filling of vacancies in membership, 100
Financial planning, 144
Fiscal:
autonomy of district, 45–47
dependence, 45
dependency and public relations, 297–298
independence, 45, 140–142
Form for minutes, 220–222
Forms of organization structure, 130–137
Foundation of legal status of boards, 63–64
Functions of:
board, policy making, 341–342
chairman, 202–204
National School Boards Association, 317–319
school boards, 138–163, 155–161, 263–266
school boards associations, state, 315–317
standing committees, 121–123

G

Gilland, T. McD., 21, 24, 27
Glen Ridge, N. J., board of education, 273–275
Grievances presented to board, 275
Grill, G. W., 222
Guidance of public opinion, 289–291

H

Handbook for school boards, 321
Harmony among board members, 260–261
Hearings, 153–154, 213–214, 287, 298–300, 310–311
for judging public opinion, 298–299
of delegations, 200–213
on dismissal of tenure teachers, 214
public, 213
purposes, 298
required by law, 214
witnesses at, 214
Hierarchy of governing authorities, 40–41
High school districts, including several elementary, 34–35
History of:
development of school boards, 16–30
standing committees, 24–25

I

Illinois Association of School Boards, resolution of, 306–307
Implied powers of board, 141–142
Importance of school boards, 1–5
Improvement of:
board members, 306–311
schools, 278–280
Incorporation of school boards associations, 315
Independence of school boards from city or county, 4–5, 39
necessary for fixing responsibility, 51
state's interest in, 49–50
under legislative control, 19
Independent school boards, 39, 44–61, 142
Index to minutes, 231–233

School board members (*Cont.*):
  attitudes, 331–335
    toward other members and staff, 346–347
    toward the schools, 345–346
  authority of, 259
  bipartisan selection of, 93
  books for, 309–310
  business relationships with employees, 259
  check list for, 334–350
  community service, 13–14
  compensation, 106–107
  conduct of, 331–333
  contributions to board's work, 348–349
  creed of, 321–323
  election of, 46–47, 81–82, 87–89
  ethical principles of, 324–335
  ex officio, 86
  exploitation of schools, 347–348
  harmony among, 260–261
  improvement of, 306–311, 336
  induction of, 110–111, 308–309
  interim vacancies, 99–100
  interrelationships, 260–261
  legal requirements, 101–102
  limitations on, 72–73
  loyalty to board and schools, 349
  methods of selection, 81
  motives for accepting, 106–108
  mutual respect among, 260–261
  need for information, 306–307
  nomination and election, 81–82
  nomination commission, 85–86
  number of, 3
  occupational group representation, 95–96
  orientation of new, 308–309
  overlapping terms, 97–99
  personal:
    characteristics, 347
    liability, 75–77
  popular election, 81–82, 87–89
  protection of the schools, 287
  qualifications for, 101–106
  qualities required for, 101–108
  relations with:
    board, 72–73, 285–288, 341
    community groups, 284–288, 345
    employees, 258–260

School board members (*Cont.*):
  relations with (*Cont.*):
    other board members, 258–273
    public, 284–288
    superintendent, 258–273
  selection:
    and term, 81–100
    method of, 81–91
    on political ticket, 92–93
    special privileges for, 259–260
    ward representation, 21–22, 93–95
School budget:
  and city authorities, 55
  an education plan, 50–51, 144
School committee in New England, 34
School control by state laws and agencies, 41–43
School districts:
  absence of, 34
  autonomy of, 49–58
  changes in, 31–32
  consolidation, 21–22, 35–38
  county, 33–34
  development, 31–32
  disadvantages of small, 35–38
  encroachment on city financing, 57–58
  foundation of control, 38–40
  governing units, 31–43
  independence of, 33, 39
  in Indiana, 33–34
  in New England, 34
  in southern states, 33
  kinds, 32–35
  legislative bodies, 164–188
  limits of jurisdiction, 55–56
  merging of, 35–38
  number, 3–4, 35
  organization, 33–35, 337
  overlapping, 34–35
  prevailing organization, 34
  relations with other agencies, 58–61
  reorganization, 3–4
  source of authority, 39
  state agencies, 64–66
  structure as corporations, 68–69
School executive: (*see also,* Superintendent of schools)
  state, 41–43
  superintendent as, 52–53

Score card for school:
board members, 344–350
boards, 333–344
Scores on check list, of certain cities,
344
Screening of applicants for superintendency, 248
Sears, J. B., 183
Secretary of board, 116–118
Selection of:
board members, 81–100
chairman of board, 112
secretary of board, 116–118
advantages of appointing superintendent as, 117
treasurer, 118–119
Self rating on check list, 344
Single trustee system, 33–34
Size of school boards, 21–22, 27–28
Sources of:
applicants for superintendency, 248
school board authority, 44–45
Special:
cases, board legislation on, 147
committees, 127
interest groups, use of schools, 280–
281, 288
meetings, 114, 192–193
taxing units, trends, 58
Standing committees, 24–25, 28
development and decline, 120–126
disadvantages, 123–126
duties, 121–123
investigations, 124–125
State board of education, 33, 41–43
State constitutional provisions for
schools, 38, 40
State control, development, 25–27
State legislature, source of authority,
44–45
State school:
authority, development of, 19–20
boards associations' work, 319–320
executive, 33
State's interest in independence of
board, 49–50
Structure of school corporation, 68–69
Suits against board, 74–75
Superintendent of schools:
abilities required, 240–242
actions subject to approval, 149–150

Superintendent of schools (*Cont.*):
administrative duties and responsibilities, 263–266
advisory functions, 52–53, 88, 149–
151, 234–235, 257–258, 266–270
announcement of vacancy, 246–247
appraisal by board, 261–262
as board secretary, 116–117
authority of, 23–24, 265–266
board's:
ethics and the, 327–328
relation to new, 273–275
support of, 272–273
caution in selecting, 244–245
changes in incumbent, 237–238
conferences with applicants for position, 251–253
confidence of board in, 150–151,
266–267
contract with, 254
co-operation with board, 237
delegated authority, 152–153
directives, 187–188
discharge of, 151, 262
effect on board efficiency, 304–305
election by:
popular vote, 261
unanimous vote, 254
employment, 129–130, 234–255, 261
evaluation of candidates for position, 253–254
executive of board, 152–153, 268,
271
functions, 235–236, 267–276
importance of capable, 234–235
interviews with candidates for position of, 250–252
leadership of, 236, 241
link between board and employees,
256
merit as basis of employment, 244
origin of position, 23–27
participation in school elections,
239
permanent tenure, 151, 254–255
promotion of local employee to
position, 243–244
provisions for dismissal, 254–255
public relations functions, 234, 278–
303
qualifications required, 240–241